Snow White
BITES
HOLLYWOOD

What an interesting life I had.
And how I wish I had realized it sooner.
—Colette

Snow White BITES HOLLYWOOD

...THEN HOLLYWOOD BIT BACK

A Memoir

JANET DAVIDSON

SNOW WHITE BITES HOLLYWOOD
. . . THEN HOLLYWOOD BIT BACK

Notice of rights

ISBN
979-8-9889999-0-4

Book design and production: John Tollett
Printed and bound in the United States of America

ACKNOWLEDGMENTS

After every Academy Awards broadcast, I, like so many young hopefuls, would go into my bathroom—hold my toothbrush to my face and accept my Oscar. Not wanting my parents to hear me, I quietly, through tears, would start with: "I'd like to thank my mother and my friends." Now I can do that without my toothbrush. However, the list has grown. First, I want to thank everyone who has found their name in my book; thank you for being a part of my journey. Whatever role you might have played, I still appreciate your being there. I know so many wonderful, helpful people and will probably leave someone out. (Anyone who accepts an award adds that line to their speech.)

People whose talent helped me shape this book: Linda Gray, John Tollett, Rebecca Partridge, Rachel Read, Jeannice Gordon, Mary-Charlotte Domandi, Alexa Bigwarfe, WPS, Joan Griffin, Ann Van Hine, Rhonda Perry, Barry Smith, Joanna-Smith-Thole, Jane Friedman, Judith Fein, Robin Williams, Pam Shepard, Shirley MacLaine, Joan Griffin, Ann Van Hine, Rhonda Perry, and dear lifelong friends, Pamela Grant, Libby Palmer, and Deborah Wilday. The cheering squad: Michael Miller, Barbara Bloomberg, Sandra Forquer, Karen Marie Jones Meadows, Debrianna Mansini, Jessie Smith, Karen Gaviola, Rany Levy, Akili Beckwith, Scottie Gissel, Cynthia Steffioni, Donna Young, my cousins Nancy and Paula, my newly found family in Ireland, The Hartigans.

Contents

Introduction: A Coming-of-Age Story 9

1 Fame 11

2 I'm An Acting Student 16

3 I Danced With a Donkey 24

4 Singing For My Supper 39

5 I'm an Ugly Stepsister 44

6 I'm an Usher . . . Ette 48

7 I Felt Pretty 55

8 I'm Looking For My Prince 59

9 Me & Sophia Loren 67

10 No Jews or Blacks Allowed 74

11 I'm a Waitress 82

12 An Ending 101

13 A Recovery 117

14 The Future 124

15 I'm a Producer 130

16 Who Is Dillon? 145

17 A Life To Get Back To 150

18 Pack the Car! Hollywood, Here I Come 157

19 I'm an Assistant Director 163

20 Caddyshack 170

21 Females Need Not Apply 176

22 Rush Week, What's That? 181

23 Remington Steele 190

24 This Is Murder, She Wrote 202

25 Me & Ten Guys Travel the U.s. 210

26 Native Son: Craziest Job Ever 214

27 Cagney & Lacey 229

28 Now I'm a Director! 241

29 Let's Try Something New 247

30 Columbo 253

31 Women-in-Jeopardy Movies 258

32 Equal Justice/Midnight Caller 264

33 The Earth Shook 270

34 Damn It Janet 276

35 You Will Never Direct One Of My Shows 286

36 If It's Tuesday, I Must Be In ...Where Am I? ... 289

37 Any Day Now 296

38 My Fatal Flaw Surfaces 300

39 A Thanksgiving Gift 312

40 The Story/My Story 323

Introduction

A COMING-OF-AGE STORY, SIXTY YEARS IN THE MAKING

In some ways, this is a fairy tale. How many Hollywood hopefuls can say they made it? I can, but it certainly wasn't the road I had any intention, education, or connections to travel down.

My earliest memories are of performing for everyone except for my father. He seemed to think anyone else was more talented than I was. But I kept on going. My first professional job came when I turned eighteen; I would be Snow White. Our small theatrical company traveled America, and I was introduced to a country I hadn't learned about in my school textbooks. These experiences began to change many of the beliefs I grew up with. Other truths would take many more years for me to face.

My dreams of becoming a famous actress were dashed early on when a stubborn case of acne scarred my pretty little face. Scars weren't allowed—at least for actresses. My parents chose not to get medical help for this—that created a different kind of scar. They didn't mean to hurt me. They were just too busy trying to save themselves.

A chance meeting led me behind the camera. Then the hard work began. Sometimes, I'd be the only woman on the set—it was a fight just to belong. But I had learned one thing as a child: how to fight. And fight I did.

Every film or TV show I worked on became a family, functioning, non-functioning, or both simultaneously. Success, or failure, depended on how I fit in. Sometimes I did, and other times not so much. Often, I misjudged power and control: who had it, who wanted it, and what they might do to get it or keep it.

My rise to director took years, but the fall took only months. Surely, I knew better than to keep poking the bear. I have been compared to a terrier with a bone—not giving in and not letting go. Always trying too hard to prove I belonged. But it was always one person and his power and control I was wrestling with. My father. How had his drama shaped me? Could I learn to escape the echoes of my childhood world and embrace it simultaneously? Would understanding help me heal the wounds, scars, and blemishes that lived inside me?

These are my memories. The people I have written about may, and probably do, see the past differently. That forms their story, not mine. I've been as honest in telling these stories as possible. I've tried to report fairly and with grace, not knowing what was behind someone's behavior, good or bad. I have examined my own extraordinary life with the same honesty and grace.

One

FAME

I am crammed in a tiny elevator with five other teenage acting students as it descends to the lobby of the building where The American Academy of Dramatic Arts (AADA) holds its acting classes.

It is February 1964, and in one month I will be seventeen years old. Our class has just presented our final student project, scenes from *Our Town;* I was Emily, the lead character. Our acting teacher seems very proud of me, or of himself as a teacher.

The feeling of satisfaction continues as my fellow teenagers chat openly in the elevator out of earshot of our instructor. He is staying upstairs doing whatever paperwork is needed to send to his bosses. I love my Saturday acting classes and will miss them dearly. They provide a wonderful escape from my parents; well, my father, at least.

The old elevator bounces a bit as it hits the lobby floor. We are used to that. Usually, we hug each other and go out the lobby doors of the Ed Sullivan Theater. Once out onto Broadway, we go in different directions toward our homes. But not today.

When the elevator doors open, we are greeted by a plethora of New York City police officers. The lobby is in chaos. All I can see are guns pointing at us.

"Who are you?" "Where did you come from?" "How did you get in?" The questions from the police are coming too fast to answer.

Finally, they motion us out of the elevator. The police seem beside themselves and as confused as we are. Then, through the glass doors, I see hundreds of screaming teenagers and police on horseback and foot, trying to protect the entrance doors. What the heck is going on? A sergeant comes to us, and he is furious. We start to explain who we are and why we are inside the building.

"We're acting students. Our class is upstairs."

The sergeant, now huddled with some other cops, is trying to figure out what to do with us. There is no way out the front doors. Somehow, they have the impression that on Saturday, the Ed Sullivan Building is closed. So, they conclude that we somehow snuck in. Things are going so fast no one has time to figure out how we could have gotten by a battalion of fellow officers, screaming kids, and paparazzi. The immediate problem for the officers is how to get us out of the building.

Attached to the lobby is a coffee shop. (Years later, this is the shop David Letterman would use for various skits during his show.) The police usher us in to wait while they figure out what to do next. None of us know what is going on. Such drama! This is wonderful for a group of acting nerds.

The small coffee shop has two entrances, one from the lobby and one from the side street. Suddenly, the side door flings open, and there are even more cops. With them are four handsome young men with lovely long hair. Everything about the four seems different and new. Our little coffee shop now holds six young acting students, many police officers, the coffee shop manager, and four young Beatles.

Now it's crystal clear what's happening. The Beatles have come to rehearse for their U. S. debut that Sunday night on the Ed Sullivan Show. For a moment, you can hear all our hearts beating as one. My eyes immediately fall on Paul.

When I come back to earth, the other three come into focus. George seems anxious; he sits at a table by himself, watching. He never speaks. Ringo asks, *"Who are ya's? What ya doin' here?"*

John picks up on us being acting students and seems to mock us. *"Sure looves, ya wanna to be famous? Ya wanna be movie stars?"* Well, yes, I do, but I keep that to myself. My fellow actors are serious theatre folk; movie stardom isn't their goal. Ringo jumps to our defense with some wisecracks, but it is Paul I'm dazzled by.

He has an audience of six young gals, and he flirts away. *"Oh John, leave them alone, they are doing what they loove to do. Right, gals?"* Paul will always be my favorite Beatle. John has a few more discouraging words for us, and this time Paul jumps back and repeats, *"Oh, leave them alone, John!"* but with much more force. I can tell that John has an edge to him. He mumbles something and slinks away. I am glad to be left with Ringo and Paul. George is still sitting by himself at a small corner table.

Everyone in that coffee shop is frightened and excited. The shop manager came to work expecting a typical Saturday. The police are caught short; they totally underestimated the popularity of the Beatles. I am amazed at the wild crowd outside. This is what fame looks like. Here I am, stuck in a room with the most famous new arrivals from across the pond. Those kids outside would kill to be me.

An officer from the lobby area comes to usher The Beatles out. With the building maintenance workers and stagehands' help, the cops blocked the glass doors so no one could see inside. The Beatles walk past the covered doors, denying all those fans a glimpse of history.

The fab four leave with "goodbyes" and "good lucks" for our fame and fortune. Their exit sucks all the air from the room. There is nothing left to do but go home and tell of our adventure. We leave by the door the Beatles had entered our lives through.

That Sunday, I find myself antsy with excitement. I sit front and center, eyes glued to our thirteen-inch TV for the start of the Ed Sullivan Show, proudly knowing that I know the Beatles. They are, in fact, sitting on my dining room table. For some unexplained reason, my father is selling their posters. He left his job in downtown Manhattan to sell advertising trinkets. This gives him more free time to visit the racetracks and gamble the mortgage away. So, the fab four with their long locks and fresh faces are just lying there on our table. Even after hearing my Saturday story, my father never offered me a poster.

A memory, really just a vision, enters my head. I was nine when Elvis first burst his hips onto Ed Sullivan's show. My father took one look and ordered me to leave the room. I have seen that historic footage and compared it to today's music stars, and it's really very mild. But my father clearly saw evil in Elvis. Or did he see sexual freedom and envy it?

Elvis and the Beatles; now, that's what fame looks like! I wondered what would it be like to have that kind of fan attention directed toward me? Movie star posters covered my bedroom walls. I hoped and prayed that some day someone would have my face plastered on their walls. But do teenagers run after movie stars the way I saw them act with the Beatles?

Twenty years later, I got my answer. By 1983, fate had stepped in and put me where I really belonged—behind the cameras. I was working as an assistant director on a new TV show, *Remington Steele*. Pierce Brosnan was just breaking into American TV. We were shooting at a grammar school in Los Angeles when our lunch break coincided with the kids' lunch break. Pierce was walking to his trailer, and I was nearby.

Suddenly, hordes of kids came his way. *People* magazine had just come out with Pierce's beautiful face on the cover. The kids waved the magazine around as they stampeded across the street. Once they got to Pierce, they were literally climbing all over him. These kids were almost as wild as the Beatles fans I'd witnessed as a teenager.

I caught up to Pierce, and we both ran to his trailer. We were picking children off him as we went. Once safely inside, he was visibly shaken.

"Pierce, your life just changed. Fame has found you."

He took a moment to let it all sink in. There was no joy in his reply. "Those were small children; someone could have gotten hurt." That is very typical of Pierce; he is kind and considerate. He continued, "I don't think I like this change."

Change. When I was young, I prayed for it. To grow up and get out to show everyone who doubted me that I could become a star in Hollywood. I had no idea that my life would be so full of changes. Some were welcome, and others I dreaded. But they all led me to a quote from the writer Colette that could not have been truer for me. "What an interesting life I had, and how I wish I had realized it sooner."

Two

I'M AN ACTING STUDENT

How am I going to get from Hollis, Queens, to Hollywood, USA? More importantly how am I going to become a star?

My first chance at stardom came to me while I was still a teen student at The American Academy of Dramatic Arts (AADA). Mrs. Lilia Skala was one of my acting teachers. She got rave reviews for her portrayal of a nun in the Academy Award-nominated film *Lilies of the Field*. One day, she asked my mother to meet her after class. "Janet, your mother and I will have a chat. Why not sit inside the classroom for a bit?"

I took a seat nearest the door so I could hopefully hear them. Mrs. Skala said some nice things about me and my talent and then went into the meat of the meeting. "They are looking for teenage girls for a new play. I think Janet is perfect for the part of one of the students. And I'd like to recommend her."

My mother was soft-spoken, and I could barely hear her. Since her back was to me, I could not read her expression. I could only hear Mrs. Skala's response to whatever my mother had asked.

"*The Prime of Miss Jean Brodie* is a new play by Jay Presson Allen. I've read it and it's quite wonderful. It opens on Broadway in the fall. I know the producers, and they know I work with teenagers here at AADA, so they asked me for recommendations."

This, it turns out, is how many actors get their roles. It's who you know and who knows you. I can still feel how my tummy twisted and turned with excitement. In my mind, my name was already on the marquee. The conversation continued.

"The production schedule would mean that Janet would have to leave Jamaica High School. She'd be tutored while the play is in rehearsal and during the run of the show." Then Mrs. Skala paused, "However, you need to do something about her skin."

Ah, there was the rub.

My pretty little face started to break out when I was around nine years old, coinciding with getting my period and all the trouble at home. Pockmarks took over my cheeks, my chest, and my back. My father yelled for me to stop picking my face, but I had gone beyond listening to him about anything. In this case, that was unfortunate because my mother was a Christian Scientist and refused to consider any medical advice about my skin.

Mrs. Skala continued, "Of course, the choice is up to you. Other parts will come her way if not this one. But Mrs. Davidson, you must see to her skin condition. It will hamper her in the future."

My mother turned towards me, and I could see I would be back with my classmates at Jamaica High School. I was crushed, then angry, then a small part of me relieved. Was I ready for Broadway?

I don't think my mother ever thought teenage acne would permanently scar me. She had lovely, flawless skin. Her Scottish skin never wrinkled; it didn't have a mark on it and never burned in the sun. I, however, burnt to a crisp. Just like my father did. So, the choice she made was to enlist her sister, my Aunt Ruth—who was a Christian Science practitioner—to help.

The mail would come, and there would be a letter from Dallas with healing pages my Aunt Ruth pulled for me to read. Passages from the Bible and from a book called *Science and*

Health with Key to the Scriptures, by Christian Scientist Mary Baker Eddy. These passages sent a clear message: my acne came from my sinful sexual thoughts and would go away if I repented. I loved my Aunt Ruth and had spent many a wonderful summer with my cousin Paul in Texas. So, I took these passages in and knew I was to blame for what I looked like.

Here is an example from the King James Bible:

> *Now the works of the flesh are evident: sexual immorality, impurity, sensuality, idolatry, sorcery, enmity, strife, jealousy, fits of anger, rivalries, dissensions, divisions, envy, drunkenness, orgies, and things like these. I warn you, as I warned you before, that those who do such things will not inherit the kingdom of God.*
> —Galatians 5:19–21

Today I think of these messages as "sin and be sorry" passages. But what was a fourteen-year-old supposed to do with this information? Oddly enough, Mrs. Skala—who was the first to call attention to my situation—was a Christian Scientist also. However, she seemed to have no problem suggesting medical help for my skin. I guess religion is personal. How one uses it—or misuses it—is on us.

The part in *The Prime of Miss Jean Brody* ended up going to my classmate, Catherine Burns, and SHE got to go to Hollywood. She received an Oscar nomination for her first film, *Last Summer.* But the critics were especially cruel to her and called her a "homely fat marshmallow, an intelligent mushroom." Soon after, she left Hollywood behind and retired from acting.

So I, too, had a physical challenge to surmount. However, I wasn't deterred from my quest for stardom; it would just have to wait until my face cleared up and stardom would be mine. I continued taking classes at AADA and also private singing classes. All paid for by my aunts. Finally, graduation day arrived. There was some family pressure to go to college, but I knew I didn't need it. What movie star needed a college degree? I would not change my mind. I would go to AADA as a full-time adult student. This decision created yet more arguing between my parents.

"Queens College is free. She can study accounting there. She's good at that."

"Bill, that's not what she wants; maybe if she continues to go to acting school it will . . . I don't know, maybe she'll change her mind."

"She's not going to make it as an actress. Why spend money that we don't have?"

"She may not become a working actress, but she loves it. And, by the way, I know better than you that there is no money. How was the track last Saturday? Win anything?"

The fighting escalated, and I removed myself from the house. Sitting by the roses in spring, our backyard was always a lovely place of refuge.

Time to mention my father was an addict. So much so that he got in trouble with the mob. I occasionally came home to find a sleek black sedan parked out front, occupied by two shady-looking guys. Other times I'd answer the phone, and a deep-voiced male would ask, "Is your mommy there, sweetie?" Handing the phone to my mother, I'd watch her pale blue eyes grow dark. I didn't have to ask who these guys were. I'd watched enough gangster movies to figure it out myself. A part of me wished they'd make good on their threats and harm my father, take him away from us. But I feared that they might hurt my mother instead.

My audition for admittance to AADA as an adult full-time

student went great! The instructors seemed really impressed. The funds my mother borrowed from her sisters were in the bank. Even a few extra dollars were available, and my mother decided it was time I left the house. She found a co-ed boarding apartment on East 39th Street in Manhattan. My father moved me in. He eyeballed the other residents. Well, especially the male ones. Was he looking to see if there were any Blacks or Puerto Ricans? He seemed to hold a special hatred for anyone with different colored skin. He once stopped the car as he saw me walking with a friend. Speedy, as our little gang called him, clearly had a darker complexion than any of us. As my father is rolling down the window, he yells at top throttle: "Get away from that spic." Whatever a "spic" was.

The American Academy of Dramatic Arts has a long history of famous graduates; Danny DeVito attended the year after me, and Robert Redford before me. I saw myself on that exclusive list. Meeting my classmates, I found a group of friends, all serious actors. We had speech classes, movement workshops, singing classes, dance classes, and many different types—or methods— of acting classes. I even learned to fence! At seventeen years old, I was the youngest at the Academy, and it showed. I began to fall behind my fellow students.

The AADA cast me in a senior play. This was a big deal. The Academy was a two-year program, and it was unusual for a first-year student to be selected so early for a speaking part in a senior play. The play was Molnar's *The Swan*, which had become a successful film starring Grace Kelly. A young actress, Alexandra Isles, was the lead in our production, and she captivated me. In real life, she was a socialite who gracefully traveled high society circles. She wore a tuberose perfume that lingered, filling the air, and I always knew where she had passed by. It seemed to me everything Alexandra touched was perfect—and unattainable for someone from Queens like me. (About ten years later, this lovely woman appeared in court as a witness against her lover, Claus von Bülow, who was accused of killing his wife. I wonder if the wafting scent of tuberose swayed the jury.)

After our dress rehearsal, the full cast lined up on stage for our director, Worthington Minor, to give us his notes. My character's name was simply The Maid, and the handsome lead actor stood behind me, undoing my apron ties over and over. I'd tie them back, and he'd untie them. I was not used to male attention, at least not from a grown man, and I was flustered and flattered. He was choosing me over the very perfect Alexandra. I felt the excitement moving through my body.

I brushed his hand away and giggled, "Stop it. We are going to get in trouble." And we did. The director's wife, Frances Fuller, the head of the Academy, was also in the audience.

"Young lady, we do not disrespect our director. Who do you think you are? What is your name?"

"So sorry; I'm Janet Davidson, first-year student."

She never raised her voice to the male actor, no, not at all. In front of me lay power and control, while behind me was the pull from another form of power and control, men and sex. I didn't know yet what the punishment would be for my disrespecting the art. A voice inside me went to those old references sent to me by my aunt of my sexual thoughts. Clearly, there would be a price to be paid.

At the term's end, our final plays were selected. They gave me two characters that I was much too young to understand. These performances would determine my fate. I could not grasp the characters they assigned to me. One play was *The House of Bernarda Alba,* by Federico Garcia Lorca, an outstanding play about sexual repression. Ha! I remember one line so clearly: "*My breast is bitter, bursting like a pomegranate.*" I didn't even know what a pomegranate was, let alone how or why one's breast would burst like one. I was embarrassed to admit my lack of knowledge to our very Russian acting coach, whose accent made him seem fierce. He didn't seem to have any use for me or my talent, and I feared Francis Fuller had talked to him about me being disrespectful. It was crushing to realize how much power one person can have and how much that one person hated me.

I felt trapped. The buoyant feelings I had when I entered the Academy slipped away. The friends I made were too concerned with their own success—or failure—to offer support. I could feel my performances getting worse rather than improving. Failure was closing in on me. I could not see a way to make this situation better. I began to fall down a dark hole, and I felt I had no power to climb back up. I thought of giving up.

At eighteen, I was facing the possibility that all my dreams, which had kept me going since I was five, might evade me, and I fell into my first real bout of depression. My mother's backup plan for me—to become a bookkeeper, marry, and have kids— was not an option. I could not stop crying. I never shared my depression with my mother, but she must have sensed it. She offered to pay for a trip to Miami with my dear high school friends Monica and Nikki. Monica was my best friend, and we were dance partners. Anywhere and anytime we heard music, we were on the floor twirling and shimmying. Nikki was a bit older and not in our classes. I can still hear her wonderful laugh.

Down at the hotel pool, we picked up a beach boy—I guess a gigolo—and he stayed with us for a few nights. When our beach boy chose Nikki, jealousy overtook me. It was clear to me I was failing as an actress and as a woman.

While we were away, the letter arrived from AADA. My mother waited for me to come home to open it. I was not asked back for my senior year. It referenced my immaturity and that I should redo my junior year in their night classes. Was this retaliation for my flirting, or was this an honest view of where I stood as an actress? I felt humiliated that all my friends went on to their senior year. Was immaturity the only problem, or was I not talented enough to be successful? I cried endless tears of shame and failure. For the first time, I thought the only way out was to end my life. But I knew I wouldn't. The pain that would have caused my mother overwhelmed my sad thoughts. I would never put her through that.

Three

I DANCED WITH A DONKEY

I desperately wanted to have faith that my future was in the hands of some higher power. I started going to a Christian Science Sunday school in Manhattan. It seems odd that an eighteen-year-old would attend Sunday school, but it felt comforting. My teacher was a wonderfully eccentric woman who had traveled and brought her world to our classes. She introduced me to some finer things in life. When she had us over to her townhouse on 5th Avenue for tea, slippers would be waiting at the entrance. We'd take our shoes off, choose a pair of new slippers, and walk on a heavenly all-white wall-to-wall carpet. I wanted this life. My tears started to fall less frequently, and I could call her when they did. With her help, I began to find the courage to go forward.

I did enroll in night classes at AADA, but they bored me because it was a rehash of everything I had already learned. At times I'd bump into my classmates who had gone on to the senior year and would see the pity in their eyes. A sharp edge began forming in my soul, a protective covering. What would happen if, after staying a whole year at night classes, I would still not be invited to continue as a daytime senior student? I was antsy and wanted to prove that the Academy had made a mistake by not promoting me. Lurking in the back of my mind was my father telling me I would never make it. I could not let him be right.

I decided it was time to start auditioning. The Pittsburgh Players were one of the three successful children's theatre producers. As the name indicates, they were based out of Pittsburgh, Pennsylvania. The professional actors mainly came from New York City. Auditions for their production, *The Dancing Donkey* by Erik Vos, were held at a Broadway theatre not in use, or "dark" as it's called.

It was scary enough to audition for strangers, but the emptiness of the vast stage made my 5'2" body feel even smaller. Looking at an audience devoid of people, I could barely see the director and producer sitting in judgment. Years later, once I started directing, I had a soft spot for actors during auditions. What drives this unique breed of humans to put themselves through this experience? To feed the hunger inside, an actor has to cut themselves open and touch places others will never even go to. Almost all actors want to be seen, heard, and appreciated. I certainly was no different.

A friend took a great picture of me. I had it touched up so my blemishes weren't visible. On my résumé, I classified my talents in the order I felt I was best: actor, singer, dancer. I would take my chosen song, give the music to the pianist, and away I would go. Everyone is treated equally; you get the standard eight bars and then "thank you, bye-bye." My "go-to" number was from the Broadway musical by Michael Stewart and Bob Merrill, *Carnival. "I come from the town of Mira"*—thanks, bye-bye. It's interesting that I would choose that number to sing. Yes, it's a pleasant song with an excellent vocal range, but the lyrics still resonate with me. *"I have to find a place; I've got to find a place, where everybody knows my name. Can you imagine that? Can you imagine that? Everybody knew my name."*

I was ecstatic when I got the call offering me the part of The Dancing Donkey's faithful companion. I got my first paying acting gig! Nothing could stop me. However, I had to choose—continue to study at AADA or take the acting job? As always, I would seek my mother's approval. Although my mother was not good with social or personal problems, she was great if I had a work problem to solve. A phone call to her just to hear her voice helped me move forward. I presented my quandary to her: stay or take the acting job? Her response was neutral, and she left it up to me.

I don't know what my father felt. Now that I didn't live at home we saw each other only when my mother asked me to come home for dinner or on the occasions they came to Manhattan. Even then, my father and I hardly said a word to each other. We had a love of baseball—The Mets in particular—in common. That was all.

I quit the Academy and went on a tour with a Dancing Donkey. I would be Sweet Ingénue, singing my heart out to save Donkey from being stolen by bad, bad guys. Who wouldn't want to have a donkey that could dance?

Before I could move to Pittsburgh to join the Pittsburgh Players, my parents demanded a meeting with the head of the company. I will call her Midge, only because I can't remember her name. Even though I was eighteen and could make my own decisions, Midge also insisted that she meet with my parents before she produced a signed contract. My parents were eager to meet her also. We packed the car and drove down to Pittsburgh.

The meeting took place at what would be my home away from home, a quaint boarding house in the Sunny Slope district. We went up the stairs to my bedroom, and I was in love. It had bright yellow walls, clean white curtains, and a canopy over the bed. I was truly a princess. I went back to the living area, and now my parents were standing, ready to leave. Once again, Midge assured them she ran a professional company and would watch over me the whole time. I think I saw a tear in my mother's eye and a fixed jaw on my father's face.

The company was comprised of, and I refer to them only by their character names: Donkey, Bad Guy, Mrs. Bad Guy, Prince, a Friar to help the Prince, and of course, Sweet Ingénue. Léon Chancerel—the great French pioneer of children's theatre, based the musical on a one-act play. The plot is simple: two scoundrels steal Donkey, then disguise themselves as good guys to sell the stolen donkey back to its original owner, Sweet Ingenue who of course needs the help of the handsome Prince, and a meddling Friar. When I met the gal who was to play Donkey, I had the thought that they had rightly given her the part as she seemed sturdy. However, she had the room next to mine, and I would hear her crying now and then because she was forced to leave her boyfriend behind in NYC. I certainly did not have that problem.

We did a few shows around Pittsburgh: one deep in coal country, one at Carnegie Mellon University, and one at a children's hospital. This allowed us to get used to each other and the show itself before heading south. It was a joy to realize how much the kids loved us. They would scream for Prince to watch out for Bad Guy and his nasty Wife.

To say I had stage fright would be an understatement; every actor does. Each actor has a different way of handling the stress. My crazy digestive system would kick in, and upon hearing the stage manager call out "Five minutes" to performance, I'd have to head straight for the bathroom—a perfect example of the mind/body fight-or-flight response. The stage manager got wise to me, and he would give me the standard five-minute warning, but it was really ten minutes before the show, giving me enough time to run to the nearest bathroom.

The physical aspect of this fight-or-flight condition started when I was a child. I hated to enter our bathroom after my father had set up camp and filled the small room with stale cigarette smoke from his four-pack-a-day habit, alone for an hour or so he could study the racing papers and select his winners. I would simply deny my need until my body was so clogged up that I could no longer control it. Of course, the more I tried to control my bodily functions, the more severe they became. To this day this chronic IBS haunts me.

Back in 1966, there were no commercials explaining the wonders of IBS drugs, and besides, there was that Christian Science non-medical world I belonged to. So, I'd just go on getting advance warnings; "Five minutes to curtain," throughout our whole tour.

In February of 1966, we headed south. I had been to Texas before to visit my cousin Paul. Other than that, New Jersey was as south as I had traveled. I did not know I was stepping into a different world.

Mr. and Mrs. Bad Guy were probably in their 40s and were real-life husband and wife. They drove the station wagon. Prince, Donkey, and I were in the back seat. Midge and Friar—who was also the stage manager—drove the van with the sets and costumes. Also in the station wagon was the couple's black cat.

We hit Atlanta, Georgia, for our first out-of-town performance. I could not have been more excited. Exhausted from the drive, we checked into a hotel in the downtown area. We ate together and then retired to our rooms. In the middle of the night, I woke up scratching, my body burning up.

Whatever was happening to me was coming from that bed. I put a pillow on the floor and covered myself with my clothes. The morning could not come fast enough. I felt that somehow, I was now contagious and might bring about the end of the tour with my disease, so I kept my nightmare to myself.

Meeting in the lobby, I noticed Mrs. Bad Guy scratching. She almost hissed at me, "Where is Midge?"

I spotted her coming towards us all smiles. Mrs. Bad Guy was not in the mood. "How dare you try and save money by putting us in this fleabag hotel? You go off to stay with friends and leave us here; this place has bedbugs! I was up all night. Don't you ever do this again, or we are leaving!"

That's what they were. I had never heard of such a thing, bedbugs!

Midge feigned total innocence and apologized over and over. But there was a show to do, so off we went. As I write this, just the memory makes my body itch. After our performance in Atlanta, we piled back into the station wagon and pressed onto Florida.

Central Florida is hot and humid. The Spanish moss lined the sleepy two-lane road. Here was the real-life version of B. Altman's NYC Charleston Gardens, where my mother would treat us to a wonderful lunch after my Saturday acting classes. This was a far cry from Fifth Avenue!

Inside the car, it was stifling. Air conditioning in cars did not become widespread until the 1980s. Mr. Bad Guy was driving, and Mrs. Bad Guy sat next to him. Their black cat was not on any tether. Donkey was by the rear back window, which was open; I was in the middle, and Prince was by the other open window.

Black Cat suddenly left the front seat and joined us in the back. Mrs. Bad Guy yelled for us to close our windows; after all, the cat's comfort was of uppermost importance. Donkey was in the middle of telling a story as she closed her window, so she didn't notice that the cat was now caught in the rising window and soon to lose its life. I like cats, but this one was friendly only to her parents.

No matter how much we didn't care for that cat, killing it was not on our agenda. Everyone in the car started yelling at Donkey. I was jabbing at her and pointing to the closing window. She got it, rolled her window back down, and it released the cat. It flew across us and out Prince's open window. However, the cat had its revenge and took a chunk of Donkey's arm with her to the Florida countryside.

The wagon came to a screeching halt, and we tumbled out to find Black Cat. Donkey was bleeding human blood. Mr. and Mrs. Bad Guy were frantic. We would be late to the theatre, and Midge would not be happy. Finally, Black Cat was herded back into the wagon, and off we went. I'm not sure who started the giggles— probably me—but soon the backseat passengers were having a good laugh. Mr. and Mrs. Bad Guy were not pleased.

Donkey's bleeding had stopped, and we prepared for the show. The theatre was in a school auditorium; most of our venues were in schools. The theatre/gym/cafeteria was small, dirty, and just as dank and humid as the outside. Our set consisted of tree cutouts, rock cutouts, some dried tree trunks, and assorted scattered leaves on the floor. We were set up and ready to perform on time. The excitement started as the children arrived, eager to cheer us on.

Like most children's theatre of the day, this show was a simple good guy vs. bad guy tale. Since Donkey is talented and knows how to dance, Mr. and Mrs. Bad Guy plan to steal it from its owner, Sweet Ingénue. To lure Donkey, they tie Sweet Ingénue to a tree. On cue, Donkey responds to Sweet Ingénue singing of love. Donkey loves this song and dances around the stage, not realizing danger lurks behind the tree. Only at this performance, I didn't recognize the choreography.

The kids love Donkey. They cheer wildly when she appears on stage. It's adorable. But this time, she is crazed and all over the stage, her hoof pointing at her knee. She came close to my ear and whispered something. I'm trying to keep singing and listen to what she is trying to tell me. Then the stage lights caught a sparkle, and I saw the reason for the new dance steps. In the dance, she kneels resting on the stage, and this stage had not been cleaned. They never were. A large nail had gone through the costume and lodged in her knee.

I'm tied to a tree. What can I do? Even then, I must have had a spark of director in me. In character, I ordered Donkey to get help while I kept singing. After the show, it was a trip to the local hospital for a nail removal, bandages, and a tetanus shot for the nail as well as the Black Cat scratch. Donkey did not have a good day.

Hot, sticky, and exhausted, we crammed back into our station wagon. We were looking forward to a weekend off before the next performance. Central Florida is a far cry from growing up in NYC.

Upon arrival, Midge deposited Donkey and me in a motel well off the beaten path. We were surprised and confused when Midge did not check in with us. Instead, she took the van away with Prince and the Friar to another motel miles away from us. Mr. and Mrs. Bad Guy got the station wagon for the weekend as they were going to visit friends nearby.

I guess Midge thought that if she left the guys with the gals for a whole unsupervised weekend nine months later, little Ingénues and Donkeys would appear. Since I had my driver's license—well a learner's permit—I pleaded with her to leave us the van. As she drove off, she assured us we would be fine staying by ourselves.

Donkey and I watched her pull away from our lonely, one-story, bright turquoise motel. At least the motel had a restaurant. Upon inspection, we realized the restaurant was closed, probably by the health department.

Conveniences such as cell phones and Uber rides did not exist in the late '60s, so we were two teenage girls stuck somewhere in Central Florida. Midge did not even leave us with an emergency phone number. For all we knew, we would never see her again. The clerk at the motel told us the town was only a few miles down the road. I had seen enough horror movies to know this motel could have starred in one. Between the bed bugs in Atlanta and this lonely, creepy motel, a part of me wanted to call my parents to come and get me. Donkey was a good sidekick and seemed to have no fear. "Come on, Janet, we are not going to let that witch win. Town is just down the road. Let's go."

Off we went down this one-lane dirt road. Miles and miles of orange trees and fallen oranges surrounded our path. Polk County is home to a huge Minute Maid orange juice factory. Most of the time, oranges have a pleasant smell, but not when they are burned in mass to make juice. It was a sickening, acrid, all-invasive smell. To this day, I need my orange juice to be camouflaged with champagne to drink. "Geez, this smell is horrible."

"Put your scarf around your face here like this." And my donkey friend tied a bandanna around my face. Now we were faceless young women walking a deserted path where some town that we really didn't trust lay ahead of us.

When we got to town, we found an open cafe and had our burgers and fries. Tired and hot, I leaned on Donkey's bravado, and we hitched a ride back to the motel.

The motel had new guests: a prison workforce—a real southern chain gang—had checked in. There were two young guards in charge of the inmates. These prisoners were nonviolent offenders. They were, however, dressed in black and white stripes—something I'd seen only in the movies. Whatever fear

I might have felt took a back seat to my sheer excitement. Talk about drama!

They were transported in one of those prison vans that holds about twelve, and they were staying overnight to rest from the roadwork they were doing for the state of Florida. I'm not sure there was anyone else staying at that motel. What a story this would be when I got home! But who would I tell it to? Certainly not my parents.

We made friends with the guards, who assured us we were safe even with the convicts loose on the motel grounds. Everyone was respectful. The guards included us in the food they brought from the local fast-food server.

Now our miserable adventure was turning into a fun time. Donkey and I chatted and shamefully flirted with the guards. Just your typical Saturday night—an ingénue, a donkey, two guards, and six prisoners.

Donkey got friendly with one of the guards, and maybe there was some hanky-panky going on. I might have been jealous. I was still a virgin and in no hurry to disappoint my mother by becoming otherwise, especially with a Florida correctional officer or, even worse, an inmate.

Midge was picking us up on Sunday. Donkey and I hatched a plan to drive her crazy and punish her for leaving us alone. We arranged with the guards to have all the inmates in front of the motel. They were just milling about, dressed in black-and-white striped jumpsuits. When Midge pulled up, Donkey and I were each sitting on a guard's lap. The chain gang just loafed around behind us at the entrances to the rooms.

The plan worked. Midge pulled the van into the driveway and immediately spotted us and went wild. She blasted the horn and got out of the vehicle. "What is going on here? Young ladies don't act this way. I could call your parents now. Get in the car!" She started to come towards us, then stopped dead in her track after all, we were surrounded by prisoners. Who knows, perhaps she was genuinely concerned for us. But we knew she wouldn't call our parents; there was no show without us. We each gave our guard a peck on the cheek, waved goodbye to the prisoners, and off we went. This was all surreal; I felt like I was in my own movie. She said nothing more to us, but we both suspected it would not end there.

It seemed we had been on the road forever. Even though life was far from perfect at home, I was beginning to miss it. Shows continued in small cities and even smaller towns. Midge had a knack for choosing bad motels. Of course, it was all to save money. One motel we stayed in—I think near Tampa—was very large, and there was a group of rooms way toward the back. That's where Donkey and I had our room.

This motel came alive at night. A "gentleman" driving around outside the back of the motel stopped and propositioned us. We ran for our room, slammed and locked the door. Turns out the owners of the motel reserved the back area for the "ladies of the night." I have no idea if Midge knew about this arrangement. Was this punishment for the chain gang incident, or did Midge not know what happened in that motel? Donkey and I spent the rest of the night with the door locked. We even propped a chair in front of it. We must have learned that from the movies.

The next day we were off for yet another show in yet another school auditorium. The tour was coming to an end. This would be one of our last performances. This school was bigger than some of the others and should have had a good sound system. Midge asked the principal as he took us on a tour about their audio system. "Oh, yes, we have a brand new state of the art sound system." He then walked us to a locked closet. "It's all right in there."

We were all confused. He went on, "It's a gift from the Federal Government, and they have the keys. As soon as they feel we have complied they will give us the equipment."

Ah! Another lesson was coming my way. Desegregation was now the law of the land, but not everyone in Florida got the message. This school, like many others, was not abiding by the law, and whatever was given to them by the Feds was locked up until the day they complied.

We were scheduled to do three shows almost every day. Two shows in the morning and one in the late afternoon. Kids were being bused in from all the surrounding schools. The afternoon performance would be for Black kids they were busing in.

The first two performances went off like clockwork. We were having our lunch when we heard this commotion outside. Soon angry voices swelled from the parking lot. We went out to see what was going on. What we saw was shocking.

Angry white parents blocked buses transporting the Black kids. The first bus was being viscously rocked back and forth by these parents. We could see the kids inside that bus were terrified. So were we.

I stood there helplessly, watching what was happening to these small kids who just wanted to see a show. The police turned the bus around, and the principal canceled the next performance.

Seeing these frightened kids, my father's words of hate jumped across my mind. Did I have these feelings as well? We moved from Brooklyn to Hollis, Queens, when I was around two years old. Queens was very segregated in those days, and I never met a Black person until junior high school. We never mingled during class or afterward. Would he have been one of these parents here in Florida blocking the school bus? I don't know. How did I feel about race relations? I hadn't given it much thought. The vision of these small, frightened children would linger with me for years.

Tension at the school remained even after the buses with the Black kids left. We all just wanted to go home. Midge disappeared for a short while. When she returned, she asked us to donate a day without pay to perform at the school these Black students went to. We all agreed to stay another night. The next day we arrived at their school to find more buses. It seemed they had bused in as many children as possible from surrounding Black schools. We ended up doing two free shows.

The performances went very well. The kids loved us and screamed their hearts out. However, there was a noticeable difference between these children's reactions and what we were used to. At all the performances in what I will call "White schools," the kids constantly screamed to warn the Prince that Mr. and Mrs. Bad Guy were on the way to steal Donkey.

At the performances for the Black children, it was the opposite. The kids yelled and screamed to protect Mr. and Mrs. Bad Guy. They wanted to let them know Prince was coming and to watch out. This seemed so screwed up to me. I could not understand how any child would want the "bad guys" to win.

Back on the road, I brought up the subject to our stage manager. "Joe, why did those kids root for the bad guys?" Joe was a no-nonsense New Englander. I was only 5'2" and he seemed shorter than I. Much like an elf—a serious elf.

He asked me what I thought was a stupid question. "If you were in trouble who would you call?"

"Joe, that's stupid. I'd call the cops."

"You grew up differently from these kids. The police down here, more often than not, are not the good guys, at least in the world these kids live in. They grew up fearing authority and those who had power over them."

"Well, who would they call for if they needed help?"

"They have to help each other."

"Joe, is it just these kids, or are all Black kids frightened of the police?"

Joe took a deep breath, "Pretty much all of them."

"That's sad to me."

That night in my hotel room I had a lot to think about. I was very young the day my father burst into our house yelling for my mother, "Where's the baseball bat?" To my knowledge we didn't have a baseball bat.

Seeing his wild demeanor my mother tried to calm him. "Bill, what is wrong? We don't have a baseball bat."

"Some of us are going up the street a [believe me, he didn't say a Black family] just moved in."

I don't remember any more of the conversation as my mother led him to another room and must have calmed him down. By the way, it was an Italian family with a cleaning person who happened to be Black. What I did take from that incident was that Black kids did not belong in my neighborhood of Queens. Until I got to junior high school, I don't ever remember seeing a Black person. How strange to think of that now.

On a microscopic scale, I could understand the feeling of not belonging. I believed my pockmarked face singled me out as imperfect. I could find proof of this in everyone's face as they glanced a second time towards me. I knew they were saying, "Poor young thing; she could be so pretty if it weren't for her scars."

We had one more adventure before Donkey would do her last dance and be turned out to the pasture. All the actors wanted to return to Pennsylvania via the Blue Ridge Highway. The problem was how long the drive would take. Mr. and Mrs. Bad Guy were Actors Equity Association (AEA) members, the stage actors' union. As members, they kept a log of our driving time. Just like truck drivers are allowed only so many hours before they must rest, the same seemed to be true for actors on the road. Midge went back in the van and warned us not to take that way home. But we went ahead and took the drive. It was beautiful.

We got back to Pittsburgh. My parents picked me up, and we all had a farewell dinner together. Back in NYC, the entire cast was called to the offices of the Actors Equity Association. The union threatened to fine the company for driving too long that day. We all spoke up; this was on us, not Midge. She should not have to pay the fine. Equity came up with an interesting solution to our problem—we would all have to join Equity. They held power over our situation. If we had said no, we might have been barred from ever becoming union members. I wanted to be considered a professional actor. And if that meant joining a union, so be it.

Most actors had to wait for the right role to come along that would allow them to join the union. Here I was at nineteen, a member of Actors Equity! Somehow that card validated me, empowered me; I would be a famous actress, a famous union actress!

But first, I'd have to find a place to live. Before I left for Pittsburgh my father came and got all my things from the boarding house I was living at in Manhattan. My mother could no longer afford it and since I would be away why hold on to it? With the little I earned doing *Dancing Donkey,* finding my own place was impossible. I would return to my parents' house. I hated this.

Four

SINGING FOR MY SUPPER

Back to auditioning. Fortunately it wasn't very long before the next job appeared—dinner theatre. Some smart ex-con must have come up with the idea of combining the two things' actors are good at: acting and waiting on tables. Hire actors first to serve dinner, then do what they love and have trained for—perform. It also saves the restaurant/theatre money. Let the audience pay the actors' salaries with their tips.

I was off to Kingsport, Tennessee. The Olde West Dinner Theatre was neither old nor in the West. Patrons pulled up to a wooden facade made to resemble a trading post. The acting company consisted of the normal numbers of villains, heroes, and, of course, a love interest. I was none of these. My part, Mad Agnes, was one of the victims in *The Drunkard*. This was the 1968 musical adaptation of a 1933 Temperance play. Agnes had been left at the alter and never took off her wedding gown, expecting her love to return. Wearing a tattered wedding gown and holding wilted flowers, I sang of lost love. My hair was teased to resemble a rat's nest, my eyes painted with dark circles, and lipstick askew. A character repeated in countless horror films. Who wouldn't want their dinner delivered by this person?

Everyone bonded nicely. During our downtime, we'd take trips around the area together. One genuinely excellent adventure came while visiting a local professor that our director,

Joe Shea, knew. All seven of us crammed into the company station wagon and drove deep into the woods. I had never met a character like this professor before; he met us at the gate, totally naked, with a feather boa floating around his neck. As we drove down the long dirt road towards his house, I was trying not to stare. He was the first totally naked man I had ever seen. I don't think I've ever seen another man, naked with a boa streaming behind him.

Joe greeted his old friend while the rest of us stood around just a bit shocked. Our host grabbed a bathrobe, flung it over his naked body, and then warmly greeted us as he ushered us into his lavish home. Once inside, vibrant green silks hung from the walls held up by golden angel sconces, all in contrast to the dark wooden walls and the huge brick fireplace. The silk drapes were broken up only by shelves of hundreds of hardcover books. And quite a few naked statutes sat on surrounding tables.

Another room was covered in fuchsia silk, so bright that the color hurt my eyes. The daybed—which was his sofa—was lush deep green and fuchsia satin with enough pillows to hide in. He had tea served in real English chinaware. Sandwiches (with cut-off crusts) were waiting for us. And there were boas of all colors to adorn ourselves with. I was just nineteen years old, and the conversation was over my head. So, I just watched and listened in awe. It seemed so sophisticated and eccentric at the same time.

Until now none of the gay men in my life were ever as flamboyant as this. My mind drifted to my beloved cousin Paul in Texas, my Aunt Ruth's youngest son. He would have gotten a kick out of this professor. Paul's coming out was difficult for him as my aunt and uncle did not approve. My, how many sin-and-be-sorry passages would they have sent to our current host?

I'm going to drift briefly away from the satin walls to continue to speak of Paul. Four years after *The Drunkard,* at twenty-three years old, I managed to get the apartment of my dreams, in Manhattan. 95 W 95 Street was a brand new building, and my studio was on the 32nd floor! Aunt Ruth visited me. After marveling at the view all the way to Queens and at how well I was doing, she sat down to have a serious conversation. "I have something to tell you. Paul is a homosexual." Of course, this was no surprise to me. She continued, "His father, Bill, did not handle that well, and Paul was asked to leave our home. Things were never the same. I can't forgive him."

I ventured into dangerous territory. "Ruth, I've known about Paul for years; I'm sorry Uncle Bill could not forgive him. Paul didn't do anything wrong."

She painfully replied, "No, not just Bill, I can't forgive Paul. I love him so much, but I just can't. Maybe it's because you are in theatre you think these things are normal, but they are not."

Ruth's beliefs, and her turning away her own son, were all part of her understanding of religion. Would it have changed anything in my aunt's mind if she could have seen how happy our gay host was? How truly generous, kind, and brilliant he was. She probably would only have seen his home as tacky and over the top, rather than a joyous expression of his personality.

Back to Tennessee and the world of satin walls and happy actors singing and dancing, stomping around to some country and western tune: I was the only one not wearing a boa, so I grabbed one and flung it over me. Dancing was my favorite activity, but I could not join in. Something always held me back. No one seemed to notice that I wasn't jigging along with them, and that was okay for now.

Whether in theatre or working on a film set, one common perception is that we performers are wild and crazy people.

While in Kingsport, we were invited to a party. We put on our finest. Todd, who played William, my smart, protective brother, went in full drag. I had never seen this before—well, at least that I knew of.

I sat next to him on the drive to the party and just stared at him. Finally, I just blurted out, "Toddy, you are so beautiful." He seemed embarrassed by the flattery. Once at the party, we realized we were to be . . . the party.

Our hostess prevailed over an almost all-male guest list. Actually, I think our female cast members were the only other gals there. Walking into her living room, I had the strangest feeling; it was almost exciting. All eyes seems to be on us—well, the women in our group. Our hostess greeted us and showed us the bar. I don't think any of us even had the chance to want a drink before the action started.

Suddenly she chose a man from the couch, brought him to the middle of the floor, and they undressed each other. Then they went at it. I grabbed Todd's hand, or he mine, and we both let out an audible gasp. I had no idea where to look, yet part of me wanted to look at this writhing, humping couple. I had never seen full nudity sex—or any sex—before. I didn't dare lock eyes with any others in our group.

Todd took me by the hand and led me out the door. We were the first to leave. A part of me wanted to stay. I was still a virgin and desperate for the courage to explore my sexuality. If I stayed, what would the others think of me? More important, from hundreds of miles away, somehow my mother would know, and it would hurt her or make her furious. So, leaving was better than facing my sexual curiosity.

It was only a matter of minutes before the whole cast was back in the car headed back home. There were many nervous giggles and many "Oh my God's." We also got a blow-by-blow of what happened after we left. Russel, the most worldly of us, shared the story that when she was done with the man we saw her with, she went to the next man in line. To say it was an orgy would not be precisely correct. She was the singular recipient of all this sex. Is this how she lived, or was she showing off for us theatre folks? Perhaps she expected us, or at least the men in our group, to join in.

The next day we heard that the party was a celebration of her divorce. All the men at that party had testified at her divorce hearing on her husband's behalf. They confessed to having had sex with her during the marriage. I was sure this could not be true but was assured it was. Perhaps that party was her way of getting her power back. Maybe she was a sex addict, something I knew nothing about. Were my urges also a symptom of a bigger problem? What was normal when it came to sex? Growing up I didn't understand anything about sex. But I equated the arguing and fighting not just to money, but some other need. I had no clue and no one to ask. The last thing I wanted was to show my innocence to the rest of the cast. Now, I think I could have confided to Todd. I would have to find my way through this valley of sexual ignorance.

Our month in Tennessee was over. Another show would arrive at The Olde West Dinner Theater. A new set of actor/waiters would arrive with a different play. *The Drunkard* ended. Mad Agnes, with her tattered wedding dress and wilted flowers, became a memory. I headed back to New York City. Once again, no job and no place to live. Now I had too much freedom to consider going back to my parents' home. I'd do what all actors do—have roommates and shared apartments. That is until I went on tour again.

Five

I'M AN UGLY STEPSISTER

I didn't have to get that shared apartment as my next tour came right away. Rockefeller Traveling Playhouse, a very respected children's theatre company based in NYC, hired me for their next *Cinderella* tour. Kay Rockefeller, owner and producer, swore she was no relation to Governor Rockefeller or the vast Rockefeller fortune. I'm sure this is true. She was a generous and kind person; if she had access to a fortune, she would have spent it on us. Before we'd go on overnight touring, we would have day trips performing within driving range of NYC. We were The Rockefeller Players, but we called them the Kay Honey Tours.

Mostly, the Kay Honey Tours were terrific. They cast me as both an ugly stepsister in *Cinderella* and as the perfect Snow White, in, of course, *Snow White and the Seven Dwarfs*. Finding seven little men—or traveling with children playing little men—was out of the question. Our little people were going to be puppets.

Kay came with us for our first few shows. She'd drive the station wagon to schools surrounding the NYC area. With her map spread out on the steering wheel, she'd find these school auditoriums; occasionally, we'd have our hearts in our throats. One time she somehow missed the entrance, and we were, of course, also late. Spotting the door to the auditorium, Kay made a quick right-hand turn.

Unfortunately, that turn led us down a long flight of steps—definitely not a driveway.

"Kay, STOP. These are stairs!"

We all screamed and held onto each other. Bumping our way down the long steep stairs, convinced we would end up dead. These short tours around NYC were to get us used to the show before we took to traveling for the whole month. Hopefully Kay would not be the driver. We landed in one piece right where she intended us to be—at the door to the auditorium.

The show went off nicely. I played one of Cinderella's ugly, nasty stepsisters. It's more fun to play these kinds of parts, but I was jealous of the gal who played Cinderella. She was the center of attention—attention that I desperately wanted.

Once we got on the road, the farthest we went was St. Louis. This short Kay Honey Tour was not all pleasant; relationships formed that I felt left out of. I was nineteen and still immature, and on my own most of the time. Not really because I wanted to, but because I lacked adult social skills. I think it appeared to them that I thought I was better than they were. When in fact, I just didn't know how to relate. I wanted to join conversations, but felt I lacked enough education to share an opinion on whatever subject they were chatting about. I desperately wanted to belong. I just didn't know how to. I resented the gal playing Cinderella. She was everything I was not. Blonde, pretty, flirtatious, and charming. And at only one year older than I, she seemed to understand sex.

I wanted to be Snow White and the star of the show, not the Cinderella's ugly stepsister—even though I felt more comfortable in that role. But I would have to wait my turn. Summer was beginning, and the Snow White tour would not start until the fall.

Back in NYC, I had time to reflect on my feelings towards Cinderella—or Libby, the actress playing her. I understood that my mother could not accept nor had any desire to accept her own sexuality, let alone mine. It's a cliche to say that married folks fight over money, children, and sex. That was certainly true in my home. Sex, or lack of it, was always in the air. My mother seemed to want me to hear her during these arguments over sex. Did she want me to feel how wrong sex was? Did she feel that way?

Fights over money could happen in any room of the house or in the car. But the fights over sex—or lack of it—happened in the living room or bedroom. By the way my mother yelled—mostly "No, stop, don't"—I always thought my father hurt her, and I wanted to kill him for making her unhappy. Literally kill him. I almost tried that once. My rage was so fierce that I took the knife I was cutting an apple with and headed towards the kitchen. As I got closer, I realized this small knife would never do any harm to my 6'2" father. I detoured into the bathroom and dug my nails into my hand until I bled.

Clearly, I grew up with some very warped views on sex and relationships. Yet, my body seemed to want this negative adventure that made me so jealous of Cinderella. She seemed to understand what being a woman was all about. I would hang on the outside of all the fun activities that the other actors took part in. My jealousy kept me from even trying to be one of the group. I knew I could not compete with Cinderella for the attention I so desperately wanted and needed.

Years later, I bumped into the gal who played the other ugly sister. Excitedly she told me that Cinderella/Libby lived only a block away. "Libby's married now and lives right around the corner. Do you want to surprise her with a visit?"

No, I did not.

Yet my "sister" persisted, and we went to see our pretty counterpart. Cinderella had left acting and married. Four years had passed, and I was now twenty-three years old and no longer a virgin. I had toured as Snow White for years, and all the traveling, living alone, and waiting tables had matured me. The door to her apartment opened, and there was Cinderella, but something was very different. Her hair was no longer bleached Cinderella blonde, but a gentle natural shade of light brown. She was warm, inviting, and above all, funny. It wasn't just her looks that had changed; I no longer felt a smidge of jealousy. I'd grown up, at least a bit.

To this day, Libby is my best friend. When my mother passed, it was Cinderella/Libby I called first. I can see us standing in front of my closet, trying to choose what I would wear on the plane to Dallas and what I could wear to the funeral. Oddly enough, Libby became a sought-out costume designer working in Hollywood. We worked together on more than a few projects. Life is amazing.

Six

I'M AN USHER...ETTE

A fellow actor suggested I try and become an usherette. That way, I could see all the Broadway shows and get paid for it. What a great idea! I now had another union membership— IATSE Local 306 Theatrical Employee—to add to my resume. We all used to wear little black dresses with white collars. It was all very formal. We answered to "usherette," not "usher," which is not politically correct today. For many years between gigs, I'd return to being an usher. Each experience stayed with me. When I got to Hollywood, I often worked with actors I had watched from the theatre aisle. I never shared that with them.

I would be a substitute and call in each day for my assignment. This suited me just fine as it left me available for auditions. When I wanted to work, I would call Barney, the head of the Local. "Barney, what do you have today?"

Barney answered me in his thick Irish accent, "Matinee at the Shubert."

"Oh, Barney, I saw that show already."

I could smell the smoke coming through the phone wires.

"You're not going to see a show. You are at work!"

"OK, sure, I'll be at the Shubert tonight." I never questioned him again. But I detected he was sympathetic and often sent me to shows I hadn't seen yet.

In 1967, Ingrid Bergman returned to Broadway starring in Eugene O'Neill's *More Stately Mansions.* She remains one of the most honored actors of any generation. Her awards include three Academy Awards, two Primetime Emmy Awards, a Tony Award, four Golden Globe Awards, and a BAFTA Award. She was not someone to trifle with.

It was a rainy night, and I was working the orchestra seating. It was my first time at the Broadhurst Theatre. Because of the rain, the regular house usherettes wanted to go home early. This was their world, and they had complete control of it. As the newest and youngest, I was left in charge. I knew enough not to seat latecomers, especially if their seats were down front. This couple came in late and wet. Their tickets were in the fifth-row center.

Looking at the seating plan, I thought we could make it without too much disturbance. As we approached the stage, I realized something was very wrong. Ms. Bergman sat on the stage floor, legs over the edge. They had taken the first four rows of the seating away. This must have been to give a more intimate feeling to the play. However, no one told me! Ms. Bergman stopped her monologue, looked directly at me, and said, "I'll wait."

Instant thoughts of pure panic filled my brain. "God please kill me now, my career will be over! She will blackball me forever." Barney never asked me to go back to the Broadhurst Theatre. I can understand that.

Rosencrantz and Guildenstern are Dead, Tom Stoppard's wonderful play, had many tryouts before its grand opening. During this pre-opening, I was there quite a lot. I loved the show. I would sit on the stairs in rapture, watching every movement of the actors.

Many times, a lovely gentleman would sit near me on the stairs. One day during intermission, he asked me what I thought. I gushed praise, but had a few problems with certain things in the writing and the performance. Unfortunately, I was beginning to have my own voice and was not shy about my new opinions. Things would fly out of my mouth without censoring them first.

A few days later, I was back at the show and noticed one thing I commented on was different in this performance. Wow, that's interesting. Then I realized the lovely man was, in fact, Tom Stoppard—the author. I was mortified to know I had voiced myself to him. I am not suggesting he took my thoughts into account, but . . .

During the late 60s, I saw many shows; it was an excellent education. It was 1968, and Broadway was changing. The world was changing. Hair was the first Broadway show I ever auditioned for. In all my voice classes I sang light opera, which is the music I auditioned with. *Hair* was a groundbreaking musical, and rock 'n' roll was their beat. I didn't fit in at all. I sang my eight bars and got my "thank you, bye-bye." However, I got to work at *Hair* as an usher.

All the ushers, being women, would meet in the ladies' lounge before the performance to be assigned a section to cover for that day. It didn't matter which theatre you worked in; that is where you would find your tribe. They all knew each other; it was a female Irish mafia.

Diane Keaton was in the cast of *Hair*. It was, I believe, a first for her. She seemed so frightened, and before the show started, she would hang out in the ladies' lounge rather than in the actors' dressing room. I guess we were less threatening than her fellow actors. She seemed comfortable with us.

However, the ushers were not comfortable with her being in their space. I was sympathetic to Diane's fear. A part of me was jealous; what I would have given to be in her shoes. Finally, one evening the head usherette cast a pitiless eye on Diane and shooed her out.

"You have a dressing room. Use it!"

After this scolding, Diane never came back to the lounge again.

During the performances, we'd see the police often. The cast would, occasionally, get naked. Male nudity was not allowed in those days, and the police would raid the theatre. In the streets, anti-war sentiment raged, and *Hair,* with its anti-war message, made its way to mainstream Broadway. The nudity was only an excuse for the cops to hassle the show. It was that anti-war message they wanted to shut down. I must admit to a certain excitement at the prospect of male nudity. I was twenty-one years old and had still only seen that professor in Tennessee's penis. So, rather than appalled, I was curious.

Sometimes they would arrest one or two cast members to make a point. I often thought the audience thought this was part of the show. The usherettes all knew when the police were coming. After all, many of the cops were Irish, and there was an Irish bond. On "raid" days, I was left almost alone by the front entrance. Nothing to do; just stand back and let it happen. I never refused an assignment to work at *Hair,* and I loved that show. And I did finally see a penis—a young one—not like the professor's back in Tennessee.

One thing I didn't appreciate while working at *Hair* was being heckled by the cast—well, one cast member in particular. During the introduction to the show, the cast members would crawl over the audience. I would always find an empty seat near the back of the orchestra or sit on the stair.

One night one of the cast members, Paul Jabara, got in my face, making fun of my being an usherette with all the old ladies. He was mean, and there seemed to be no stopping him. The audience went along with it thinking it was also part of the show. My savior from Paul's heckling, and his bullying, was cast member Lamont Washington. He saw and heard Paul go at me, and from the other side of the orchestra, he was at my side with lightning speed. He banished Paul and had a few choice words with him. Lamont then asked me how I was and let me know he'd always be there if that should happen again. Still, the audience thought this was all part of the show.

Sadly, Lamont died in a fire in his apartment later that year. To this day, I can see the photo in the *New York Post* of him standing at his window while on fire. He was only 24 years old, an incredible talent, and for me, a prince. Who knows what his future would have been?

Young talent—like Lamont—had the benefit of being able to see Broadway up front and close with the aid of a free teaching program for the arts. NYC paid for busloads of students to attend specific Wednesday matinees of various shows. After the performances, the actors would come on stage and answer questions. I always liked to work at these performances; I learned so much from these experienced actors.

It was 1969, and soon I would be twenty-two years old. Al Pacino and Hal Holbrook starred in *Does a Tiger Wear a Necktie,* written by Don Petersen. I remember the Q&A for that show. Al wasn't on stage, and a very fatherly Hal Holbrook filled the gap until Mr. Pacino appeared. As I recall, Mr. Pacino had nothing to add to the conversation. He seemed exhausted. This was his Broadway debut, and it's an emotional and draining play.

Around that same time, I had another meeting or two with Mr. Pacino. He hung out after and between the shows in a nearby pub. I filled in for a friend of mine more than a few times, waiting tables at this pub.

Al had a friend he'd meet there, a charming, good-looking guy way out of my league. So when this good-looking, charming, out-of-my-league guy paid attention to me, my head spun. He invited me to his home, a boat docked at the 79th Street boat basin. I must have known there were private boats all over Manhattan. In school, we had to take the Circle Line Cruise at least once a year. But the concept of living in Manhattan on the river...wow!

I remember the black satin sheets, the boat gently rocking, and the guard walking with his dog up and down the pier while playing his harmonica. This was the most adult I had ever felt. But I sensed it could be dangerous, so I lied and said I was still a virgin and hoped it would mean something to him. After all, I put myself in this situation. To the charming, good-looking guy's credit, he left it at kissing and rubbing.

He gave me a package in the morning and asked if I would deliver it to Al that night. Later at the restaurant, it appeared to me that Al was not in great shape. While I passed his table, he swayed, and his head dropped dangerously close to his soup. I pulled his lovely black mane of hair up, and his face followed. I left the package with him.

That was my last day at that restaurant. I never saw or heard from the charming, good-looking, out-of-my-league guy again. And that is a very good thing, as I suspect he was not always a prince charming. I can only speculate as to what was in that package.

Barney called and told me he had a full-time job for me. I didn't really want to tie myself up, but at the time I had no acting tours booked. A new movie opened at the Cinerama Dome on 44th and Broadway. None of the regular usher-ettes wanted to take this job. Barney, our union boss, told me in no uncertain terms I was to work there. The Dome had a French Quarter theme. We had to wear high heels, fishnet stockings, and a black satin French maid's short— very short— outfit with a hot pink bodice, no wonder the regular ladies didn't want this job. The film was *2001: a Space Odyssey.*

2001 was a stoner's dream and my nightmare. Smoking was still legal in theatres, and it was never specified what kind of smoke. And the pot was the least of what some of the audience was ingesting. We all dreaded the end of the film.

"Janet, it's your turn."

"Ray, I was at the screen for the earlier show while you were having lunch at Horn & Hardhat."

"Janet, who's the boss?"

So, I dutifully trotted down to the screen. Toward the film's end, as the capsule hurls through space, the first three rows try their best to join the expedition. Like zombies, they would hurl their bodies toward the screen. A Cinerama screen works with louvers from top to bottom, like a huge vertical Venetian blind. If even one of these louvers got damaged, the following screening would be canceled while the technician fixed the screen.

The first zombie comes towards me, and I go right up to him. "Back, get back to your seat!"

"UU ggg UUU ahh." They had their own language.

"GET BACK TO YOUR SEAT!"

Fortunately, whatever they were on did not entice them to make me their dinner. But wearing the French maid outfit, the smell of pot, popcorn all over the seats, and giant roaches gave me the creeps. I'd be leaving the world of a union usher behind me.

Seven

I FELT PRETTY

Summer stock theatre was a great tradition, one that isn't as common anymore. They would hire a company of actors whose talent and range meant they could appear in each of the five scheduled shows. In some shows you might be the lead, while in the next you'd be a background player. Some of it is pretty amateurish theatre, but for me, it was glorious. I had auditioned with my standard eight bars, and expected the usual, "bye-bye." But no, I got the part. I was going to be Maria in Playhouse on the Hudson's version of *West Side Story*.

The theatre was only an hour or so away from NYC, so my whole family—aunts, uncles, cousins, and my father's crazy mother—came to see me in all the shows. Like many small theatres this was originally a movie house. One row of seats were taken out and a long table put over them. Each row seated about ten people, and there were probably nine rows. This kept attendance to under ninety-nine, which was an Actors Equity limit for special consideration; i.e., low to no payment for actors. Dressing rooms were downstairs, actually dressing ROOM.

After each performance my parents attended, I would wait to hear which actor my father thought was better than I. He never failed me. Sarah sang better, Ruth acted better, in general they were all just better than I was. He may have been right in his assessment, but what father doesn't support his daughter, even with a few white lies? Was I so geared up to hear the worst that I cherry-picked his critique of me? I came across a photo of my family sitting in their seats ready for the show to start; his expression was one of a proud father. Why couldn't he show me that face?

My best reviews came during *Gypsy* when I was in front of the curtain as Miss Cratchit. I'm on the phone pretending to talk to the boss in the light booth—a short, sweet speech intended to give the set people time to change sets.

Crash! The stage manager peeks his head out enough for me to see and whispered, "Keep going, the set fell down."

I went on well past my scripted lines. Improvising as I went, I have no idea what I actually said, but the audience ate it up. I felt as though I was five years old again entertaining the audience unscripted, just my imagination working overtime. The review for the show gave me a whole paragraph on my wonderful, funny performance. No mention of the set collapsing.

It was a beautiful sunny day and we were supposed to be in rehearsal, but no one was inside the theatre. I found them sitting outside on the lawn. It was June 6, 1968, and they were in a high state of distress. Most were in tears. Cynthia was yelling into space, using every curse word she knew. I walked over to them and asked, "What's up?"

Ruth, through her tears, replied, "They killed Bobby Kennedy."

Just the name sent me back to my high school drama class where I was performing a monologue when the news came of JFK's death. I remember being pissed that my performance was interrupted. Since I was born a card-carrying Republican, all I ever heard from my family was how frightened they were of this powerful, very Catholic family, and the Democrats. Just as back in high school, here on the lawn of the theatre, the appropriate response was beyond me.

"Oh, wow." And then I added, "So, are you ready to rehearse?"

Cynthia turned her rage to me. "You selfish fucking bitch." That was pretty harsh, even from this gal who I already knew didn't like me.

"Sorry . . ." I stammered. "Who killed him?" They all just glared at me.

Once again I was out of step with the appropriate human response to this tragedy. My consciousness hadn't been fully awakened yet. I really had no idea what Bobby Kennedy stood for, or why I should care about his being killed. Somehow I had forgotten the injustice I saw while performing for the Black school in Florida. I had only one goal in life, and politics/social injustice didn't play a part in reaching that goal. Eventually, the mourners came back to the stage to continue rehearsals. But now, the rest of the cast and I were estranged. Except for Ruth and my roommate Rebecca, who both stood by me. Ruth and I became very close as she was cast as Anita, and we had so much rehearsal time together.

The entire cast lived together in one huge house. Rebecca, my roommate, was beautiful, talented, and a bit strange. I'd met no one like her. She would have crazy dreams, wake up, and draw strange figures all over the walls. One morning she almost set herself on fire. She was steaming her face over the stove and the towel around her head caught the flame. I grabbed it off her head and threw it into the sink. All the while, she just smiled the most peaceful smile I've ever seen. She finally confided she was so frightened of performing that she was taking just about every drug there was. Her dreams and odd drawings were a result of these different drugs. I worried about her. And her drug use left me with no desire to even try pot. In fact, I became a bit "holier than thou" about it all. Probably supported by my Christian Science upbringing.

She was not the only one terrified of performing. Playing Maria terrified and excited me. But my name was on the marquee! This was stardom. One memorable performance, I somehow forgot the lyrics to *I Feel Pretty* and just kept muttering "I feel pretty" over and over until I got back on track. There was a reviewer in the audience that night who wrote I had a sweet but light voice, especially apparent in the *I Feel Pretty* number. Sometimes the critics go your way and other times they just don't. I kicked and screamed to no one that my voice wasn't light, I just forgot the lyrics. But we were on to the next play; my time as a star was over.

Many years later, after I changed careers and put my rear behind the camera, Carol Lawrence was a guest star on an episode of *Murder She Wrote* and I was the 1st Assistant Director. Carol was the original Maria on Broadway. While standing around shooting the breeze, I got the courage up to tell her I'd played Maria.

I confessed to her, "I can't hit those notes anymore."

"Neither can I, baby." I detected some sadness in her reply.

By late August, our time at Hudson Playhouse was ending. Politics had taken over, and the cast was glued to the news from Chicago of riots surrounding the Democratic Convention. I still didn't get it. My mother's family was still holding on to the righteousness of the Vietnam War, and I just followed along. Time and many miles of travel around America would start to alter my beliefs, ones I had accepted without question.

Eight

I'M LOOKING FOR MY PRINCE

September 1968 finally arrived, and the *Snow White* tour I'd been waiting for began. Once again we had performance dates in and around NYC before we took off for the heartland. This was a great way to get in rehearsal time while Kay Honey could watch us as she wasn't coming along on this tour.

Our station wagon seemed huge to me; it was green with wooden panels on each side. A small truck followed with all the sets and costumes. We left NYC behind and entered yet another new world for me: middle America. Pennsylvania would be our first stop. As we entered our destination, we saw a sign on the road welcoming us to the birthplace of a famous WWII flying ace. Now, it seems Pennsylvania was the birthplace of many WWII flying aces. As far as I know, this ace was no more notable than all the others, but he was from this small town.

We pulled up to our hotel and parked next to a row of Harleys. Once inside, we were greeted by the drivers of said Harleys. It seems our arrival was widely anticipated. We all felt as though the circus had arrived, and we were the elephants.

After introductions, the lobby emptied, and we were left with just two men wearing chaps, leather jackets, and Marlon Brando caps.

"Welcome to your home away from home." They were also the owners of this hotel. Looking towards the door they added in unison, "Is this everyone?" These men seemed to expect a theatre company comparable to the NYC gay men's choir, not our straggly *Snow White* group.

Our performance at the local high school was set for the next day. As I was unpacking, Bob, who was about to become my favorite puppeteer, knocked on my door. Bob was short with reddish hair, something I was not usually attracted to, and he was gay. No matter; I was developing a crush on Bob, or perhaps I had a crush on Sweet Pea, one of the seven dwarfs he manipulated. Here he was at my door with a hammer, nail, and towel.

"Bob," I asked in my sweetest way, "what's up with the hammer, towel, and nail?"

"Do you see the door has been split in the middle. Probably by an axe. All our doors are split just enough to allow a peeping Tom to watch us."

How gross! "So what are you doing?"

Duh, "I'm nailing this towel over the slit so no one can see inside the room."

Now Bob had positioned himself to be my savior. What other surprises did this town hold for us?

That night Fairy Godmother, Wicked Queen, and I went out to dinner while the guys went to a few local bars. There were no Harleys out in front of the S&W restaurant we went to, only a row of horses attached to their buggies.

I had never met an Amish person, and now they were all around us. We were definitely out of place here—women in long black skirts, men with equally long beards, and what seemed to be endless numbers of kids populated the S&W. Folks were staring at us. We quickly ate, left, and went to the movies.

We saw *Wait Until Dark*. I longed to look like Audrey Hepburn; I even got a short haircut and a perm, hoping to look like her. After the film, we took our time and strolled back to our hotel. Safely in our rooms, we all made sure our towels were still hanging in place on our doors. I didn't hear or see the guys until the next morning.

Turns out the guys had gone out drinking and dancing. They probably asked our hosts where to go for the night. Who knew that there were three bars in this small city, and two were gay bars. WWII flying ace, Amish by the score, and two gay bars!

Bob was particularly out of sorts that morning. It turns out a fight had broken out at the last bar they went to. Two women got into it, and one came back with a knife. One slash at the victim's breast and it was cut clean off, according to Bob. I didn't want to admit that I didn't know there was such a thing as gay women.

Now the others continued the story; Bob had fainted away and could add nothing more to last night's adventure. Ambulances, police, and our NYC stage crew and actors were in the middle of it all. As in many places we went, the drama was not ours to create, only to witness.

Performing at the high school was so odd, knowing this small Midwest city harbored major secrets. Did the Amish know about the gay bars? Did the kids know what their parents were up to at night? The gay bars, the hotel, and the dinner at the S&W would make an excellent beginning to a successful horror film. I could see it all. After all, at around seven years old, I remember writing an idea for a movie I called *The Fog*. In 1980, John Carpenter made a film called *The Fog,* I should ask him for some residuals. HA.

Kay asked us to stay another day; *Snow White* was such a success that the school wanted more. Or was it the hotel owners, the bar patrons, or the buggy drivers? Bob was the loudest "no" in the group. My experiences were leading me to believe that NYC got a bad rap for being outrageous. Middle America seemed to me to hold its own in the crazy department. Onward to the next small-town America.

We headed west to Illinois. We never played really big cities like Chicago, only the smaller ones off the interstate. Most of the time, the shows were at school auditoriums or gyms. But sometimes, we found other venues.

The venue in Springfield was an active movie theatre. We set up the stage behind the screen while the film was still running. One of the pitfalls of performing in a movie theatre is the greasy stale-smelling popcorn, and the ability of the kids to throw it at us. While we were setting up, we slipped and slid all over the stage on ancient popcorn, trying not to disturb the kids watching the film.

Once the movie was over, the button was pushed to raise up the screen, but it got stuck. Now the show would be delayed, and the kids—and their parents—were getting antsy. The theatre manager was beside himself, worried that we might ruin his precious screen. This was his theatre, and he was in control of it. Mind you, this screen was already filled with holes and various edible splatterings.

Even during the performance we were still sliding all over the floor. Our shoes would be forever slick with whatever they put on that popcorn. At all the performances, once the kids get into the show, it's magic. As the Wicked Queen displays the apple to Snow White, encouraging her to take a bite, all the children get into a chant, "Don't eat it! Don't eat it!"

They go on and on until Snow White can't resist any longer and takes a bite, which horrifies the kids. At this performance, one little boy way up in the back row got in between the appropriate chant with, "OH EAT IT, SNOW WHITE!!!"

The Wicked Queen and I could not go on. Tears were rolling down our faces. It could not have been a more perfect ending to our exhausting day in Springfield, Illinois. On to Indiana.

We hit Indianapolis, home of the Indianapolis 500, which meant nothing to most of us. After all, we were "artists." We took a city tour, and it was some sort of parade day. There was an electric energy in the city. It soon turned very dark. Rounding a corner, we came upon a part of the parade none of us wanted to see.

There had to be fifty men, all in some sort of Nazi uniform— swastikas on their raised arms. They were marching and shouting—what they shouted, we could not make out. This group was hell-bent on being angry, about what I had no idea. We all felt that violence was about to break out at any moment, and we returned to our motel rooms for the rest of the night.

It had been almost twenty-five years since my father returned from Germany, having fought in WWII. I wondered what he would make of all this.

We'd gone as far west as we were scheduled to go and we headed east towards home. On the way back through Illinois, in yet another small town, we spotted a pagoda-style home that turned out to be a Chinese restaurant. Wow, we were hungry for a slice of NYC, and nothing spelled hometown more to us at that moment than Chinese food.

Parking the station wagon and van, we noticed we were the only cars there, but it was late; perhaps the patrons were all home now. The host/server greeted us was an enormous smile. He was Chinese, so we were in for an excellent authentic meal. He seated us and took our orders. Not only were we hungry actors, but we were also tired and road-weary actors.

The food seemed to take forever. I went to use the restroom, which was just beyond the kitchen. As I passed the kitchen, I saw our host/server, now changed into a chef's outfit, cooking all by himself. Something about his demeanor tugged at my heart. He seemed indeed overworked but so happy, ignoring the fact that he had only one arm. Something from way back in my memory was fired and awake.

When I was very little my father, mother, and I would travel by car to surrounding states. This was before I was fully aware of the troubled life they had. And possibly they didn't understand the hard road their marriage was traveling toward. On one trip, I think to Martha's Vineyard, we stopped at a small coffee shop for breakfast. We sat at the counter and ordered, I must have been no more than six years old. I noticed the cook/waiter had only one arm. I'd never seen a person without an arm or leg before, so for me it was a bit creepy. My father knew instantly that here was a fellow WWII survivor, and he asked the cook where he had served. Then they had a conversation about the war, where they'd been, what they saw. I was too young to understand, but what I did understand was how important this little meeting was for my father. I never again heard him mention the war; I wish now I had asked him to talk about it and everything else in his life.

I wonder how our current host/server/chef/dishwasher had lost his arm?

When I got back to the table, our traveling players were becoming antsy; where was our food? I relayed the fact that our host/server was also the chef, in the kitchen all by himself. One trait most actors have in common is that they are sympathetic creatures, especially toward the underdog. This knowledge not only calmed them, but made each one want to volunteer to help in the kitchen.

Soon the host/server/chef appeared with the first of the dishes. Because he had only one arm, the service took as long as it did to prepare the meals. Every actor is also a waiter and each one of us so wanted to get up and help, but we suspected that our host was a proud man and that would have hurt him. We all finally had our meal and could not wait to dig in. But now we had a bigger problem: the food was horrible. One of us went to the restroom only to spot our host/server/chef adding bus person and washing dishes to his chores. We could not send these plates back still full of food.

Someone went out to the car to retrieve a garbage bag. One of us stood lookout for our host/server/chef/dishwasher as we emptied all contents of the plates into this garbage bag. When he returned, we gushed at the food and how we had eaten it all. His smile was worth it all. We tipped him significantly; after all, he had many hats to wear.

Sneaking out with the garbage bag, we piled into the station wagon. Miles away, we stopped and threw it in the trash. We found a hamburger drive-thru and chowed down. We left Illinois this time with our overly dramatic hearts broken and concerned that our acting was not good enough to fool our host/server/chef/dishwasher. Soon we crossed the boundary of this tour and were back in NYC.

By the end of this tour, we were at odds with each other. There were no more performances scheduled. We were all experiencing an actor's worst nightmare: unemployment. We said our goodbyes and escaped the station wagon, each to our own apartments, me to a new set of roommates. A strange but common phenomenon happens to actors on tour: we become dependent on each other. During my absence, life had gone on for all my friends—gone on without me. They were happy I was home but were otherwise busy. Not knowing who to have dinner with, I ended up calling another cast member. It turned out the same phenomenon happens in the film world. An artificial family is created for a short period of time. A family that is sometimes closer than blood relatives. No wonder so many relationships are formed during location work. It's so intense, lonely, and frightening. We cling to each other, not really knowing if we even like each other.

"What are you doing tonight? Dinner? Great, let's meet." There we all were together again.

I think the vision of America I saw on the road started to mature me. I saw things so differently from what I was brought up with. The next *Snow White* tour would not happen until the spring school season, so back to auditioning I went.

Nine

ME & SOPHIA LOREN

I registered with Central Casting in hopes of getting some work as an extra on film sets. The phone rang, and there was my first film job. I would be a stewardess. It was ironic to me as I had applied and was rejected by Eastern Airlines. It turns out no flight attendant in their world would have bad skin. This would be a Sophia Loren/Carlo Ponte film. The Italian title was *Mortadella,* but it was released in America as *Lady Liberty.* It was 1970, Sophia Loren was a massive movie star, and her husband Carlo Ponte was a prolific producer. After all her magnificent performances, this film was an expensive disappointment for them.

My first day started at 10 p. M. I took the approximate hour ride on the E train (the same subway I took my whole life back and forth to get to my home in Queens) and arrived early; I was always early. Then I sat around in the TWA terminal for hours. This is an everyday activity for extras on film sets.

Mr. Ponte insisted on bringing in an entire Italian crew. Of course, the local IATSE (International Alliance of Theatrical Stage Employees) demanded a whole American crew as well. So it was a sizable multilingual affair. At that time, the union regulations insisted on a meal break after six hours, putting our lunch at 4 a. M. The Italian crew had pasta and wine, and the American crew whined. That was not their sort of breakfast. So then, after a few days, there were two lunch lines—one for the Italian crew and eggs and bacon for the Americans.

I loved airports as much as my father did. Crazy as it seems, we also loved the smell of jet fuel. We'd drive to La Guardia airport, go to the observation deck, and dream. We both seemed to want to get away as fast as we could. I knew where I wanted to go. I wonder what world he hoped to escape to. But for now, I was content with just sitting in the VIP lounge of the new TWA terminal.

Soon they got around to calling us into wardrobe to be fitted in our uniforms. Oh, my goodness, I checked myself out in the mirror as a stewardess. Everyone else seemed blasé, but I was beside myself. I was so excited. I loved my time on stage, but film was my magic carpet ride. Eventually, we were bussed to the hangar where the just-arrived jet awaited its film debut. Since this was an actual working TWA plane, our time working on it was limited.

The easiest way to shoot on a plane is to use a mock-up. It's a shell built on a stage with a complete interior. In the 1960s–'70s, the film work in NYC was sparse compared to today, so they had no mock-up planes sitting on sound stages; we had to work on an actual Boeing 707. Working on a real aircraft created lots of challenges for the crew. All the equipment is first hoisted up to the tiny plane doors, then carried down narrow aisles. Think how long it takes passengers to board a plane! Crews with lights, cameras, and sound equipment—well, that takes forever. But I was having a load of fun and learning as I got paid.

Back then, I had no idea what an Assistant Director did. There are many descriptions of what a 1st AD does. I like this Google explanation: "The 1st AD is the director's right hand. They plan the filming schedule, working with the director, director of photography, and all heads of departments to ensure an efficient shoot. Because they run the shooting set, they have gobs of responsibilities. Including making sure the background actors are placed correctly, although it's usually the 2nd AD that places the background actors." I could never have imagined that years later I would make my living as a 2nd, then 1st AD.

On the first night of shooting, one of the assistant directors lined up all the "stews" for inspection. Then suddenly, one of the female extras was chosen and taken away from the rest of us. The remaining "stews" remained sitting in an area of the hangar with space heaters and were out of the crew's way. Then the gossip started.

"Well, we know who will get that job," commented one of the other stewardesses.

"What job?" I was clueless.

She went on, "See what a slut will do for a speaking part."

Speaking part? I was totally lost. I was about to be educated. A speaking part was available, and the AD could suggest to the director which of us to give that part to. I was still so naive that I needed it spelled out for me. One of the more seasoned extras did just that.

"She'll do him or one of his friends, and then she'll have the speaking part."

Do him? What the heck!

This seasoned extra looked at me as if I was from Mars. "SEX, don't you get it?"

Getting a speaking part meant you could join the Screen Actors Guild (SAG) and put more money in your paycheck. The Snow White in me was shocked and frightened at the same time. What was I getting into in the film world?

The next night the plane was late arriving from wherever it had been. So the director, Mario Monicelli, had time to line us up for a look-over. It turned out the speaking part was still open.

Suddenly I was asked to come forward and say, "Welcome to New York." Then I was told to give my information to the AD; I was getting my SAG card.

I felt my fellow stewardess' glaring at me from behind. Especially that gal who thought she had it in the bag. I was also confused. Did this mean I had to do some sort of sex act? The joke would have been on the recipient. I was still sexually lost. But no, it was all legit.

That same night Ms. Loren's makeup artist called me to where he had set up his station. I was sure he would talk to me about the scars on my face. My acne was somewhat under control, but the pockmarks were forever; they were not going away. Once while entering a dimly lit bar, a man (I hate to give him that much credit) lit a match to my face and shouted out, "Who let the sponge in?" Try living with that all these years.

But this Italian man, who painted Sophia Loren's face each day, only wanted to show me how I could make full use of my "lovely eyes." He never mentioned my skin. He explained the secret of how he applied Ms. Loren's makeup to give all the attention to her eyes. He could do the same for me. I had no idea if this was a come-on, or a man genuinely interested in making me beautiful. Possibly, he was just bored like the rest of us, waiting for the camera to roll. When he was finished, I admitted I did look pretty.

Finally, the night came for me to say my one line. "Welcome to New York." I was a star. When I dragged my friends Michael and Alice to see the film, my line had been cut out, and if you blinked, I was gone from the screen. My friends consoled me with dreams of next time. However, I had my SAG card, and no one could take that away.

In the film, Ms. Loren gets off the plane and heads to customs with her big ole mortadella (ham). This took three days of filming. On the second day, I was walking with three other stews, and Ms. Loren had caught up to our group when we wrapped for the night. We would resume in the exact same spot the following evening. When we came back the next night, we took our precise places from the night before, only there was a man with us who had not been there before. I knew enough about filming to realize this would be a mismatch. As a kid, I was always bossing— or directing—my friends around. I guess that since I could not control my home life, I would try and control the life outside my home. And now I couldn't shut up and accused the interloper of not being there the night before. He angrily disputed my claim.

I was so sure of myself that I called the 2nd AD over. One of their responsibilities is to have the right actors in the right place. Once again, the new person asserted his position in line. The 2nd AD chose to believe this man over the girl, me.

I was so sure of myself that I had the 1st AD called over to finalize the dispute. He brushed it aside; surely, a young female extra could not be correct. Lighting was completed, and we waited for Ms. Loren to join us for the filming.

She waltzed out and greeted each of us individually.

"Good evening, good day, good evening, and you, sir, were not there."

Ha! Vindication.

I knew I was right and felt such a surge of power. How I knew this and how important this incident would become for me was a mystery. I had a talent: I was very observant. I could not see how this talent would fit into a world that only had places for men. But I got such a rush from being right. I understood something fundamental to the film world without ever being taught.

During my time in the early '70s as an extra, I saw few, if any, women on set. Even hair and makeup artists were men. The DGA (Directors Guild of America) directing team members were always all men. What was there for me to aspire to? I did not see myself getting to do any of the jobs except acting, and that was certainly an uphill battle.

"Welcome to New York" got me into the Screen Actors Guild, and I started looking for a film agent. I had new professional pictures taken and sent them to every agent I knew. I'd get many interviews, and each went the same way. Those pictures of mine had been retouched, and when the agent saw me in person, they reacted the same way. "You have to do something about your skin."

I did a few more films as an extra, but I knew the doors that had barely opened would be closing on my film acting career. All this failure began to play on my nerves, and the digestive problems that started on that first children's theatre tour worsened. I developed spastic colitis, IBS, as it is called today. A horrible thing for anyone to have, it became a living nightmare for me.

I'd start for an audition fresh and clean, and soon I would be headed back home to change clothes. My bowels had their own life, and I would lose control on buses, subways, and waiting rooms. I had to have enough money to take a quick cab home, praying I would not embarrass myself. Still unfamiliar with doctors or wanting to please my mother, I sought healing. I started to follow Christian Science practices for myself.

I knew all about mind over matter and the power of belief in a higher ability to heal, which is a tenet of Christian Science. When I was seven, I tried to stop my mother, father, and grandmother's argument. It had gone on for far too long and was getting out of control. The only way to stop them was to be even more dramatic than they were.

I marched into the kitchen, screaming and shaking.

"STOP, STOP FIGHTING!"

They did. Their faces showed how worried they all were about me. I won, but upon leaving the kitchen, I blacked out and fell hard to the floor. Now I had their attention. However, there was a price to pay, and I did not walk or eat for five days after that. My parents placed me on the living room sofa, and all was calm in the house for those five days. I had some sort of phantom paralysis.

When I came around, I asked for a steak and iced tea. My mother was fine with that. My father said since I had not eaten in five days, I should start with something easier to digest. Anything I wanted, my mother tried to supply, so she went off to the A&P to buy my dinner. The fighting resumed, but now it was over my steak. Was this the beginning of my problems? Or did it start when my father would take residence in our one bathroom for hours? This was his place to smoke and read the racing papers. When he'd finally emerged, I could not bear to enter until the smoke and his presence cleared out. I taught myself not to need the bathroom, but nature will have its way.

Ten

NO ᏠEWS OR ᏝLACKS ALLOWED

I enjoyed being Snow White. Perhaps I related to her sad family situation or her never feeling good enough about herself. For the hour or so that I was on stage, I was "the fairest of them all." The shiny apple she is asked to bite-what a great metaphor for the Hollywood promise I still clung to. The Wicked Queen wants youth, beauty, and eternal life. Almost everyone in Hollywood has bitten that apple. Sometimes we get the sweet, tasty side; sometimes, the bite is bitter and poisonous. But, at this point in my life, I still had stars in my eyes. The reality of Hollywood would take years to show itself to me.

We were to be off again on tour from NYC to the South. Back in the same green station wagon with its faux wooden panels, we passed the New Jersey industrial section off I-95, which anyone who's ever been there recognizes that odor. Although I was looking forward to this tour, I was conflicted. I had gotten a job as a stand-in for Ruth Gordon on the film *Harold and Maude,* which became a classic. A stand-in job is just that. During the lighting, the star is elsewhere while the crew lights the set with someone of the same height and coloring. So, Ruth and I were similar.

I decided to turn it down as I felt obligated to Kay Rockefeller. Kay was with us for part of the tour. She was driving, and I got to bragging.

"I just turned down working on a new film with Ruth

Gordon." I thought everyone would feel sorry for me, but happy I was with them.

Kay very sweetly responded. "Oh, too bad, I had another Snow who could have taken over."

That shut me up. Understanding I wasn't the only one in the whole of NYC who could be Snow White, wow.

Our first performances were in North Carolina. Wake Forest University was, to me, a dream. What struck me first was how clean it was. Sparkling brick buildings with green, green lawns. It just felt comfortable and inspired. For the first time, I thought I had missed something by not attending college. The faculty members always invited us to join them at their homes. We had a lovely tea; yes, the crusts were cut off the sandwiches at one professor's home.

Kay and this woman had a great relationship. I listened to their conversation, hoping their brilliance would rub off. Kay mentioned to her friend that she dreaded the last few stops we were headed towards, and her friend nodded in agreement. I tried to understand her reluctance, but understanding lay in the future for me. Unlike some other places we played, here at the University they never treated us as anything but equals. They respected theatre, even children's theater. And who could resist the delicious Moravian cookies the region is famous for?

We only had one new crew member, and he was one of the puppeteers. But he soon fell in line with the others in teasing me. Bob was still handling the strings for Sweet Pea. For me, most of Snow's deathbed scene was anything but sad. The puppeteers who hung over me, dancing their string counterparts up and down my body, would do anything to get me to laugh. Many a time, they won. I would place the wilting wedding bouquet over my tummy to hide its rising and falling as I giggled away. All those tinny puppet feet tickled. They'd whisper all sorts of nonsense.

"Cinderella is fooling around with your prince."

"I hear Goldilocks is gay; she cut her hair off to look like a guy."

"No, she got her hair caught in the lawn mower."

"I heard that prince of yours is cheating on you with Dumpy."

When the prince finally showed up to kiss me out of my death slumber, they'd chant in unison, just as loudly as the kids, "Kiss her, KISS HER!" Then all the smooching sounds they could think of rang in my ear. Including most of the boys going, "UGH."

Each tried to tickle me with the puppet, blaming the puppet as if it had a mind of its own. I guess working in children's theatre, one has to tap into one's own childhood. And they did that very well.

Bob, my knight in shining armor, was back on tour and still operating Sweet Pea. I had not seen him since the last *Snow* tour, and we resumed our friendship. Somewhere along the line, I began to confuse Sweet Pea—who loved Snow very much—with Bob, his handler. It appeared that Bob also began to confuse the two as we always hung out together. From town to town, we sat next to each other in the station wagon. We'd even have dinner together. One day Bob's best friend took me aside to explain that Bob was through and through a gay man and not interested in me, at least the way I wanted him to be. The thing is, he had to take Bob aside to explain to him that the friendship was getting confused.

The other puppeteers got the word, and their job now was to separate Bob and me. In those days I think the concept of bisexuality was off limits. Life seemed very black and white— no gray area was allowed, although it surely existed. This estrangement was sad for both of us. It was, after all, Bob who had come to my rescue after discovering the peephole split in our hotel room doors. It was Bob and I passing the long, tedious hours driving from town to town with endless conversations. I was the one who didn't laugh at Bob's fainting after the breast-cutting event. Would Sweet Pea love me as much now that Bob and I were separate? Which was my biggest fear—losing him or Sweet Pea?

I began to resent gay men, thinking other men were taking all the good guys. But I loved all the guys on the tour and adored Paul, my gay cousin. I was simply jealous that it appeared gay men had an easier time meeting gay men than I had meeting a straight guy. But that wasn't true either. I had female friends meeting men all the time. I think I wore a sign that read "pious virgin, watch out." Sex was so confusing for me. I began to feel very alone with no one to confide in.

We hit Alabama, end of the line. We had four days of performances booked in Birmingham. Kay had left the tour after Wake Forest, and Henry, our stage manager, was in charge. He was older; well, when you are just 20 years old, everyone is older. I'm sure he started out as an actor, but found continued work stage managing.

"Henry, I thought we were booked to perform in Birmingham. Why are we staying in Decatur? It's like over two hours away!"

He took a deep breath and launched into the explanation as he knew it. "Kay could not find rooms for us in Birmingham."

I think he hoped this would be enough for me.

"That's crazy. There have to be hotels closer to our shows than this one."

He took an even deeper breath. "Of course, there are. But they wanted Kay to sign a letter that there were no Jews or Negroes in our company, and of course, she refused to sign it."

I showed my ignorance, "We don't have any Jews or Negroes in this company, so why couldn't she just sign the damned thing, and we could stay in Birmingham."

"Listen, you are lucky you have work. Kay never wanted to take this show here."

"Why?"

"It's the whole 'skin as white as snow' thing. That line represents what is beautiful about Snow White. And it's out of step with the times. The Daughters of the American Revolution sponsored this tour. Kay begged them to sponsor a different play. They were determined it be Snow White. If you don't understand this, well, I can't help you."

My not understanding of our situation must have seemed to the rest as borderline bigotry on my part, or at least a profound ignorance. I still had a lot of growing up before me. I learned and grew up a bit more with each mile we traveled.

On every drive down and back to Birmingham in our green station wagon with New York plates, we were randomly stopped by the police.

"Henry, what is going on? Can't you drive better?"

"It's not me; it's us. Terrible things happen here. We are targets driving a station wagon with New York license plates. In 1964, three activists were pulled from their station wagon and brutally killed."

Five years had passed since those Mississippi Burning murders. It wasn't just that we were considered East Coast "N" lovers, every guy in that car was gay, and they knew a different but still violent fear of those traffic stops. An officer would come to the driver's door with his hand on his holster; Henry would roll down the window and politely asked, "What's the problem, officer?" Usually, I'd be in the middle next to the driver. I learned to lean over and smile my best Snow smile at the officer.

We were stopped by some men who were not in any uniform.

These were the most frightening times. We often got out of the car and did some dog and pony show to prove we were just actors, not agitators. Henry had our itinerary, which he'd pull out to prove we were just doing children's theatre, not raising awareness. After all, we had the seal of the DAR with us.

Before the tour was over and we'd make our way back to NYC, we shared a short vacation on the beach in Panama City. It was my twenty-first birthday, and the gang had planned a surprise for me. Stubbornly sitting on the beach, I was in denial that the wind and waves were picking up. I never wanted to come in from the beach.

When I was very young, I was alone on a dock at the lake we were visiting. I saw my Father on the land waving furiously at me. "Get back here! A storm is coming! Come on, jump in, swim!"

Nothing could get me off that dock. Finally, he took a rowboat and came for me. He wasn't angry. I think he was frightened.

Here I was a grownup—well, I could vote now—woman refusing to leave a beach that a hurricane was headed directly for. Finally, the group talked some sense into my stubborn head. Reluctantly I acknowledged that, yes, a hurricane was upon us. We got into the Big Green Boat, as we now called the wagon, and moved on to a higher, drier country.

Once safely on dry land, they produced the cake and gifts they had intended to present to me on the beach. Twenty-one, legal age, stuck in a small motel, exhausted from the storm and the drive to safety. Indeed, a coming-of-age event.

Once again, we headed home to NYC.

I toured on and off as *Snow White* for five years. During these tours, I could watch and feel the country changing. Each performance of Snow White starts with Snow as a child after her mother has died. She is brought out on stage and handed over to the Wicked Step Queen. In each city, a young Snow White was chosen from the girls in the school we performed at. A remarkable thing happened at the last performance I was to do back in Winston-Salem. The classmates chose a little Black girl to come on stage as Snow White. They cheered her on, oblivious to the "skin as white as snow" line in the play. We were all so struck by this change that had come about in those five years. We had a hard time going on with tears welling in our eyes.

My very last performance of *Snow White* was a twofer (two shows in one day). The morning show was at the Willowbrook State School in Staten Island. This horrendous institution was meant to house 4,000 children with mental disabilities but had 6,000 residents, all kids.

Not too much later, the conditions at Willowbrook hit the headlines for appalling and criminal medical practices. It was something out of a horror film. None of us wanted to get out when our station wagon pulled up. It was a huge building with a haunting grey facade, and hundreds of tiny faceless windows. We heard screams from inside as we approached the steps to enter. I was not the only one who didn't want to go in. We were met by a man in a doctor's jacket that was dirty.

Kids, many of whom looked to be of adult age, shuffled into the auditorium. It was chaos. As we performed, the kids began to calm down. We realized how important just showing up was for these kids. Many of these children at Willowbrook were there because of their violent actions. And many more were there because doctors persuaded their parents to lock them up for their physical and mental challenges. Yet they were all lumped together. We were there in 1972, but it wasn't until 1987 that the scandal of Willowbrook could not be hidden any longer. It was shut down.

We were all horribly affected by our time at Willowbrook and never expected how different our second performance of the day would be. We arrived at the United Nations' shiny, pristine building on 46th Street and 1st Avenue. We parked at a loading dock and were greeted by a handful of dignitaries who ushered us into our dressing area. This performance would be for the diplomats' children. Everything about the UN spelled importance: it was sparkling clean, almost antiseptic. But kids are kids, and they loved us. Even though I do believe for many, English was a second language.

I was almost 25 years old; I wanted my children's theatre days to be over. Deep inside, I knew my career was going nowhere. I could travel forever, moving from Snow to The Wicked Stepmother as I aged. I didn't want that. Packing up and moving from one small town or city to another isn't glamorous. It's exhausting. Coming back home and starting life all over again is risky. Friends might have moved on during my absence. I wanted to stay put, get my own apartment, and create a life for myself. I saw how that was not in the cards if I continued traveling so much.

I thought I'd hung up this vagabond lifestyle forever. How ironic that years later, I'd find myself packing up and traveling from one place to another when I signed on to the world of film.

And by that time, I had a promise to fulfill—a promise I made to my mother.

Eleven

I'M A WAITRESS

Between acting tours, I not only found work as an usherette but also, alas, as what else...a waitress. It's impossible to talk about being an actor without talking about waiting tables. I found out that waiting tables is hard work. The wages are low, the stress is high, and the only way to take home some cash is if the customer tips well. And the only way that happens is if you are friendly, calm, and patient. Shamefully, it didn't hurt for me to wear a short skirt.

Fortunately, some restaurants saw the value of hiring smart, talented, good-looking actors to serve their patrons, while others would shut the door in one's face as soon as they realized all the prospective employee wanted was to be a famous actor. My friend and fellow actor, Ruth Saada, recommended me for a wait job at Chips Pub. Ruth was Anita to my Maria when we did summer stock. Chips Pub was located across the street from the ABC news broadcast center on Columbus Avenue; ABC is still there, but not the bar. It was a typical NYC watering hole; long and narrow, nothing unusual except for the patrons.

Before and after the on-air reporters delivered the local tragedies on both the 6 p. M. and 11 p. M. newscasts, they would stop in the pub. We could watch them on the TV located over the bar and know instantly what mood they would be in when their feet crossed the threshold. The 6 p. M. star news-caster was Roger Grimsby. Often, I thought his name served him. He could be quite grim.

I was beginning to have some social and political thoughts that belonged to me and not ones handed down from my family. However, I would not dare to enter a political discussion with any newscasters. Some reporters were content to be "regional" reporters. Others, like Roger, were bitter that their careers didn't take them to the mother ship—network news. One thing they had in common was that they were journalists, not actors pretending to be journalists. And, of course, they were all men. That did not change for many years.

Chips Pub also had a group of regulars who were not working at ABC. Two of these were brothers who owned a private detective agency. They were in their fifties. It was one big happy, familiar family. The brothers seemed like nice unremarkable guys everyone knew, including all the on-air personalities. They always wore dark suits with ties and white shirts. The only thing that set them apart from the reporters was their size. They were a bit chubby. Occasionally, they would disappear for a few days or even a week. We were used to them disappearing and reappearing without notice. I thought they were out finding missing husbands, etc.

One snowy winter night, one of the brothers—I'll call him John—called me over to him. "Janet, you look cold. It's too cold here in New York. My brother and I are off to Puerto Rico for the weekend. Sally over there is coming with us." Sally was another waitress there; she was in her late twenties—I liked her and trusted her. "So, come with us."

John took a sip of his beer and continued in a casual manner. "Hey, no strings attached. You can have your own room. We have a little business to attend to, and then we will gamble, eat a good dinner, swim, and relax."

By now, his brother Alex had joined in. "Seriously, if you are concerned, we can call your father and get his permission."

Oh yeah, that would be the day. And I'm sure they were banking on my not wanting my father involved. Swimming in mid-winter was beyond tempting. I said give me a day, but I knew I'd go. I trusted them, and Sally told me they were harmless. Sex with an older chubby man—no, that wasn't a picture I could form in my brain.

Sally, the brothers, and I arrived in Puerto Rico. The sun was so warm and inviting. Our driver passed this beautiful beach, and I almost cried joyfully. But we passed the beachside hotels. We checked into a hotel that was not exactly the resort-type environment I expected. But since I'd never been to a resort on the beach, I had nothing to compare it to. It seemed huge to me. Sally and I sat as the brothers checked in. Then we went off to our rooms. There were only two rooms, one for each brother. I was naive in thinking that we would have separate rooms.

"John, I thought you said I'd have my own room."

"They were booked up, but you can take the bedroom. I'll sleep in the living room."

You bet your bottom dollar you will. Well, that's what I was thinking. I didn't say anything.

"Come on, change, and let's eat and then go to the casino."

I wasn't sure what to wear to a dinner at a resort; I'd never been to one. I had a little sun dress with me—it was blue, which always worked well with my eyes. John had a leisure suit on. Since he knew this hotel that must have been appropriate.

We all met in the lobby and then proceeded to dinner. Sally had a dress with some sparkles on it. That made me feel under-dressed; however, both brothers were in those casual leisure suits, both the same color, dark blue. It was a tense and quiet dinner. This restaurant was very plain; it felt more like a cafeteria. The brothers seemed agitated. I attributed this to their wanting to get on with the gambling. I know how gamblers get when they think they are missing the "big one." After all, I grew up with this. So I chalked up their emotions to the need to gamble. We had a quick dinner, and then they accompanied Sally and me to the casino.

I had never been to a casino. The ones in the Bond movies provided the fantasy look I was expecting. This was not that. The smell of stale cigarette smoke was the first thing I noticed. Then the noise. Machines zinging, bells going off, and the sounds of happy people and desperately unhappy people. A cacophony of ear-splitting sounds. Even the carpet made me dizzy. Years later, I found my fantasy casino on a trip to Europe that included Monte Carlo. It was ornate, with crystal chandeliers, velvet curtains, gowns, and tuxedos. This cavernous room was nothing like that Monte Carlo casino. This supposedly fun experience had at least two things not working in its favor: I hated gambling and smoking, both courtesy of my four-pack-a-day gambler father. Why had I agreed to this?

The brothers handed us a wad of bills and told us to have fun. Then they were off. I fully expected them to be back within minutes. They came to gamble, so where were they going? Sally and I hung out for a while, anticipating their return. She was having a much better time than I was. The smoke, the noise, and the anticipation that they would be returning soon got to me, and I retired to my room.

I decided it was safer to take the sofa. No confusing signals that way. It was late, maybe 4 a.m., when John got back. Gone was the pleasant gentleman I'd been assured of. He wanted payment for my "vacation." This could have gone badly. He pushed just so hard, then stormed off to the bedroom. I lied and said I was still a virgin. That seemed to help him make his decision to leave me alone. I was left on the sofa. Sleep didn't come at all. Now it all seemed stupid and slightly dangerous.

Maybe I liked that part. I couldn't understand how this older man would think I'd be interested in him. I had a lot to learn about men.

Our weekend adventure came to a close early the next day. We checked out, had breakfast at the airport, and took the first flight home. We were there for about 24 hours, and as far as I could tell, the brothers never got to gamble even a dime. Maybe that's why they were both uneasy and in a sour mood. I was not hungry, so I wandered away from breakfast. I bought a tiny oil painting of the beach in a small airport art gallery. The closest I would come to the water on that trip. I used the money I had not spent at the casino for this trinket. For some reason, this upset my date, and it was a silent and tense flight home. Where had these brothers been all night?

About eight years later, after I moved to Los Angeles, a friend sent me a copy of the latest New York Magazine. There on the cover were the two brothers from NYC. The article exposed who they truly were; they were not mild-mannered private detectives but major CIA agents.

They traveled to hot spots and did whatever it was under-cover agents do. Their MO was to take women with them as beards. That way, they were just two brothers taking their lady friends on vacation. Thank goodness I was not named in the article, but I was indeed in those pages.

The article detailed just a few of the many trips they had taken. One, a trip to Egypt, and then another, a quick trip to PR. While in Puerto Rico, the brothers took a boat to Cuba for a meeting. It also told of the two young women who accompanied them—how they gambled throughout the night, waiting for the brothers to return. I have no idea what the purpose of this visit for them was. But in the late '60's and early '70's, we, as a country, were always messing with Cuba.

I remember feeling quite ashamed that I had been so naive and gullible to be used. I was not given the option to be a CIA operative. I'm not sure I ever would have agreed to that. I wondered if the newscasters that hung out with us knew who the brothers really were. I will never know the answer to that.

My life pattern was becoming apparent. Go on a tour, come home, get a new restaurant job while continuing to usher on Broadway, audition, and start the circle all over again. Now I had enough money to have my very own apartment on the Upper West Side—a studio apartment on the lobby floor with a backyard. I passed a pet store on my way to work at my new restaurant. There in the window sat the soon-to-be love of my life. Sam, a black Yorkipoo. And my new apartment was perfect for us.

Columbus Avenue was going through a revitalization period, and this smart young couple opened a hip restaurant very near my new apartment. The day chef was Jacques, and Robert handled the night shift. Both were friends from their hometown near Paris.

They would meet and chat, in French, between shifts. I waited tables there at night. I don't believe either was genuinely interested in me other than to have another notch in their belts or beret. Nonetheless, the flirting was very ego satisfying.

Jacques lived on the street behind mine. His apartment building also had a backyard garden, and a fence separated us. He would be on his balcony waiting for me to let Sam out. His robe tied loosely; he'd flash me his naked body. I don't understand why some men enjoy doing this. This just delighted him, and I really couldn't have cared less. The more I didn't care, the more he did it. Now Jacques professed his love for me everywhere. From his balcony, passing on the street, and, worst of all, at the restaurant.

Then Robert got in on the act. Even though he was married to a gorgeous French woman, Robert's ego forced him to make his play. I admit I was dizzy with all this attention. He was probably the first of many unavailable men I was attracted to. That would become a pattern for me. I don't think I ever wanted him to leave his wife. I seemed oddly comfortable with competition even as I professed to hate it. I understand now that not having good role models growing up meant I didn't trust falling in love and being loved. The best way to avoid that trap was to fall in love with unavailable men. When, really, I was the unavailable one.

French women are not to be trifled with, so it was wise of me to leave Robert alone, which meant finding a new restaurant to work at. Waitressing was becoming more important to me than acting. Or I should say, having money was becoming more important to me.

My little basement studio on West 95th Street was heaven—no roommates, just good friends, my little dog Sam, and well-paying waitress jobs. I was enjoying a newfound sense of stability. A life I could control—or thought I could control. The goal of fame seemed less important than living away from Queens and my family. And I hated auditioning. But how could I just give it up? Acting was all I thought I knew how to do. My mother and I spoke on the phone almost every day. On one occasion, I called with a specific need. I wanted her permission not to go to an audition that day. I wanted her usual encouragement, but what I got was, "Well, what do you want to do?"

What did I want to do? Each audition terrified me. I don't know which was worse: being rejected or having one of my "accidents" on the way to an audition. I began questioning whether performing was worth what I put myself through. Auditioning is dreadful, and I wasn't sure getting the part would be a reward. The constant proving of my talent and that I was worthy of calling myself a working actress plagued me. And I was always dealing with how I looked. Now, my father's negative voice was replaced by my negative mental nagging.

To top it all off, my new waitress job at Roast Beef N' Brew (RBNB) was fun. This restaurant was on the ground floor of an office building on the corner of 59th and Madison Avenue. The restaurant was managed by a very large restaurant corporation—a corporation rumored to be mob-related, but rumors constantly plagued the restaurant business. By now, I was a member of three unions: Actors Equity, Screen Actors Guild, and Theatrical Employees Union (ushers). With this job, I became a union waitress.

I had never been to college, but in my fantasy, Roast Beef N' Brew was what it would have been like — just without the textbooks. All the wait staff and bus staff were around the same age. Some were actors, some were writers, and some were actually going to college. We were, for the most part, friends.

I met my first Black friend, Latisha—a beautiful young model. Although NYC is a melting pot, each borough had its own demography. Growing up, my section of Queens was populated by all-white folk. There were Black students at my high school, but we never mingled.

One of the waiters I became close to was named Bear. He was just that—a bear of a guy. He was the sweetest man and seemed to have a crush on me. I didn't feel the same for him. I do not know this for a fact, but rumor had it that there was a sort of high-class brothel on one of the office floors above us. Some ladies who reportedly worked upstairs would hang with us when they got bored or were otherwise unoccupied. Bear fell deeply in love and ended up marrying one of these gals.

Eduardo, one of our busboys, was from Argentina. To me, he was exotic and adorable at the same time. He seemed to feel the same about me. The kitchen was in the basement, and coming back up the stairs with a loaded tray was tricky.

"Hey, let me carry that for you." Eduardo seemed to be right there all the time.

"Thanks, Eduardo."

Then I'd hear his friends start to almost giggle at his blatant antics. Soon he asked me to go to lunch with him. I could not break through the barriers my family had installed in me regarding "others." Did the slur my father used—"spic"—when he saw me walking with my Puerto Rican friend also apply to Eduardo? And why did I still care what my father thought? So I passed him up, and he quickly found affection with Joanie. She and I were both the actresses in the group. And I admit I was jealous when I saw how loving he became towards her.

Then a new night manager appeared. He had a boyish charm. And with his good looks, he was dangerous. Mr. Black ended up being my first consistent sexual partner. I was now 22, supporting myself, and falling in love. Yet, each time we had sex, I could feel my mother's disapproval. Of course, she knew nothing of the relationship. And never would.

Eveline, one of my best friends at RBNB, saw this mistaken romance with Mr. Black coming from a mile away. She was the most practical gal I'd ever met. She was bold and frank and always in the right place at the right time. The apartment she lived in was a result of her excellent timing.

We were chatting one day about our apartments. She told me this story—true or not it's a great story. "I was passing the funeral home when this person fell out of one of the upper floor windows. I saw my chance at a vacant apartment, and I went inside and applied then and there for that newly vacant space."

"Wait a minute; you live on the top floor of a funeral parlor?"

"Yeah, it's not like I see dead bodies. I go in a different door and up to my rooms."

Then I'd see a twinkle in her eye. "What, what else?"

"Well, sometimes I visit Roger, the mortician, and we sort of fool around down there." She never had a thought about living above dead bodies. My imagination went to a dark place, and I needed to move off this conversation.

"Ugh, no more stop!"

However squeamish I was, I never turned down traveling the city in the hearse she convinced her landlord—the funeral director and sometimes romantic partner—to lend us. It's impressive how traffic gives way to a long black wagon out of some sort of respect for the contents. I never gave it much more thought other than how convenient it was until one night, there were three of us out on the town: me, Eveline, and a body in a casket.

"Eveline, why is there a casket in the back?"

"It was a busy day."

I am not buying this. "Is there a body in that casket?"

She knows I'm about to vomit. "NO, are you crazy? You think I would steal a body?"

This seemed like a bald-faced lie to me. Why would anyone store an empty casket in the hearse? Her eyes would sparkle when she lied. She got a giggle out of scaring me.

She would tease me endlessly over my infatuation with Mr. Black. "Janet's got a BOYFRIEND." She was like a six-year-old. I knew deep down she didn't like him, but I was sunk, head over heels. Even on my off days, I would find ways to end up at the restaurant to spend time with him.

One night I used the excuse of picking up my paycheck to see him. On the way in, I noticed a car parked outside. It caught my attention as it was in a no-parking zone, and the auto was older, not the Madison Avenue limo type. For some reason, I noted the license plate number.

Standing with Mr. Black, flirting away, I suddenly felt a pistol in my back. The gunslinger says, "Just act cool, and everything will be alright."

Mr. Black was given a bag and told to collect all the money from the registers. I was to stay with the gunman as a hostage. Did I expect Mr. Black to wrestle him for the gun? Not really. But being an actress, I went into performance mode.

Turning my head a bit, I told the gunman, "I'm going to cry."

"Be cool, and nothing will happen." The gunman and I went back and forth with this performance art until I did start to cry. I don't know if the patrons (only a few left that night) knew we were being robbed. It was so quiet, our hearts beating louder and louder. My tears were threatening to erupt into sobs, and my gunman was getting nervous. He pulled the hammer back to shut me up, and the noise almost sent me to the floor. Both of us were losing control.

He called Mr. Black back, took the bag full of money, and was gone. I fell into Mr. Black's arms; that sounds so romantic. He sat me down and got a glass of something to calm me. He then went into manager business mode calling the robbery in. First to the restaurant's headquarters and then to the police.

When the police arrived, they asked how much the robber had gotten. I could tell by the number of patrons each night roughly how much cash would be in the register. The amount that Mr. Black reported to the police was way in excess. I was about to provide a more exact amount when Mr. Black shot me a look—my first lesson in insurance scams. I gave the police the license plate number as I remembered it. I sort of felt sorry for the robbers. If the rumors were true and RBNB had some shady connections, then these guys had surely hit the wrong address.

Late in June of 1971, during an Italian American Civil Rights League rally at Columbus Circle, Joseph Colombo Jr. was shot. The Colombo Family was one of the "Five Families" reported to belong to the American Mafia in NYC. There would be no questioning the shooter as to who he was working for, as he was conveniently killed at the scene. Joe Gallo and Carlo Gambino, from rival Mafia Families, were brought in for questioning and quickly released. Everyone knew that the Colombo Family would take care of this themselves.

The Italian American Civil Rights League offices were at 635 Madison Ave, between 59th and 60th Street, above RBNB. So, our restaurant was a convenient and friendly place to hold a backroom meeting. One night in July, our manager asked Joanie and me to stay for a private dinner after the restaurant's regular hours had ended.

Ten men came into the restaurant, wearing expensive black suits. Neither Joanie nor I knew them, but the new night manager did. Mr. Black had been moved to manage the lunch crowd. Our new night manager was also Italian and spoke the native tongue to our guests. If the bling these men were wearing were any indication, Joanie and I would be in for a good night's take-home.

In the beginning, this was a quiet and severe group. As the beer and wine flowed, they got louder. Every time Joanie or I entered, they were silent again, almost on cue.

"Joanie, am I crazy, or do they shut up when we enter the room?"

"I noticed that also. Who are these guys anyway?"

I said, "I think they are the Colombo family, and we should just shut up about it."

Soon their business was too important to contain their voices, even when we entered the back room. By the tenor in their voices, something big was in the works, and they were in disagreement about it. Joanie and I locked eyes and, as if we were deaf, just went on serving. Close our ears and collect the hundred-dollar tips coming our way. The night ended peacefully, which seemed to be the end of the story.

But vengeance can take its time. Almost a year later, Joe Gallo was spectacularly gunned down in Little Italy. That night at RBNB vividly came back to me. Once you are in the sights of the mob, it might take a while, but things get "sorted out" eventually. Everyone suspected it was the Colombo family behind the bloody shoot-out. The episode was now closed.

I thought of when my father had gotten in trouble with the wrong people. The day I picked the phone up only to hear a deep voice ask for my mother. Handing the phone to her, I watched as she got very still, the color draining from her face. The fight my parents had that night was a doozy. Now I realized who the big black cars belonged to that were occasionally stationed in front of our house. I don't know what would have happened to my father, mother, and I had my mother and her family not helped pay my father's debts. My mother kept working so hard. Bills, legal and illegal, had to be paid.

I must have learned my work ethic from her. I would take extra days at RBNB, or was it to see Mr. Black? My apartment on West 95th Street was filled with beef bones I'd bring home from the restaurant at night. Jacques no longer lived in the apartment on the other side of my yard. My little dog, Sam, was living the high life with all these bones, sometimes bigger than she was. It somehow didn't occur to me that the bones kept going missing.

Sam and I were tucked in tight for the night when a crazy commotion woke us both. The noise was coming from the kitchenette area. I got up, and as soon as I did, a huge rat popped out over the stove, then another. I grabbed Sam as she was smaller than these NYC monsters. Then a third came out from under the oven. They kept coming. What does a 22-year-old do without a parent or even a super to call? I called 911. I can hear you laughing.

Two young police officers came to help me.

"What's the problem?' the older of the two baby police officers said.

"Rats—you can't see them now, but they are huge, and they were all over my stove and sink."

Their smirks stopped as the rodent gang popped back out.

"Oh, SHIT!" Neither of these young officers seemed to have ever seen creatures this big before.

"GET BACK!"

They pushed me back toward the garden door and took out their guns. They were aiming at the stove.

"Wait, what if the bullet ricochets off the metal and hurts her?" Or did they mean harm themselves?

So, what would any two young police officers do when faced with this harm? They called for backup.

Sirens screamed down West 95th Street, waking all on the block. It's the emergency squad. In walked a sergeant who had seen everything. He looked around my little apartment and at Sam and me.

"What, what we got here?"

I will never forget the look on his face when he heard, "Rats, sir!"

The sergeant excused himself as he took the two young officers to the hall. No need to do that; I could hear him yelling at them a mile away. "We don't answer rat calls!!!"

One of the youngsters spoke up. "But there are hundreds of them."

"That is not our problem."

The other one spoke then. "She is alone with her small dog."

The sergeant was totally over these two, "NOT OUR PROBLEM."

He came inside to talk to me. "We can't help you, but the guys will stay here until you and your pup can pack up and go somewhere else."

By now, all the occupants were in the lobby, and my neighbor said I could stay with her. Then the sergeant added, "Tomorrow, you can call the Rat Patrol. The number is in the phone book."

No sleep that night, as I listened to the new tenants rummage through my whole apartment. Books falling over, curtains ripping, and whatever mischief rats get into when left alone.

The next morning, I entered my apartment through the back door and was horrified at what I saw. With one eye on me, mama rat finished my chocolate cake.

I called the Rat Patrol. "I have rats!"

She asked, "Yeah, what's the address?"

I gave her my address, and the next thing I heard was, "Goodbye."

"What! Aren't you coming to get them?"

She couldn't even muster a chuckle. "We don't do that."

I reply, "Well, what do you do?"

"I've made a note of it." Click. Now what? I know I'll call the owner.

I was away from my apartment for five days, staying with friends. I returned each day to get some things I'd left behind, only to see the increasing horror that my home had become. Calling my landlord never worked, so I had to take things into my own hands.

At one point, I went to my parent's house to stay for the night. They had aged, and things felt very separate and strange. Queenie, the dog my father had bought when I was nine, was now ancient and neglected. Her belly and tail were covered in ticks. I showed my father this, and he was upset that he hadn't noticed. He quickly went to work on her, taking off the ticks. In the morning, I showered and realized I had a tick sucking on my vagina. Was this a punishment, as I had just lost my virginity to Mr. Black? I pulled it off, packed up, and went back to Manhattan. I was no longer a kid and would have to take control of my living situation myself.

My landlord turned out to be a 5th Avenue lawyer, a bona fide slumlord. He would not see me. The actress in me came out, just as it had when the robber had a gun to my back. I was sobbing and hysterical, and soon I was ushered into his office; seems I was making a fuss in the lobby. I was beginning to understand what it takes to get things done.

The wall behind the stove was fixed with a metal sheet that those damned rats scratched on each night. The workers found many restaurant rib bones stacked in the wall at the entrance to the rat's home. So that's where those tasty bones went. Sam and I moved back in.

I had applied and was approved for a yet unfinished new apartment building across the street. My space would be on the 32nd floor. It was a fantastic apartment filled with light and views all the way to Queens.

I felt safe that my new friends could not follow me in the elevator. I stayed in the old garden apartment until my new space was ready. The hole was now fixed, and I felt it was okay to be there until moving day. CRASH! The ceiling, which had been peeling down, now fell down, and guess what came down with it? First one, then at least three more. I was grateful they didn't have suitcases with them. But I packed up mine and once more went to my friends, Michael and Alice, on the other side of the city.

Now that Joanie was getting Eduardo's help with her trays I was forced to go down to the kitchen with the orders and up with the tray full of beef and potatoes. I prayed that I wouldn't fall or the tray didn't drop. The restaurant wanted us to do all this in heels. I fought with both Mr. Black and our new night manager. I wanted to wear regular solid clunky, but safe shoes. All I got was "no." We had to look a certain way; no one cared if we fell and broke one of our bones. I took my complaints to our union, who found in my favor. We could now wear sneakers or any footwear we'd feel safe in. This was the first real stand I took against injustice. After all, the guys didn't have to wear heels.

We had to put up with Mr. Camisa, the head of the kitchen. He was as irritable as they came. Returning a not well done enough beef could mean it might be flung at us as if he thought we were the ones complaining, not the patrons. If it is too rare, pour juice over it; pound some red ketchup into it if it is too well done. By the time we got back upstairs, the meat was probably cold, and down we'd go again.

This back and forth never ended, and no one was paid enough to endure Camisa or those stairs. So when the restaurant offered coupons, a sort of buy-one-get-one deal, I got a brainstorm. The voucher was good if you ordered a specific combo from the menu. I bought all the papers containing these coupons. I cut out the coupons and stashed them in my apron pocket.

Now a kinder waiter taking cash from a customer who didn't have a coupon would pull one out of her pocket and offer it to the customer. I rolled the dice each night. This was a cash-only scam, and cash was king in those days. When someone paid for their meal and didn't have a coupon, I would cash them out myself, pocket the money, then later present that check to the cashier with the coupon from my pocket. Now half of that paid bill was cash with my name on it. It was a dangerous and stupid scam considering who might own the restaurant. At any moment, a manager could ask me to empty my pockets only to find checks not yet cashed out with the cashier and unused coupons. It was also theatrical.

Sometimes a night would go by, and I could not pull off the scam. No one would order the right combo that didn't have a coupon. Mr. Black would stop by my apartment occasionally, and I would gather all the evidence of my coupon searching. I didn't trust him with the knowledge of my scam. I should not have trusted him with my body either. I was almost caught by our new manager, who demanded to see what was in my apron pocket. My acting skills came in handy. I had a sudden bathroom emergency and ran past the manager — "I'll be right back." I bet on his forgetting that he wanted to see the contents of my apron. No, he was waiting for me; however, he only wanted to get his opinion of me off his chest.

"You are just like a bird; all you do is eat and shit." Wow, that was close.

Close enough to teach me a lesson. Realizing the restaurant's possible connections, I decided to drop the scam. However, I'm not sure I had the proper remorse for my cheating.

In a cash world, pulling off these sorts of scams was easy. I saw it for myself one night while attending the movies. I bought my ticket and entered the theater. I offered it to the usher, who took my whole ticket.

"Aren't you supposed to tear that in half?"

Here's how it worked: the box office would sell a ticket, and the usher taking the ticket was to rip them in half. The patron was to get one half while the office got the other, so they had a check and balance between tickets sold and money in the cash box. This scam was basically the same as my restaurant one. The guy who sells the ticket works with the usher taking the ticket, and by not ripping the ticket in two, they could resell it and pocket the cash.

Once again, I asked this usher to tear my ticket.

"What's it to you? Mind your own business. I'm doing my job."

This usher was a tall, dark Italian guy and very handsome, probably an actor. His heavy New York accent gave him a rough edge. But I stood my ground.

"Here," as he tore my ticket in half, "ya happy now?"

Being an usher was just a stepping stone for this handsome man. He became a very famous actor. But not all rocky starts have such a happy ending.

Twelve

AN ENDING

Finally, the day came when my new 32nd-floor apartment was ready, and I could leave the rats behind. My mother and father helped me move across the street. They seemed impressed when they saw my new apartment—a studio with all one side windows with a view of Central Park and beyond. I could even see Queens from up there. Sam wouldn't have her backyard anymore, so we went to the park more often. It was sunny, clean, and perfect. Things were looking up. My job was fun, I made good money, and Mr. Black was still in the picture.

One sunny morning my father called to tell me that my mother was going to Texas.

"Why?" I asked.

"She had a little accident and wants to be with her sister Ruth for healing."

"What kind of accident?"

"Well, a few days ago, she was showering and fell."

A few days ago, and he is telling me this now.

"We are going to JFK tomorrow. Do you want me to pick you up?"

"No, I'll meet you there."

I took the E-train to JFK and met them at the American Airlines terminal. Her hand in mine was so small, like a child's hand. I kept picturing her showering and then falling onto the floor. Our shower was inside the tub, so she would have fallen first onto the hard side of the tub, then to the floor. I had to erase that picture from my mind. A question formed inside my brain: what made her fall? My mother and I had never had an intimate conversation. So, it was not unusual for me to not just ask her why she fell. Just my realizing her nakedness in the shower seemed an intrusion on my part.

I was getting what I always wanted: my mother was leaving my father. This, however, was never how I imagined it. We walked slowly to the gate, my father trailing behind us. I could tell she was hiding some discomfort, some physical pain, from me. We stood and waved goodbye as she boarded the plane. My father and I parted ways without speaking. His 6'2" frame seemed diminished. Here was a broken man. And I felt sympathy for him.

How could this be the same man I tried to kill? When I was around 13 years old, I was sitting in our living room when the usual fight broke out in the kitchen. I was eating an apple and had the paring knife in my hand. I could not take it anymore. I snapped, and with a force, I'd never felt in me before, I headed into the kitchen, my goal to kill my father.

As I rounded the hallway towards the kitchen, his size became a reality for me. They were mid-argument, and I realized how stupid and useless this would be. He'd never laid a hand on me, and I don't think he ever struck my mother either. Still, I chickened out and darted into the bathroom, dug my nails into my hand to give me some release from my fury. I stayed there until I heard him start to babble incoherently. Then he flung himself down the stairs and out to the car. He would do this, babble and throw himself down the stairs often. I guess this is what he had to do to exhaust himself and burn off the fury.

Heading back to Manhattan on the E-train I wondered if my mother thought about her mother. After my beloved Grandpa

Gardner passed away, Grandma Gardner stayed with us for a while. But she was frightened of my father's mother. And she had a right to be. Grandma Davidson had a temper—frankly, she was nuts. One day at her apartment, she was wildly arguing with my mother about how my Mother had ruined my Father's life. She picked up a knife and held it to my mother's throat. She had my mother against the wall, screaming at her. My father took the knife away and calmly said, "Let's eat."

So, Grandma Gardner was right to be frightened. Uncle Louis whisked her away from our house and put her on a plane to Texas for her safety. She passed away while there.

My mother was still in Texas six months later, and I missed her terribly. We spoke on the phone all the time. She'd ask me to go to dinner with my father, and I tried to accommodate her. On occasion, we'd go to dinner in Manhattan. Eveline, my friend from Beef N' Brew, would come with us sometimes; he liked her. Without her there, I had nothing to say to him. I never asked Latisha, my Black friend, to join us. I wonder what he would have thought or done if I had.

Latisha was not only a beautiful model, but she was also very interested in filmmaking. So many of my fellow waiters took classes during the day, and Latisha urged me to sign up for filmmaking classes at The New School. While there I made a short film about the dating life of two small city dogs for my final exam. It was staring my dog Sam and my friend Libby's (Cinderella) dog Ping. I had not heard the old adage "never work with animals or children." But we had fun, and it's a charming short film.

I acted in one of my classmate's projects. When we screened our work for the class, I was amazed at how pretty I was on camera. They say that the camera loves certain people, and I was one. Only I shrank from the shots where the light caught my scars. That was all I could see—a pretty face ruined by pockmarks. I had to do something about this.

Since my mother was still in Texas, this was my opportunity to get help. I had given up all hope that I would be healed by prayer. I consulted with a highly recommended plastic surgeon who suggested dermabrasion. This skin-resurfacing procedure uses a rotating (wire in my day) brush to remove the outer layers of skin. Rarely had I ever been in a doctor's office, let alone a hospital. I was frightened but determined to get rid of my pockmarks.

After surgery, my friend Ruth popped her head into the hospital room and quickly popped back out. Just as our time back in summer stock, we remained close. Struggling actors— or successful waitresses—we confided in each other. Our choice of apartments spoke miles about who we were. I lived on the family oriented Upper West Side, she in a one room walk-up in Greenwich Village. That seemed so edgy and exciting to me.

I heard Ruth retching in the hallway. I should have asked the doctor more questions; what would I look like right after the operation, and how long before I could see people? Ruth came back into the room.

"How bad is it?" I asked.

From our time doing West Side Story, I knew that Ruth was an excellent actor, and I watched her "actor preparation" to portray the "everything is all right" good friend.

She took a deep breath, "Does it hurt?" It didn't.

"Not yet, but it probably will. How bad is it?"

"You haven't seen yourself yet?"

"No, they will not allow it."

"Well, it's blood; not great, but I'm sure the results will be worth it."

Please God, don't make me go through this without results.

We chatted as best as possible; my mouth would not open entirely. Ruth left, and unfortunately, I looked in the mirror.

Then I started retching. My face was an open sore of bloody goo.

This procedure was painful and debilitating and initially, while I was still very swollen, things looked a lot better. But ultimately it did little to improve my skin. I hoped for a miracle that I would wake up with skin as white and perfect as Snow White's. Instead, I ended up with a lifelong obsession with my looks. Subsequently, I have had three more operations on my face. But I still see the marks. I will always see those marks. Each scar holds a memory of my childhood. And, after all, I know where to look for them.

It took about a week before I could go out in public and put my life back in order. I began to feel guilty that I had this operation, which my mother would have opposed. I was racking up a long-distance phone bill calling Texas, so I had used that as an excuse for not calling for a week or so. Now I needed to speak with her. I needed to see her. I had to go to Texas to see her. I asked management for time off so I could fly to Dallas.

I enjoyed a wonderful few days with my Mother and my Texas family. Aunt Ruth's son Paul was like a brother to me. When we were young we did everything together whenever I visited Texas or he came to NYC. We especially enjoyed going to open houses and discussing the furniture placement. He had moved to an apartment in Dallas and I visited him and met his "roommate." He understood that I knew this was his lover, but we still never discussed it. It was clear Ruth was not about to discuss Paul with me. In fact, his name rarely—if ever—came up during my visit.

My mother seemed to be doing a lot better. I had done enough investigating to understand that she must have had a stroke. Now, it left her walking with a slight limp. I was concerned that she might ask me why my skin looked better. What would I say? Oh, I had an operation, or, oh, a new cream came out on the market. If she noticed, which I don't think she did, she never said anything to me. Now that I think of it, she never talked to me about my skin. Her skin was perfect. She tanned a shade of brown/gold without ever putting any lotion on. My pockmarked, sunburnt skin was just out of her vision. During our last day together, I blurted out, "I'm thinking of leaving acting."

Where this came from, I don't know. I thought perhaps she'd say, "Oh, no, you are too good to quit." But what I might have wanted was her permission to quit. Her money, her asking her family for more money, afforded me my classes. She came with me on Saturdays when I was too young to travel alone on the subway. She fought with my father over my desire to act. I thought she was as invested in my future as I was.

What I heard was this: "My work is done; I can leave now. You are going to be okay."

I don't know how I expected my mother to respond, but that answer never crossed my mind. Was I her work? I could not process this. The car was waiting to whisk me to the airport. My mother stood at the screen door and waved bye to me. While on the trip home, I put it all out of my mind, except for a brief phone conversation to let her know I was home safely. I couldn't know that those would be the last few words I would hear from her.

Thinking she was well on her way to healing, I gladly went back to work at Roast Beef N' Brew. I knew I had another conversation that had to take place. My periods were horrible but on time. Now, I was late. I thought I was so in love with Mr. Black that I was not frightened by this lateness. In my fantasy world we would walk down the aisle, have this child, and live happily ever after. And I'd still be a star someday.

That was all a fantasy. When I told Mr. Black I was late, I heard this from him; "Oh no, not you, too."

What the fuck? I went directly to Eveline, knowing she would have the scoop. He was also with a waitress from the day shift and the hatcheck gal (who was married). Somehow, we all were late. What a busy guy, and what a wrong choice on my part for my first intimate relationship. I still hoped he'd choose me, but it became clear that his choice would be the afternoon shift waitress.

I didn't have much time to worry about all this, as less than a week after I got home from Dallas, the one phone call came— the one you never want.

"Lynn, it's Uncle Louis." My family called me by my middle name, as my mother was Janette. "Your dad asked me to call you. He's right here. Ah, umm, your mother passed last night."

It took a second. Nothing has ever been that quiet.

"Are you there? Are you OK?" Silence from my end.

"Your dad wants to go to Dallas, and we can buy the tickets for both of you this afternoon. Aunt Violet and I will pick you up and drive you to the airport."

Somehow, I said yes, and asked what time. Then the rage came.

I flung the phone across the room. "NO, NO, NO!"

It was so violent that my poor Sam ran under the dresser to avoid the screaming. My neighbor came to my door. I didn't open it but said I was okay.

Is this what she meant by saying she could leave? Why didn't I ask her what she meant when she said she could leave and that I was okay now? By not asking her what she meant, did I somehow permit her to leave, to die? Then I remembered her telling me that my father wanted her to come home. That he was going to travel to Texas to bring her back to NYC. I now had even more reason to hate him. The pain, despair, and rage I felt now had an object I could direct it all to.

Sitting in my new apartment, high atop Manhattan, the late February sky was as bleak as my soul. My little Sam knew whatever was happening to me was too big for even her love to heal. She stayed under the dresser. I pulled myself together and called Libby to come over and help me pack for the trip. We had become best friends and I needed her now.

She must have run to my apartment, and we stood holding tight to each other. When the tears stopped long enough I spoke up. "Libby, I need something to wear to her funeral."

We stood with my closet doors open.

"What does one wear to a funeral? I've never been to one."

Libby sighed deeply as she scanned my wardrobe. "How about this one?"

It was a simple dark purple dress with a v-neck. "Okay, what else do I need?"

I don't remember as Libby took over and packed my bag for me. Then she spotted poor Sam who had come out from under the table, but clearly knew something was wrong.

"I'll call the kennel. Oh, I guess I have to call work also." I managed to call work and explain I'd be gone. They were wonderful about it.

Libby asked, "Do you want me to come with you to the airport?"

"No, thanks, I told Uncle Louis I'd take a cab to the airport. I'll drop Sam off on the way."

I know I did all these things; I must have. However, I don't remember any of it beyond the first phone call.

Flying to Texas for the funeral with my father was something out of a bad sitcom. He could not stop crying. American Airlines had, in those days, a steward whose only job was customer service. He came to us and kneeled next to my dad's aisle seat. "Can I help you with anything?"

I leaned over my father and told the steward, "No, we are on our way to Dallas. My mother just died."

He sincerely hung his head, "Oh, I'm so sorry. Can I book your flight back home?"

Trying to get him away from us, I then said, "No, thanks. We don't know when we will be coming back."

The best one came: "American Airlines would be happy to bring the casket back for you." At that, my father lost it, and the steward went away quickly.

I have never cried or laughed as loud as that week we spent in Dallas. My father was useless. He could not even choose the casket. I was 23 and in charge. Uncle Louis paid for the airline tickets, and I guess her sister Ruth paid for the funeral. I know my father didn't have the money.

The coroner's report said she'd had a massive stroke. I blamed my father for how hard she had to work to keep us together. And for all the stress of arguing about sex and money. All that was true, but the secondhand smoke was probably the actual killer. And that gave me something else to blame on him.

I'd only seen funerals in the movies. I was sick with food poisoning and could not attend my Grandfather Gardner's funeral. This Texas funeral was certainly different from the film versions of funerals I'd watched. No one wore black, and the cars were white, unlike the black hearse in which Eveline and I rode.

My father insisted the casket be open, at least for a while. I dreaded this. I refused to look at her. I kept my back to the casket, but someone in that direction called my name, and I turned without realizing I would be facing my mother in her coffin—the one I picked out for her. I was now face-to-face with her. If I were brave, I could have touched her. All my aunts quickly came to my side. But I didn't have the hysterical reaction they thought was coming. When I looked closely at my mother's body, I knew she wasn't there. No bodily function, fluid, or organ could have brought her back. What made her my beloved mother was gone.

My mother was cremated. I asked my father if I could have her rings. The answer was no. I tried so hard to make him see they would burn up and the gold probably stolen. No. It might have made me feel better if he had wanted the rings. But that wasn't the case; he wanted them to burn up with her earthly body. I didn't think I could hate a person more, but that week I hated my father even more.

For his part, he could not understand how the family could be in tears one minute and the next laughing so hard about some tiny thing. He moaned and cried the whole time, which seemed phony to me. I have no idea what he felt during this sad time. I hoped he felt guilty. Guilty for all the shit her put her through. Emotion was a manipulative process for both him and his mother. It was always show time, always theatrical and bigger than life. Who were they both beyond the stage curtain?

My father might have taught me some acting tricks. He had a flare for drama. Besides flinging himself down the stairs all the time babbling incoherently, he also had many imaginary illnesses. He'd complain about symptoms from terrible diseases, trying to enlist my mother's sympathy. It always backfired. It didn't help that he would name a condition he knew nothing about, like rickets. Clutching his chest and head falling to the table, he'd yell, "I have rickets!" or cancer, anemia, liver disease (although he never drank). This would send my mother and me into peals of laughter. Dejected, he'd grab the racing paper and sulk to the bathroom or the closet, his hiding places.

When I first arrived in Texas, my stomach erupted into violent spasms. I started bleeding uncontrollably. I thought I had simply finally gotten my period. I sat with Aunt Ruth for spiritual healing. Her take on it was my umbilical cord was being torn away. It took me years to realize I must have had a miscarriage. That would be the last hint of pregnancy I would ever have.

Returning home to NYC and to work, nothing felt the same. Everyone was sympathetic and kind, but it could not penetrate my sadness. Libby made dinners for me and was a great support Thankfully Mr. Black had been transferred to another restaurant. Eveline told me he had chosen the waitress from the daytime shift, who was pregnant. At least I didn't have to see him each day. And it was a blessing that I would not have to worry about having his baby.

Within a month, I quit the restaurant. Was I quitting just the restaurant, or was I going to fulfill the promise to my mother to leave acting? I was profoundly grieving over my mother's passing and saddened by Mr. Black not choosing me. I was so alone. My body was healing from the miscarriage, but my soul was lost.

Because my mother had asked me to, I attempted to communicate with my father, but he asked me not to. I reminded him too much of my mother. He continued this charade of grief. Over and over, he threatened to kill himself. I was tempted to hand him the knife. I never knew what was real with him, so I didn't trust anything he said. He was a broken man, but he'd been broken for years.

If I quit my quest for stardom, would that amount to the total loss of my identity? Who was I if I wasn't performing? I was a failure as an actress, a woman, and a daughter. The weight felt like boulders rolling downhill to the ocean, and they would take me with them.

If I gave up acting, would waiting tables be the only thing I could do? It's hard work, and I knew that if I continued, my body would give out at some point. I needed to find something else to do. The trouble was I didn't think I had any other skills. I was in no shape to even look for other work.

At some point each day, I wrestled with the concept of suicide. The thought would take over, and I began to see ways to end my pain. I would stand behind the pillar when the subway arrived at the station. Sometimes even hugging it to prevent me from dropping to the tracks.

Weeks after my return from Dallas, I was attempting normal life. While doing my laundry in the 1st floor communal laundry room, a woman in our building jumped to her death. How quickly the body fell before me. It lay in the courtyard for eight hours. There was a massive explosion at a ConEd station, and it seemed no coroner was available for a single Black woman who lay in the playground on the upper West Side.

That incident shook me to the core. It seemed horrible and enticing at the same time. I took my laundry to my apartment, and the window called to me. I'd lean out the window and take in the body below me. Looking down from the 32nd floor, the dead woman looked at peace. She lay uncovered for hours until someone from the building put a blanket over her body.

Soon I was thinking how easy that would be, to just jump. I became obsessed with the thought, fearing that I would fulfill this madness. I hid under my desk and pulled the phone beside me on the floor. Then I called my neighbor to come over to my apartment. She sat with me until the feeling left me, at least for the moment. One thing I have learned throughout my life is the value of good neighbors. My little Sam never left my side. I have come to understand those stories of someone dying and taking their pet with them.

Sometimes, when these feelings overtook me, I shook them loose by thinking of my mother and how devastating my suicide would be for her. Did I believe in an afterlife? Would I meet her if there was such a thing? I kept waiting for a sign, something to hold on to. My Aunt Ruth called and asked what I wanted for my birthday, which was a week away.

It was a cold and exceptionally wintry March, and I said, "All I want is a perfect day." And that is what happened. March 16th , the temperature went into the high 70s. Coats were being flung off, and it seemed everyone was out in Central Park. The next day it snowed. Was it a sign? I don't know, but I was grateful for that day.

A friend recommended a therapist to me. He was a young man who was also a minister. I made an appointment with him. It was not easy to bare my soul to him. But I tried, and little by little, things began to lighten up. Then the sadness would blanket me again. On our first visit, when I was laying out the background of my childhood, he looked at me with great concern and said, "I'd like to talk about your mother."

"My mother was perfect. It's my father we have to talk about."

"Maybe," he continued, "but it's your mother we need to talk about."

"My mother was a saint."

"I'm sure, but let's chat about her."

This did not sit well with me. I refused to see that my mother was responsible for any of the bad parts of my crazy childhood. Life would have been perfect if she had left my father. That was all I was willing to talk about. But the question had been presented to me, and it swirled around my brain. After all, she had left him, and look how that turned out. I thought it was only my father I didn't understand, but I didn't know her either.

I recounted a joyful tale of playing shopping with her. She would pretend to send me on an errand. I would leave by the back door, walk around to the front door and come home with pretend groceries I had purchased. One day she sent me to get chocolate pudding mix, and I actually went to the local A&P, a long walk across busy streets. It didn't seem to occur to anyone on Jamaica Avenue why a four-year-old was there alone. But the store manager knew my mother—perhaps because she owed him money—and he called her to say I was in the store looking for pudding.

The therapist wanted to hear more stories. I took a deep breath and launched into how I found out about menstruation. There was blood on my panties, and I thought I was dying. I could not worry my mother about this, so I hid my underwear or washed it myself. I was only nine years old. My best friend, Gail, who lived around the corner from us, saw my blood one day and asked about it. I said I fell on the seat of my bike.

"You didn't fall. You got your period."

Now, I have to point out that Gail and I were best friends until we went to junior high. She was brilliant and skipped not one but two whole grades. The separation was too much to hold the friendship and it fell apart.

So she was indeed the right person to learn these things from. I asked her, "What, what's a period?"

She took me to her mother's closet and pulled down a box of Kotex. "See, you have to wear these each month."

It was the biggest, ugliest boat of cotton I'd ever seen. "No. I just hurt myself."

In retrospect, I think Gail told her mother, and she called my mother. A few days later, I was walking towards my bedroom. We were living in the downstairs section at the time. My bedroom was approximately 6x9 feet. It had a twin bed and a vanity. It also had a closet, and if I swung the closet door wide open it acted as a door without much privacy. Their room was next to mine and for some reason had no door either. So as I passed her room I saw my mother in tears. She was holding a soiled pair of my underwear. I tried to tell her it was just a bike accident. Even then I knew this intimate situation was just too hard for her to face.

"Mom, there is nothing to cry about. I'm fine; it didn't hurt too much."

"You didn't hurt yourself on your bike. I know that. This is going to happen to you every month." At that point she started to cry some more. "Your life is over, and there are things you can't do now."

"Like what, Ma?"

"Swimming is out, and your dancing will have to stop while this is happening."

These two things were my happy place, so now I was crying. She held me tight. Ultimately she bought me the Kotex along with the elastic with hooks one needed to keep it secure. And she bought me new underwear. I have no idea if she told my father about it.

She never actually explained what was happening to my body. I knew this bleeding thing had something to do with sex. But what was sex? I also realized their fights were not just about money but also about this sex thing. My hormones began to talk to me, and I responded. She found me masturbating one day and took a hairbrush to my backside. That is the only time she ever laid an angry hand on me. I could sense my father wanted to stop her, but I belonged to her alone by then.

I shared the "sin and be sorry" passages I'd been sent with this therapist, and began to connect some dots. My mother's connection with sexual intimacy was so horribly damaged, and she had passed this down to me. I resented him asking me to turn my back on her. How could I turn my back on this woman who was everything to me? I didn't want to entertain any flaw in her character, yet the evidence stared me in the face. She had passed down her fears, her most intimate fear of sex.

He prescribed some lithium for me to take. I begged him to commit me somewhere. He assured me he'd be there for me whenever I called, and going to a hospital would not be wise. I was frightened that I could not control my urge to kill myself. It was the spring of 1971, and having had my birthday I was now a 24-year-old orphan with pockmarked skin, no career, no boyfriend, and an empty apartment. An unwanted motherless child. This seems so dramatic to me now. But I have no doubt this is what I was feeling. Not unlike so many young women and men at that age who don't see a tomorrow that ever could be bright and happy.

Thirteen

A RECOVERY

My aunts knew how I was grieving and gave me money to travel to Europe. I don't think any one of them knew the depth of my unhappiness; they just knew how close I was with my mother and wanted to give me something to take my mind off her death. In late spring of 1971, I found an American Express bus tour to five cities in Europe. Sam went into the boarding kennel. She never fussed about this. I treated myself to a cab ride to the airport.

Before my adventure could start, I was invited to my former roommate—Alice—and my dear friend Michael's wedding. We all met at the Grosvenor House, a boarding house in Manhattan that I lived in during my days at the American Academy of Dramatic Arts. It was a lovely wedding, I think. Both the loss of my mother and my sense that I was losing my friend Michael made enjoying the celebration less than perfect. But I could entertain everyone with my tales of my upcoming European trip.

The adventure would start in London and end in Spain. I was nervous about traveling alone but also very excited. My only time on a jumbo jet was during filming with Sophia Loren. Now, I looked for where the cameras were hidden. But then, this wasn't new for me; I always felt there was a camera on me, watching me. Who or what held this camera? Well, I never questioned that.

Off the plane at Heathrow Airport, I quickly spotted the American Express sign held high by our group leader. As I looked around at my soon-to-be fellow travelers, I saw I was the youngest person on this tour. I was lonely and cried most of the time. I dutifully sent postcards back to my father. After all, my mother had asked me to try and stay in touch with him. Years later, I realized he had served during WWII in many places I visited. Another thing we could have had a decent conversation over.

It was a bleak and cold April in London, a perfect choice to brighten my mood. The group went together to museums and points of interest. I found I wanted to go my separate way. The women on the tour were almost all my mother's age, which was painful. How I wish my mother could have been with me.

In England, I learned that the Indian culture thought pockmarks were a sign of God. I was quite fawned over at a restaurant in the Indian district. In Paris, three young Algerians found me sitting in a café and we became friends. These guys— or their parents—owned the sweet shops in a few of the metro stations. I don't know why I trusted them and traveled with them, delivering the sweets their family had prepared. What an adventure to be in the Paris Metro stations at 4 a. M.

In Nice, I met a South African who worked as an exterminator. We sat at a café and chatted. He explained that his father was a wealthy farmer in South Africa. But he wanted nothing of the life his father led, so he left and now had a new career. We drove the Grande Corniche in his small VW, with a rat sculpted on the hood. (I could have used this guy in my old New York apartment.) We ended up at a magnificent casino in Monaco. A valet took the rat mobile away to park next to the Rolls Royces! We weren't dressed in tatters, but certainly not in the splendor of the other patrons. This stop was certainly not on our mid-priced American Express tour.

My eyes lit up as I saw all the glamor of the gambling world before me. I realized that I might have the same problem as my father did. I carefully limited myself to losing $10; after that, I'd have to walk away. It helped that I did not speak French, and my exterminator had to get the rat VW back to Nice.

While in St. Michele, I met up with Alice and Michael on their honeymoon. They were so happy and their happiness was contagious. Michael always had the ability to make me laugh and be happy. Before I became a union usherette, he and I would do something called "fade in." We'd mingle with the crowd during intermission and then slide inside for the second half. He could always find good seats. Of course we only saw one half of all the Broadway shows. I know there were moments in my life when I wondered why he chose Alice and not me. But I loved them both too much to let those thoughts linger. They seemed so brave to me. There was no safe bus tour for them; they were hitchhiking! The three of us left St. Michele with our fingers in the air, and a lovely gentleman picked us up.

The group always had planned things to do, but I so wanted to spread my wings. And besides they were all so much older than I. Many of the women tried to comfort me once they knew why I was on this trip. Off on my own in Madrid, I had my camera taken from me. Well, just the film. I was on the train, and we were passing such poverty that I photographed it. The police saw me, marched over to my seat, and demanded my camera. I was frightened and didn't speak a word of Spanish. The passenger next to me explained in English to hand my film over. I fumbled and took the roll of undeveloped film out and handed it over to the police. Unbeknown to me, I must have taken a picture the government didn't want the world to see.

The final stop was a summer resort in Malaga, Spain. This was what I needed. Water has always been a healing balm for me. The hospital I was born in, Brooklyn Doctors Hospital, was torn down to build the base of the Verrazano Bridge. In many ways, I was born on the water and am a Pisces; it is my happy place, In the water or laying on the sand, I could feel tiny pieces of me were healing. I watched the ocean ebb and flow. I swam in the beautiful pool, met some young children who spoke English, and we laughed. I tried all sorts of new food, watched new dances, and caught the eye of some men watching me. I was growing up.

That trip was healing in many ways, and I was grateful for the chance to feel my freedom and loneliness all at once. I always thought my mother would be there for me. When I was born, she was 38 years old; in her day that was quite old for marriage and giving birth. When I reached my 40s, I began to see in my body had become so similar to her body. I noticed things I found myself doing that I remember her doing. To some degree we do become our parents. But in losing her so early, I didn't know who she was. Who was she besides my mother? What did I inherit from her? All questions I would only start to consider much later in life.

All the way back from Europe, all I wanted was to be reunited with my precious little Sam and tell Libby all about the trip. I had dinner with Libby, and we laughed over my adventures. I knew I needed a job. Would I go back to waitressing? If I were going to give up on my acting dream, I would have to get a job in the 9–5 world. I hit the want ads and found my next adventure, far away from acting. Or so I thought.

Vidal Sassoon was at the height of his career. Starting in London, he revolutionized the hair industry. Now he brought his talent to America. I became a receptionist at Vidal Sassoon's new 5th Avenue hair salon. His haircuts were all the rage, and celebrities and average women wanted a Sassoon cut. Vidal had a big personality and an even bigger temper. He could go from charming to furious instantly if things didn't go his way.

One day, he was standing outside the salon, yelling at the window. I have no idea what he was raging on about. Suddenly he threw his cane into that plate glass window. I was neither amused nor frightened. I'd seen these dramatics throughout my childhood.

From my position at the front desk, I could see the bustle of 5th Avenue. I spotted a lovely redhead coming towards the salon. I knew right away who she was. Jamaica High School had two final performances, one a comedy and the other Shakespeare's Troilus and Cressida. I was Cressida, and this lovely redhead was the lead in the comedy. She won best actress and got the coveted back page of the yearbook as "Best Actress." Here she was, headed my way. I didn't know if she would recognize me, but she did.

"Janet, is that you?" Now we would have to chat about our careers. The one I had just given up."Did you ever continue with your acting?"

My ego jumped out of my mouth, "Of course, I've traveled to every state east of the Mississippi performing."

Now I didn't confess these were mostly children's theatre productions. It was my turn to be the "best actress." That triumphant tale of her adventures I was waiting to hear never came. I should have suspected something was off by her outfit. While we were all wearing miniskirts, she wore a print dress with a white lace collar and white gloves.

"Oh, I'm so happy for you," she said, "I had some problems when I got to college, and I didn't act again. I left college altogether."

It stunned me. We left Jamaica HS seven years ago. What had she been doing all that time? When she appeared after the haircut, she looked as lovely as ever. Her long curly red hair was shorter, not quite the bob Vidal was famous for, but still stylish. She came to the front desk. From her purse, she took out a single pre-signed check. After staring at the check for a few seconds, she looked at me with a combination of sadness and embarrassment. "Can you help me? My mother gave me this signed check, but I've never filled one out before. This is my first time out without her."

My heart leaped from my chest to my throat. I calmly took the check from her and filled it out. What was I to say to this woman?

I had been so angry and hurt when I lost the "best actress" title in high school. I now felt horrible about making such a big deal of my minor accomplishments traveling the country and acting in shows. I showed her how to fill in the amount due.

I guess we were the same age, 23, but she was stuck in time, still at home, not moving forward. I watched as she took out a hand-drawn map she would use to find her way home. The steps were counted out for her from the salon to the stairs that would take her down to the subway entrance. Then from the stairs to the platform, onto the right train home. I suspected her mother was, at this moment, not far away, watching her lovely, wounded young daughter. Making sure she was safe.

I never mentioned to the lovely redhead that after graduating, I went on to the American Academy of Dramatic Arts in Manhattan and never graduated. That I also could not take the rejection and left acting. I think we both wanted to believe in my success. This encounter left me so shaken. We were both rebuilding our lives after great disappointment. That takes courage, and I began to see I had an extra dose of it.

Sassoon was a rest stop to find my way out of acting. Soon I was offered an even bigger job with Vidal Sassoon. It meant traveling and opening salons across the country, which sounded cool. But I turned the job down. I explained that if I wanted to stay at a hair salon, I would cut hair, but I had no talent or desire to do that job. I might have harbored some residual fantasy that I'd act again and needed to stay in NYC. It just didn't feel as though Vidal was my future.

Vidal was the kind of man you didn't say no to, at least when it came to his salons. I was reminded of Vidal when I worked for another famous hair stylist, Jon Peters, who produced *Caddyshack*. They both had an amazing arrogance and sense of celebrity that I could never understand.

After Vidal fired me, I wondered what was next. Once again, my friends came to the rescue. Another ex-Sassoon gal was now working at a small production company answering phones. She needed a sub for a week or two, and I was lucky enough to be able to fill in for her. It turned out to be my future.

Fourteen

THE FUTURE

Sitting at my little reception desk at Langley/Sann Productions was a blast. This was my introduction to the world behind the camera. I'd be on their shooting stage when things were slow at the reception desk. I watched them create advertising wonder.

That is where I rubbed elbows with the lovely Kim Novak, a genuine Hollywood star. She had a string of hits with Alfred Hitchcock. *Vertigo* was my favorite. As a kid, pictures of friends I would someday meet covered my walls. Elizabeth Taylor, whom I never met; Rock Hudson, whom I had already met while ushering; and Kim Novak, whom I was now encountering. So, this was what working in commercials was going to be like. Wow!

Bob Sann was the producer in the company, and he saw something in me that made him think I'd be good at this racket. But their company was fully staffed, and I needed to find my place. Enter my mother's wisdom in making me study accounting in high school. A job opened in a large, very prestigious production company in the accounting office, and I got it.

Griner/Cuesta was at the top of the advertising production world. Our office was physically divided between the creatives making the commercials and the accounting office busy collecting the money and paying the bills. The reception desk separated them, and the receptionist guarded entry to either side with a vengeance. However, the casting office was next to the accounting office, on the non-creative side. I assume this was to keep the actors from annoying the people who might hire them.

Far too often, I wandered down to the casting room. I became dear friends with Carole Pfeffer, the casting director for this company. She was brilliant in every way. She enjoyed having me help her with the casting process. The head accountant did not take kindly to my adventures in casting.

Carole had black hair, black eyes, and extremely white skin. She'd wear heavy dark rimmed glasses which she really needed to see the world. The fact that she would choose me to be friendly with amazed me. She was the funniest, smartest person I've ever known. When Harvey, our accountant, would demand that I stay behind and do the job I was hired for, she'd pop into the accounting office and would put on her best, sweetest personality to get him to let me "help" her in the casting sessions. He'd give in, and as co-conspirators, we'd head off for the casting office. There she'd be behind the camera as I read the offscreen lines to the actors. She'd fill me in on what she liked about certain actors and what she didn't care for.

But soon, Harvey had enough and gave me an ultimatum. Stick to accounting or find another job. I chose to leave. I hated accounting; I wanted to be part of the creative side of the office. I became involved with a married man who worked in production there, and folks had begun to realize what was happening. So, my leaving was a good idea for both of us.

I got a job at another prestigious production company, N. Lee Lacy, as a PA (production assistant). They occupied every floor of a beautiful East Side brownstone. I remember Chevy Chase lived next door, and in person, he didn't seem to be the happy comic we saw on *Saturday Night Live.* I would end up having three encounters with Mr. Chase: one on the stairs of the brownstone, then in 1976 on SNL, and then working on *Caddyshack*.

Money and drugs flowed during the mid to late '70s. I was never interested in drugs and sometimes not even in the money. I'm pretty sure I had a reputation as a wet blanket. Not only was I disinterested in drugs, but I also still carried my Christian Science teachings with me even though I didn't practice the religion at all. For me, it was about the work. With each commercial I worked on, I learned more and more about filming. It was an exciting time. I hardly thought of acting and performing anymore.

The budgets to produce these commercials were getting bigger and bigger. Each company would compete to hire the most prestigious cinematographers and the best crews and use the newest equipment. Soon celebrities were eager to work in a commercial; the work was easy, and the pay was great.

One day at N. Lee Lacy stands out over all the others. It was a reshoot we had to do for a shampoo product. The ad agency didn't like what Lee had done with their gem of an ad, so they demanded he reshoot it at his expense.

I was excited because this would be one of my first times working on set as a junior producer. The day dragged on endlessly. Lee kept lighting the shot and then relighting the same shot over and over again. At one point, three stage lights were visible in the shot. What the heck was he doing?

I went to the 1st AD to see if he could get Lee to focus. We were wasting tons of money, and it was our money, not the advertisers' funds. I was afraid I would be a failure on my first time out alone on the set.

The 1st AD, Ted Zachary, turned to me, "Don't worry. It's Lee's money. He knows exactly how much he has to waste. Once he feels he's made his point, he will light it correctly, and we will go home."

What an ego Lee had. What game were they all playing? Was there a rule book on how to succeed in production? Why was I there if I had no power to change the course of the events of the day? I had to find a mentor to help me.

Maggie Condon was one of the producers for N. Lee Lacy. She was a beautiful, sophisticated woman who moved confidently in the world. I envied that. She was brought up in the world of jazz music, as her father was a famous bandleader. Manhattan was her playground. She had one glaring fault: she lost things. Sometimes simple things like pencils, time cards, or her coat, and as her production assistant, I was always busy finding her lost items.

One day, she dropped an envelope with over one thousand dollars in it. I found it and decided it was a good teaching moment. But she was frantic, and I could not hold back any longer. I confessed that I found the money; she was grateful, but I'm not sure any lesson was learned. I probably could have stayed; my work was well received. I felt I had learned all I could while at that company. After only one year working there, it was time to leave. Find another company that I could grow with. Once again, in hindsight, I don't think I liked Lee very much. That's really not a sustainable reason to leave a good job.

Since I said goodbye to acting at age 25, three years later at 28 years old, I was moving pretty quickly up the ladder. I had no time to waste. I was hired as a freelance producer to do some of the wacky commercials they did back then on *Saturday Night Live*. I didn't see much of Chevy Chase during the filming of these commercials. His star was certainly on the rise. I hardly saw any of the cast. I'd come in around 9 a. M.—which is late for a film person—and sit tapping my fingers until someone in the know would arrive, and we could go to work. I was so bored, and I'm not good when I'm bored. By the time their creative juices flowed, I was ready to call it a day. Most of them came from standup comedy, and that's a nighttime world. Film, unless it's meant to be a night shoot, is the stuff of early morning time.

However, I was very ambitious and this SNL gig seemed to be headed in the right direction. I am not sure where my ambition and courage came from. My mother didn't have the courage to leave my father. My father seemed not to have the courage to see me. I tried one more time to have dinner with him. He came to the apartment only to tell me he could not eat as he had throat cancer. After all his smoking, this seemed possible. Even though he didn't appear sick at all to me. Strangely, I started to cry. Then I woke up.

"Who gave you this diagnosis? What hospital are you going to?" I wanted proof.

"No one, I just know it."

My tears stopped. How dare he use me with his phony physical problems. I'd gone from hearing he had rickets to cancer. "You DO THIS all the time! Go to the doctor if you think you are ill."

"I've been and he said it's a matter of time."

Well, it's always a matter of time, no matter what is wrong. He saw how angry I was; he couldn't get away with babbling and throwing himself down the stairs. I was on the 32nd floor. So he left in silence.

Not long after this visit he sold the house in Hollis. Before he moved out, he called to see if there was something I might want from my childhood that would still be at home. I did not. After the sale, I remember someone from the IRS asking if I knew where he might be. He seemed to owe them for years of non-payment. I laughed and told them he certainly had nothing to give them. I don't know where the money from the house sale went, perhaps to pay off gambling debts. He must have used some funds to move into a small apartment down the street from where the Trumps grew up. Only once did I visit that apartment.

He never had cancer.

Fifteen

I'M A PRODUCER

It was a wintry cold March day, but the view from my window seat was blue skies and palm trees as my plane landed at LAX. After leaving N. Lee Lacy, I had enough work credit to apply for a producing job. This was a dream job at Mason-Stearns Productions.

Bill Mason was the award-winning director, and his friend Neil Stearns was the executive producer. Bill was Black; Neil was white. Back then, things were very different for Blacks. What it took for Bill to become a sought-after director in the '70s was not just talent but hard work—exceedingly hard work. And an amazing ability to put his ego aside.

His partner, Neil, has to be given credit also. Going out daily to "sell" a Black director to mainstream advertisers could not have been easy. And they trusted me with their company. Working for them I would have my first of many trips to Los Angles as a commercial producer.

White advertising executives hired Bill to take their ad campaign and make it "Blacker." Bill hated this. He just wanted to use his directing talent, period. We often worked with Burrell Agency out of Chicago, the leading "Black" advertising agency. The experiences I had working with this talented group would start to solidify the changes in my beliefs that started while touring in children's theater.

One day, we were heading uptown and needed a taxi. Suddenly, Bill and the ad execs left me alone at the curb with my arm out to hail the cab. I turned, and they were in a doorway. What the heck!

When the first cab stopped, and I opened the door, they approached the car and whammo, the taxi sped away. I was mortified. These incidents occurred often. Once on the New Jersey Turnpike, Bill was driving and his wife Evelyn sat beside him; she was the stylist for the company. I was in the back with two female (white) ad execs. Bill always drove perfectly, and after this incident, I understood why.

A patrol car with a siren whirling and lights flashing cut us off. Bill pulled over, and the officer came out with his hand on his gun holster. He ordered Bill out of the vehicle and spread him over the hood. Those of us in the back seat went nuts.

Evelyn, Bill's wife, was calmer. She had been through this before.

The second officer came to the window to ask us white gals, "Are you all right? You are safe now, you can tell me who this man is, and you are safe to tell me the truth!"

On and on with this stupid, ignorant chatter. The advertising agency producer sitting in the back with me started screaming at the cop. "We are working with Bill. He is our director. We are making commercials."

After examining Bill's credentials, the officer finally backed down, and Bill got back in the car. All the times our station wagon was stopped when I toured the South, I was never as afraid as when this officer pulled Bill over in New Jersey. I had no fear for myself but for Bill.

Bill tried hard to make light of it, but we all knew he was devastated. These incidents happened over and over. Each time, they broke my heart. Bill was such a wonderful man; he didn't deserve this treatment. No one does.

Bill was a director member of the Directors Guild of America, and by contract, he had to work with a DGA assistant director. Often, this additional hire made me nuts as I felt I was already doing that job myself. I had a small group of guys that I usually hired. New York suddenly had a lot of film work, and none of my "regular" hires were available. On a recommendation, I called Pat Curtis.

A woman answered, and I said, "Can I talk to Pat Curtis, please?"

"I'm Pat," she replied. I was taken aback.

"No, I mean the 1st assistant director Pat Curtis."

"That's me."

What? A female assistant director!? How could that be? I hired her right away. Bill loved working with women, so this was fine for him. Realizing that a woman could become a DGA assistant director, I started applying for membership in the union. I was turned down each time for various reasons. One was that I didn't have a college education.

There were some directors, and a few agency producers, that loved working with women. But certainly not all. Our company was growing and signing more directors to take the load off Bill. While working with a new director on a commercial in LA, I heard a refrain that would echo throughout my career. He was driving, and I was next to him in the passenger seat, and he asked when Blair, the 1st AD I had hired for him, would be joining us? "Well, she is still on *Hart to Hart,* but..." I didn't get to finish.

"You hired a fucking woman to be my AD!" He crossed two lanes of the 101 in Los Angles and swerved to the side of the highway.

Yup, you asshole. That's what I wanted to say. He insisted that I fire her right away.

"You can't do that. There is no reason to fire her; we'd have to pay her full salary plus some."

That shoot was hell. He now hated both Blair and me. I never wanted to—and was sure I would never—work with this man again. He didn't stay at our company. When I got back to NYC, I told Bill all about the incident. He had some choice words for that director.

We had some great projects. Next one up was a commercial with a young NBA player who was a star even in his rookie year. During filming, he bent down to pick up his co-star—a child around 6 or so. We all heard his knee snap. He went down to the ground but managed not to drop the child. Earvin Magic Johnson was sidelined for 45 games with a torn cartilage. He supposedly tore this while practicing. We prayed that was the case.

On one occasion, I had to step in and direct one of the commercials because the child actor hired for the spot was terrified of Bill. I can only speculate on what happened with his parents to make this boy so frightened of a Black man.

Bill tried so hard to win this child over. Finally, to get things done, he came to me and asked me to direct the child. I can say this was my first time directing, and the circumstance gave me no pleasure.

Speaking of children, one of the more disappointing people we worked with was Bill Cosby. Sitting on the steps to a brownstone and surrounded by adoring children, he seemed a likable guy just giving Jell-O-Pops away to the neighborhood. These kids knew him as Fat Albert, and loved him. I'm sure they, and their parents, were so excited to get the gig and meet the man. The man they met, Mr. Cosby, was anything but joyful. The kids begged for his autograph; they would not leave him alone. Mr. Cosby paid zero attention to them. I would go so far as to say he was nasty to these kids.

Bill went to him to get him to sign some autographs for the kids—or at least say something nice to them. That never happened. Mr. Cosby's time was over, and he was finished with the whole event. Character does come out . . . eventually.

Fame usually changes people—some for good, others not so. Gordon Parks, the hugely famous Black photographer, was hired to do a commercial for the United Negro Fund. Our production company was engaged to produce the ad with him.

Gordon arrived in Los Angles a bit before I arrived and was already checked into the Beverly Hills Hotel. I had never stayed there before and was excited to stay at such a landmark. I am not fussy, but my room was a broom closet. I would be working out of this closet; I just wanted a little more space. I went downstairs to see if I could change rooms.

They were firm; they had nothing else. Gordon happened by and saw me at the counter. He came over and acknowledged to the receptionist I was with him, or he was with me. Suddenly, there was a perfect room.

Gordon was incensed. He asked me where else WE could stay. I knew he loved staying at the Beverly Hills, and I didn't want to make him leave, so I said it was fine. I would stay there. He would not have it. He immediately checked out, and we both went to stay at a much lesser address. No one was going to be mistreated on his watch. What a wonderful man.

Many New York production companies loved staying at the Beverly Hills Hotel or the Beverly Wilshire, as long as the budget would allow. Mason/Stearns was on a tighter budget, and we often stayed at a nearby motel. However, the days ended up in one of those hotels' iconic bars.

One Saturday night, I was showing off to a friend, and we went to the Polo Lounge at the Beverly Hills Hotel for drinks. The maître d' I knew was not on duty that night. Our drinks came, and they were terrible. I complained to our waiter, who whisked them away and told us to leave. What? I mentioned the other maître d's name, and it didn't matter. Never in all the times I'd been there had something like this happened. Of course, I was with a group of men all the other times.

The next time I saw the maître d' who I knew, I asked him what that was about.

"They didn't know you."

"I realized that, but why treat us that way?"

Seeing I did not understand this, he repeated, "They didn't know you."

He saw he was going to have to explain it more explicitly.

"Some girls there on Saturday night pay for their tables."

I was dumbfounded, still not understanding.

"They pay us for a table, and then they get to stay there all night or until they get picked up. They work the house."

It was clear now. They thought we were also there to "work the house" and had not paid the price for admission.

Bill Mason, his wife Evelyn, the agency producer, and I went to the bar at The Beverly Wilshire Hotel one afternoon. It was early, maybe around 4 p. M., and the bar was pretty empty. There was a man sitting by himself on a stool at the bar. He was not the type to inhabit a bar like this. Scruffy beard, hair uncut for many a month, and clothes that might have come off a Goodwill rack, and yet there he was. He turned his barstool and angled it so he could watch us. However, he was not just watching us collectively but staring at me.

It became extremely uncomfortable. Bill grew annoyed and asked if I was okay. I said I was, but Bill remained upset. Finally, he said he would speak with the man at the bar.

I'm not sure if the vagrant at the bar heard Bill or just realized his time was up. He took one last swig of his drink and went to stand up. Something in the way he did this made me realize who it was—Steve McQueen.

He was still one of the biggest stars in Hollywood. The Hollywood gossip rags printed that he had left his current wife and was living at the hotel. To this day, I wonder, if I had realized who it was sooner, would the outcome of the evening have been different? I was not immune to being flattered by a Hollywood legend.

Hollywood is filled to the brim with legends. Many of them were realizing that doing a very financially lucrative commercial would not be beneath them. Some of these stars were before my time. But they carried with them an aura of grandness.

Our entourage drove through the gates of a Bel Air mansion. The first car was a Mercedes, owned and driven by my assistant. With him was a new director that Mason/Stearns had added to their lineup. He was an Englishman and had an interesting but quirky personality. Sometimes I had trouble understanding him, and it was not just a language problem.

Driving in, the barren landscaping was the first thing that seemed out of place for the glamor of movie stardom. Not a tree or shrub in sight. The next lightning bolt came when Zsa Zsa Gabor trotted out to meet us; her arms were full of her small Shih Tzu, complete with a red lipstick kiss mark on its head. She went straight for the Mercedes, not my rented Toyota.

With me in my Toyota was the advertising agency producer. Seeing Zsa Zsa head straight to the Mercedes, he told me, "I can't drive with you anymore!" When we got up to the rest of the group, she plopped her dog in my arms. After all, I was the only woman in that group, so I must be the assistant. I remember I made a mental note that Hollywood would not be kind to a female and to get a Mercedes.

I never understood Zsa Zsa's fame. She was undoubtedly beautiful. She had a sister, Eva, and they were known as the Gabor Sisters. Everywhere they went, paparazzi followed, much like the Kardashians today. With their broad Hungarian accents, they were perceived as exotic, and they both knew how to marry well. It wasn't until 1993 that she had a big hit with the TV show, *The Beverly Hillbillies.*

This was the first of three cross-country stops we'd take filming a commercial for the post office. After Bel Air, we would move on to Atlanta to film Ray Charles and then back to NYC.

Zsa Zsa led us through her mansion. Since no one told me to put the dog down, he was still in my arms. I was a bit taken back by how uninteresting the interior was. To me nothing was particularly grand or even well-appointed. As we moved along, she pointed out interesting facts about the house. The most important one was its former occupant, Howard Hughes. I knew the name but didn't know anything about him. Zsa Zsa, speaking in her thick Hungarian accent, launched into a complete history lesson. It felt as though she had done this often.

"Howard was one of the world's most influential and richest people. He was a billionaire." She let out a little laugh. "But *darlinks,* he was *krazy.* He never left the house. He thought the plants and grasses were trying to poison him. So, he had them all taken out. Can you imagine that!"

I wondered why she hadn't replaced them. Then Zsa Zsa showed us evidence of his reclusive life. With a flip of a switch, the house completely shut down. Impenetrable steel plates now covered all the windows and doors.

As we stood in the master bedroom, Zsa Zsa told us how Howard had paced the room and worn the carpet into a complete circle. As she continued, I was only half listening; a portrait over the fireplace had caught my attention. It was a large portrait of a young woman. I knew I knew her.

"Zsa Zsa, is that your daughter, Francesca Hilton?"

She looked rather surprised and replied, "How do you know her, *darlink*?"

I explained to her how, back in high school, I competed with her daughter in the yearly Shakespeare competition at Hofstra University. Her daughter Francesca attended an all-girls private school. While I was stuck playing Cressida in *Troilus and Cressida,* Francesca got to be Richard III.

"I lost the best actress award to your daughter."

"*Darlink,* you are better off," Zsa Zsa told me. "She is 300 pounds and in a mental institution."

These were her exact words to me. I will never forget them.

The crew followed her to the kitchen, where she had made Hungarian stew for us all. I lingered, trying to process a piece of my past. Coming home from the competition, one of the other students felt it was my fault that we lost "best of." At this moment, in Zsa Zsa's bedroom, I realized that I was never going to win that competition. Not while I competing with one of the wealthiest families in the world. I think Hofstra got a new stage donated to them shortly after the event.

I wanted to call my mother and share my new insights that my high school loss might not have been fair. I missed her all the time. Maybe she would have passed the information on to my father. That's who I really wanted to communicate this to. I could have called him and told him. Even if that had at that time occurred to me, I would never have acted on it. With him still in Queens, those 3,000 miles apart seemed perfect to me.

I wonder what he might have said to others about my acting ability. I don't know why Zsa Zsa was so cavalier about her daughter. Or how dreadful Francesca's life had turned out to be. Was acting Francesca's dream, or, like me, her escape from the reality of her home life? Or did she just want to be loved? After all, isn't that what all actors want? Heck, what everyone wants. Just like the tears, anger, and resentment I had spent on my redhead high school friend, whom I met again at Vidal Sassoon, I was face to face with an equally sad story about another perceived winner from my past. If the world is divided between winners and losers, I began not to see the difference. Each have their own pain points.

Here in Howard Hughes' bedroom, he didn't feel like a winner to me. His presence still filled the room, and that presence woke me and moved me to loosen the grip my feet had on the floor as I stared at Francesca's portrait. I put the pup down and followed the others to the kitchen.

A note on Francesca's life: she was often in and out of recovery. She passed away penniless a year before her mother died. She was never 300 pounds.

Our new English director was quite a character. I'm unsure if drugs played a part in his odd sense of humor or if I was missing something that the British might consider funny. Half the time, I had to guess what he wanted to accomplish, and the other half, I think he was hoping I would achieve it for him. He amused Zsa Zsa to no end, and she giggled at his charming ways.

When that job ended, we barely had time to unpack when our English director and I were back in a plane and headed over the pond to London. We were to interview Dame Barbara Cartland and do a commercial for her latest romance novel. In her life, she wrote over 700 romance novels translated into 38 languages.

Much later, she also became famous as Princess Diana's somewhat batty step-grandmother. However, at the time, I did not know who she was. On the plane over to London, I read two of her books. I considered the books nonsense. Nothing could have prepared me for the woman herself.

We were to drive to Barbara's estate for a preliminary meeting with her. This magnificent home was formerly Beatrix Potter's residence. As we drove in, the land unveiled itself as something out of Ms. Potters' imagination. Rabbits scurried away from our car. This must have been Beatrix's inspiration for her many children's books and certainly the *Peter Rabbit* series. We met a few of the English crew members at the front entrance. We were buzzed in, and a formally attired butler met us at the door. All out of *Downton Abbey!*

Barbara was delayed a bit as she was having her picture taken by Cecil Beaton, the world-renowned photographer. Soon, she glided down the stairs in her pink chiffon gown. Her hair was teased and piled high on her head. She wore tons of makeup spread over her face. In her very high-pitched, very English accent, she asked us to lunch. "James has prepared *sanWhiches for Uss.*"

Sitting at the head of the table, Barbara held court. This dining room was far from lavish. The furniture was older than she was, and we ate on beautiful delicate china. The forks and spoons made that great tinging sound as I stirred my coffee. Out of nowhere came what would be the luncheon conversation. "*I THink Jewissh men are the BESST LOovers, don't you?*"

The whole crew stared at me, and I don't think any of them were Jewish. This could make or break my relationship with these guys. I was always being tested, but not usually by another female. What would I say? I was seated to her left, and the only other woman there, and now I was incredibly uncomfortable.

Coffee—I'd deflect and reach for the coffee directly behind me. As I reached back I could feel Barbara glaring at me. "James will get that for you."

"Barbara, it's right behind me I can get it."

"*Sooo AmerIcan.*" She reaches under the table and there was a buzzer. At first she was gentle. When James didn't appear she went full on crazy on the buzzer. And then started screaming, "JAMES!"

I think he was as old as she was. He did not respond, and soon, the silverware and dishes were dancing around the table as she banged harder and harder on the buzzer. The poor man emerged from the kitchen buttoning up his jacket, and she demanded that my coffee, which I no longer wanted, be poured. The whole lunch episode was bizarre. I still don't know what to make of it all.

Shoot day came, and Barbara was again delayed. This time her pink chiffon gown was even more elaborate. Jewels, perhaps real ones, hung heavily around her neck. Once again, her hair was piled high on her head and teased to the heavens, but now she added a tiara. I noticed one of her false eyelashes was coming undone as it precariously fluttered while she spoke. Who was going to tell her? Of course, it fell to me, the only other woman. She simply put her finger up and slapped it back on.

While the crew moved the equipment into her home, I took the time to take in the living room. Once again, it wasn't that lavish palace I fantasied royalty lived in. Her home was all pink. The wall-to-wall carpet was deep pink shag. Our contract was to shoot only a 30-second commercial. The ad agency decided to tack on an interview with Barbara. We were not prepared for this at all. It was suggested that I do the interview.

By now, I had spent enough time with Barbara to be able to write up some questions that sort of made sense. Barbara wanted to look into the eyes of the interviewer. Being I was much shorter than Barbara, the crew had to build a walkway for me.

They took about ten apple boxes (grip equipment used on all sets) and laid them out to form a runway. As I asked my questions, the camera moved in sync with me toward her. Soon, we were close enough for me to realize that her eyelash was coming undone again. I had to call on all my past acting skills; I so wanted to just burst into gales of laughter. It was all so ridiculous. But this was a job, and I'm a professional. We finished with a flourish, and everyone was happy.

She gave me a little gift: a preserved leaf from a 400-year-old tree that Queen Elizabeth I had planted. It didn't look all that different from any other oak leaf.

"The *Gyppp-sEEss* make these." She had the most dramatic way of pronouncing things.

"*Theeey,*" indicating the Gypsies, "came with the *prop-EER-tty*. Beatrix seemed to like *tHeemm*. I . . . let *theem con-tin-UUe* to live here."

She was getting tired, and her eyelash had by now removed itself. She excused herself and disappeared upstairs.

We started to wrap up, and as the apple boxes were collected, I realized they had been recently painted, and the black paint had not thoroughly dried. There on the pink shag was a ten-foot-long outline of the boxes. A back design that surely would drive Barbara wild. I imagined that poor butler scrubbing all night. We got out as soon as we could. I was always curious that we never received a complaint about the paint. I wonder if that poor butler cleaned it all before Barbara saw it.

An unexpected perk came along when I called the office back in NYC. I told Neil Stearns we had wrapped up with Barbara, and I was coming home. However, due to the excellent exchange rate and my good producing skills, I had $1,000 left over from the budget. He was feeling very generous and said, "Stay there. Enjoy the week, on the company." Wow! I decided it was time to search for my mother's family. I flew to Edinburgh, rented a car, and drove throughout Scotland.

Driving on the wrong side of the road was a feat, let alone driving a stick shift. Fortunately, there was little traffic on the roads I took. It was a week of wonder. My beautiful trip ended in Glasgow, where I met aunts, uncles, and cousins from my mother's side.

I found the Davidson tartan and bought my father a traditional Davidson tie. After turning in the car, I went to Glasgow Airport for a short flight back to London. I found myself being detained by immigration.

A very nice Scot looked over my U. S. passport. He kept looking me up and down. "Ms. Davidson, can you come with me, please this way."

Did I have a choice? I just followed him to a small room, he knocked, and a policewoman opened the door.

"Body check," as he handed her my passport.

I still didn't say anything. My mother's parents had thick Scottish accents, and I never found that threatening. It wasn't until the policewoman asked me to go behind the screen and take off my clothes that I got very nervous.

"I'm going to miss my plane. What is wrong, officer?"

As I complied, she reviewed my clothes and came around the curtain. "Don't fret, lassie. I'm not about to hurt you."

She didn't touch me, just had a good look over. "OK, lassie, put your clothes back on. I just have a few questions. You arrived in Edinburgh over a week ago. Where have you been during that week?"

"I rented a car and drove around. My grandparents are from here."

"You drove by yourself?"

"Yes, I dropped the car off this morning here at the airport."

"Are you sure you didn't just cross the sea and come from Ireland? You look very Irish to me."

Irish, what the heck is she talking about? "I'm not Irish."

"Well, you look Irish, and you can't account for a week here in Scotland, so we had to check. Things are bad these days, and lots of you Americans seem to favor the gangsters in Ireland." She paused. "Hurry and get dressed. Sorry for the time. We can't be too trusting."

I dressed and left quickly; after all, I had a plane to catch. The incident lingered in the far recesses of my mind. I had no idea what they were talking about. It wasn't until years later when I could see Scotland from the Northern Irish shores while traveling Ireland it clicked and I understood why I had been detained. In the late '70s, the IRA (Irish Republican Army) were being watched, and they could not fly directly to London without being caught. So, they rowed to Scotland and went from there to carry out their war on the English. It was a bloody dangerous time.

It would be years before I would come to find out my father was 100% Irish. I was born with black hair and blue eyes, the same coloring as his. I wonder how many other traits we share.

Sixteen

WHO IS *DILLON?*

Upon returning to NYC, I called my father. Since I had found the Davidson name on a tartan there, I connected him to Scotland. In hindsight, my father never said anything about his heritage; I made the assumption that Davidson was a Scottish name—he must be Scottish. Surprisingly, he agreed to see me, and I was oddly excited to visit him. Before I drove to his new apartment, I thought I'd drop in on my grandmother in Jamaica, Queens. Before my mother passed away she warned me, "Watch out for your grandmother, she will outlive us all." Perhaps I was checking in on how much longer I'd have to wait.

I wanted to get that visit over with quickly. I found a parking space right in front of the apartment building and as I walked towards the apartment building, I could feel eyes watching me from above. Heads appeared from many windows. They were all looking at this white gal coming onto their property.

Finally, one shouted out, "It's Peggy's granddaughter. Leave her alone."

Yes, Grandma Davidson was the last white woman in Jamaica, Queens. How did a woman so bigoted end up surrounded by people she looked down on and feared? She would swear her tub was dirty because one of her neighbors came in and used it, that they were the cause of the mice in her apartment, that her checks were missing, loads of batshit crazy stuff.

Well, like mother, like son. This is where my father's attitude came from.

Sitting in her one-room apartment, I watched a mouse scurrying across the floor, competing with roaches for crumbs left behind. There was no bed, just a sofa to sleep on. However, it was—if not clean—tidy. She had once worked as a house-keeper, and I could see she still tried to keep a tidy house for herself. She was taller than me at one time, but now she seemed shorter. She might have been pretty in her younger days. But there were no pictures to prove that. She was agitated and got very quiet. Then she leaned close as if what she was going to say could not, or should not, be heard by anyone else. I felt as though she was always in my face. My earliest memories are of her leaning in so close that I'd always have to pull my head back. I thought she was trying to devour me. So, once again my instinct was to pull my head back. "Do you think your father is the way he is because of what I did?"

I rolled my eyes. But this was strange and out of place. To my mind she never took responsibility or blame for anything.

"I don't know. What did you do?" My curiosity was piqued, but I wouldn't let on so my tone was very mocking.

Now she started to cry. "Well, your father is not a Davidson."

Period, end of sentence, and end of the story as far as I was concerned—just a madwoman rambling on. I have no idea why she let me in on the dark secret of hers and my father's life. Or if there was even any truth to it. Either I appeared uninterested, or she decided not to say anything more. However her tears were still flowing and she was getting even more agitated. Maybe there was a memory there that was indeed painful. I hated being touched by her, and can never remember volunteering a touch towards her on my part. I sensed a touch coming my way. I needed to get away from the mice and roaches and that touch.

I decided to change the subject.

"Grandma, I'm telling you again, you have to leave this apartment. I'll find you a good residence and help pay for it."

By now the dam was broken and she was in full-on crazy mode. How fast this 95 year old got to her feet still amazes me. Perhaps my mother was right and she will outlive me. She's waving her arms in the air and shouting at the top of her lungs. "No, don't you dare. Get out!"

Okay, that's exactly what I wanted to do. But before I could leave she grabbed me and violently turned me towards her. I tried to loosen her grip, but she was damned strong. Now she hit me—well, tried to, but I had enough time to duck. This prompted me to fling my soda in her face. Seeing her dripping in Coke brought my rage down. I was physically fighting with a 95 year old crazy person, and I carried this woman's DNA! I did slam the door as I left. I'm sure the neighbors had a lot to chat about.

I got in the car and calmed down. Arriving at my father's new apartment in Jamaica Estates, I was surprised by how nice the building was. His studio apartment was small but efficient. He looked older and thinner. We chatted about the trip, and then I gave him the Davidson tie I purchased in Scotland. He looked at it and, without a word, quickly put it down. I felt rejected. Here I was, trying to be a good daughter; then, the earlier conversation played in my head—could my grandmother have been right? "Grandma said a crazy thing today."

"What did she say?"

"Oh, that you weren't a Davidson."

He went silent; his gray eyes looked towards me, but he wasn't looking at me. Then, he started to cry. He cleared his throat, and his voice was soft. "I'm not."

I didn't know this man. No matter how much I hated him, I

could feel the small, heartbroken child sitting next to me. This was unlike the hysterical tears he shed at my mother's death. This was something very different. He continued, "My father's name was D-I-L-L-O-N," he spelled it out for me. "No one knows this. I never even told your mother."

I could not believe what I was hearing. I sat very still, I wanted to hear this story. Throughout my childhood he'd been a good storyteller; he was quick to recite a poem, or a joke, at the drop of a hat. But this one didn't come from memorization—this was from the depths of his soul.

"I had a brother who was a year older than I, and he was Thomas Davidson's son."

This was confusing, but I didn't want to interrupt him. I'm trying to put pieces together as he's speaking. So, Davidson wasn't his father. I wondered when he knew that Davidson wasn't his father, and where was this brother? "Davidson knew I was not his child and left your grandmother. He would visit on my brother's birthdays and holidays. He brought presents for him; I got nothing." Then he mentioned his Grandma Kelly, who I'd never heard of. "I lived for a while with my Grandma Kelly. She was the only person who ever loved me."

I'm sitting beside him, and he seems to acknowledge that he knew neither my mother nor I loved him. Well, at least that I didn't love him.

The confessional was over. He got up and changed the subject. "Want a soda?" This trait of changing the topic in an instant was definitely in our DNA.

Woo, wait, what am I hearing? I didn't press him, and I wish I had. I was still stuck on this new name: Dillon. Now, I had this stranger in my head, a stranger who was my grandfather. I thought he stopped the conversation as the memories were painful, and he was unwilling to visit them. Or was he trying to judge my reactions to his life?

My heart went out to him for the first time, but I didn't show him that. Instead, I headed back to Manhattan. The conversation bounced around in my head. Dillon; well, that's an Irish name. My grandmother's maiden name was Hartigan-he was fully Irish. That meant I was at least ½ Irish. Dillon: who is he, and how did he fit into my father's life? At that time, I didn't have the energy or desire to sort out what I heard. My father's side of the family was always a question mark. I have strong memories of my grandmother's sisters, but even they disappeared from our lives when I was in my early teens. Well, I'll have to do a Scarlett O'Hara and I'll think about it tomorrow. After all, I had a career to attend to and a life to get back to.

Seventeen

A LIFE TO GET BACK TO

New York was experiencing a little resurgence of film production. Now that I was home from my job in the UK, I had to
get back to work. I wanted to get back to work. I visited the
set where Mason-Stearns was shooting a commercial with Joan,
who had taken over for me while I was in Scotland.

Through the office wall, I could feel a presence watching
me. This was a new crew member for us; boy, was he cute. His
jeans could not have been tighter, and his body was lovely. Bill
Mason always teased me about the "guys" in the crew. He could
do this because he knew I didn't cross the line of business and
relationships. At least, not any longer; I'd learned that lesson.
But this new guy meant trouble, and even Bill could see that.

I was distracted by Kevin, and soon afternoons were spent away
from work, holed up in my apartment with him. Although Kevin
was not married, he was seriously involved with another gal. He was
very honest about this. But he wasn't forthcoming about the fact that
I was not his only "on the side" person. This was the first time since
my falling in love with Mr. Black, back at RBNB, that I wanted—or
thought I wanted—to have a full-time man in my life. In retrospect,
I'm glad that neither of these men wanted me full-time either. I think
there is, at least for me, a great confusion between sex and love. Girls
growing up in my time had to have these two relationship compo-
nents go hand in hand. No love, no sex. The next generation was able
to separate sex and love. I envied that.

My relationship with Kevin tempted me to stay in NYC. But the draw towards Los Angeles was even bigger. I found myself loving being there so much more than my hometown. Bill Mason and I were a good pair—me as producer and him as director. That confidence tripped me up, and I few times I over-stepped my boundaries. Neil would remind me that I worked for him. And that I seemed to forget it was his company.

Gradually, a wall was built between Neil and me. At times I felt we were becoming enemies. Which was so sad, as in our hearts, we both only wanted the best for Bill. Our next job was once again on location in LA, and I was thrilled. Neil was with us on this job; the tension building back in New York spilled over and the night before the shoot we had a full on argument.

Here's where writing one's life down on paper gets tricky. I've made a choice to bare my soul and be as honest as I can with the events that shaped my life; the people I write about might not be as willing. I have tried to be fair and understand where the opposite side was coming from. Consider their point of view. I could choose to leave this incident out, but then you'd be wondering why I suddenly left a job I loved. Putting all the pieces together, I was trapped.

Neil was asking for some cash that I, as producer, carried for emergencies. Or in this case, to pay for a piece of equipment that Bill requested to work with and the vendor wanted cash on delivery. The next morning, I canceled the equipment before we got to set. When Bill asked about it, I simply said, "Ask Neil." Would it have been safer to simply take the blame, tell Bill that I forgot to order it? It didn't matter; the result would be the same. There was no way out of that trap.

When we returned to NYC, Neil called me into the office. Bill was crying, and I knew what was about to happen. I knew enough to let it be, as Bill needed Neil much more than he needed me. I felt like a child sitting between a parent I loved very much and one I didn't trust—an all too familiar place to be in.

If it wasn't that incident, it would have been another. I've never fully understood or perceived power, and whoever has it will win the day, especially in a man's world.

My heart broke as it sunk in. I would never work with Bill again. For two years, this was home; for the most part, I loved every minute.

I was also frightened of starting over at a new workplace—if I could find one. I was a thirty-year-old woman, and there was no family home to return to. I was indeed on my own and had to support myself. I called everyone I knew to say I was now a freelance production manager. I immediately got a response from Leslie McNeil, who I didn't know personally but by reputation as a first-rate producer at Lear Levin Productions.

My phone rang and a joyful voice told me she'd looked over my resume and wanted me to "come on over."

I met Leslie at the front door of the West Side brownstone the company occupied. That joyful voice came from an equally happy face. Lear lived on the upper floors, and the office was below. Sitting on the sofa in the reception room, she asked me what my dream was. To this day, I can't recall ever having such an insightful interview.

I confided that I wanted to live in LA but would always be available in NYC. To my utter astonishment, this was her reply: "I want to have a baby." Well, that was interesting, and certainly a first in an interview. However, this honesty between us formed the basis for a lifelong friendship, and the statements of our desires would end up being very profound.

Leslie offered me a small, easy job that had to be done immediately. They had a significant commercial planned to shoot in the next two days. Everything was set, but they needed to secure the permits in the town just north of the city.

I returned to my apartment on the Upper West Side, got my little old Toyota out of the garage, and drove north towards the suburbs. Once there, I discovered the town the scout they hired had chosen did not allow filming. How had a professional location scout spent a week getting the filming locations without checking first to see if the town would approve it?

I have always taken the position not to say something is impossible until I found out it indeed was not possible. I spent the remaining day at a nearby town that did allow filming, replacing all the locations for the commercial. When I called in, I reported the bad news first but then gave them the good news. They were impressed. My career as a freelance person was under way.

My relationship with that cute tight-jean guy Kevin continued. It was anything but healthy for me. He'd say he was on his way over, and then I'd not hear from him for days. I allowed myself to be treated as a convenience. I couldn't stand up for myself and demand more. If I did, he'd surely leave.

I realize now that I have always been in relationships that were "threesomes." It was either me, a man, or his significant other. Or it was me, a man, and my work. For me, ultimately, work came first. In my day, I never met a man who enjoyed playing second fiddle to a woman's career. The men in my life always wanted me available for them on their schedule. This was just not possible with my crazy work hours, out-of-town locations, and the devotion I had to the work itself.

There is an interesting side note to the Kevin relationship. I alluded to his perfect body, and it was. However, his face was also pockmarked like mine. I realized how different it was for men than women. Perhaps some of his friends spoke unkindly behind his back about his appearance, but I doubt it. It never crossed my mind to even talk to him about his looks. Certainly, in Hollywood, leading men were allowed to have flaws on their faces and bodies. That was never true for a female. I sometimes see a young person afflicted with acne and want to hug them. With today's care, this no longer has to be a stigma for life.

I began to see Southern California as a new beginning, away from Kevin, my father, and all the old business relationships. Now, I was a freelance worker. What was to stop me from exploring a new territory?

...THEN HOLLYWOOD
BIT BACK

Eighteen

PACK THE CAR!
HOLLYWOOD, HERE I COME

Soon my little dog Sam, my dear friend Carole Pfeffer—the casting director from my days at Griner/Cuesta—and my new used Toyota were on the road across America to Los Angeles. At a monthly rent of $195 I figured I had enough money saved to keep my rent-controlled apartment looking over Central Park for a year; LA was never a sure bet for anyone. I found an affordable furnished apartment in Studio City and struck out for fame.

Once again, I called everyone I knew and said I was now available to work in Los Angeles. I didn't get producing jobs right off the bat. I had to go backward and do production assistant jobs at first. Being a PA is a job that is taken advantage of way too much. Everything that no one else wants to do is given to the PA. They are first on the set and last to leave. But I was grateful just to be working in my new home city.

In the '70s there was a lot of money and drugs flowing on film sets. Many top directors and directors of photography started in commercials. Celebrities realized that it was not shameful to appear in commercials—indeed when the money was so lucrative. I worked with many of them. I remember a Lincoln car commercial with Nancy Sinatra. Her hit song *These Boots Are Made for Walkin'* would play as the car door opened and a pair of men's well-made Italian shoes hit the ground. The camera then panned up to find that it was her dad, Frank Sinatra, dressed in the most elegant suit I'd ever seen.

Every hard-core New Yorker on the set craned their neck to glimpse Frank and get a picture with him. I don't know if my reluctance to have my photo taken with a celebrity was because of how I thought I looked, shyness, or arrogance. In any case, I have hardly any pictures of all the stars I worked with. Someone would say to me, "Jump in," and I'd say, "No, I'm busy," or something like that. This was unfortunate. I would love to have those memories now.

Frank Sinatra wasn't the only Rat Pack member I got to work with. On another job, I was to meet Dean Martin at LAX. I walked across from the terminal we were shooting at, and there he was by himself in the parking lot. We went to cross the street, and as I was checking the traffic, he launched himself into the road. I had to put out a hand to keep him from getting hit. Dean joked that he knew what he was doing; he had "guys" all around him. These "guys" might have been his protectors years ago when there were rumors of Mafia connections, but this day at LAX, there was only my hand to keep him out of oncoming traffic. I felt so sorry for him. Hollywood was not kind to men or women who had outlived their perceived fame.

Brawley, California, southeast of LA, is one of the hottest spots in the United States. I was hired as a PA for a commercial to advertise American Motors' newest small car, the Pacer—a car that went off the market almost as soon as the TV ads were finished. It was considered one of the 50 worst cars ever made.

On film, Brawley can replicate the Sahara Desert with its miles of pristine white desert sands. The commercial seemed to tout that the little car could withstand this brutal weather like a camel. We had a camel with us to prove it. The first thing that went wrong was all the plastic wells in the car melted in the heat. I brought this to the ad exec's attention, whose response was, "Well, how many people would be in 130-degree heat?" Wasn't that the point of the commercial?

Then the next incident was where I almost lost my life. The camel was fed up with filming and broke away from the handler. Fortunately, the talent, Peter Brown (who had a successful western series on TV), was not riding him at the time. We watched as the camel broke over the dunes and onto the road.

We could see a passenger car headed towards the loping camel and waited to see them jam on their brakes. I can only imagine what the conversation in that car was. However, the dangerous part for me was that the camel had left his footprints all over the pristine white sand. Enter the helicopter.

The next day, I was assigned along with another PA to monitor the helicopter hovering over the sand, smoothing it out. This should have been relatively easy to do from the safety of the jeep. Soon we realized that the helicopter was not just smoothing sand out but bringing things up—water bottles, soda, beer cans, dead things.

My new job was to run in after the helicopter left, scoop up debris, and call the pilot back in for another round while I sat in the Jeep. One time somehow, our communication failed. I did not need to look up. I heard the whirl of the blades approaching, and I knew I was in trouble. I tried to use the radio to let the pilot know I was still in the sand. He saw me, but it was too late.

At 125 degrees, a helicopter hovered above my head, blasting sand at me. I barely made it back to the Jeep. I could tell by the look on the other PA's face I was in more trouble than I even realized. He doused me with the water we had in the Jeep but that wasn't going to do the job. "Water, more water," was all I could get out.

"The only water nearby is the canals," he tells me, "and they are filled with scorpions."

Through my sand-filled mouth, I whispered, "Don't care."

He quickly drove to the canal, and I jumped in. Steam hissed off my body, and I left a ton of sand behind for the scorpions to enjoy.

I was totally out of breath and nearly heaving the contents of my stomach when I finally took my seat in the Jeep. Once I could find my voice, I demanded to be driven to the main filming unit. The 1st AD was in charge of sending the helicopter my way, but not until he got the all-clear from me over the radio. I marched up to him.

Still wiping fine sand off my very red sandblasted face, I started yelling at him for releasing the copter too early. He must have known he made a big mistake, but he covered it by treating it as a joke. "Come on, what's a little sand? We're all out here in it, not just you."

He made it sound as though a girlie couldn't take the heat. My fury had no words for him. I was done with taking orders from jerks. Then and there, I promised myself that somehow, I would be the boss from now on. And, when I got there, I would run a safe set.

(A note about safety on the set and the responsibilities of a 1stAD: while I was still living in Santa Fe, NM, they experienced the most tragic event possible: the loss of life. This sad tragedy was avoidable. But the dirty secret of the film industry's working conditions—cutting corners financially—was exposed. In my entire career, even though I worked with guns many times, I only held a gun once. That was when the person in charge of weapons asked me to, as they needed a female hand to fire the pistol in a close-up shot. On-set safety is the responsibility of the 1st AD, and it weighs heavily on all responsible DGA ADs to facilitate the safety checks in front of all crew members and actors. It takes time away from filming, and sometimes it was a challenge to take this time.)

Even though I now lived in LA, I got much of my work from my old buddies in NYC. Leslie McNeil and Lear Levin had a job in Arizona. They needed to find a hidden bridge built under the river's surface that could not be seen but could be found by those who knew where to look. I traveled with the head of the Arizona Film Office to Sedona. After a bit of a search, there it was—the perfect river crossing.

It was, in fact, so hidden that the driver missed it. As our scout car sank into the river, all my photographs for the day floated away. We crawled out of the back window, and he radioed for help.

Soaking wet, we were driven to the small Sedona Airport, put on the smallest plane ever, and flown back to Phoenix. I did feel sorry for my guide from the State Film Office and hoped he would keep his job. I was grateful that I was working for Lear, who was very understanding when I said I had no pictures of anything. Although I wish I would have taken one of the sinking station wagon. Lear would have to take my word for what would work for that particular commercial. I could hear the whole office—with good humor—laughing at my fate.

Lear had sent me to New Mexico to scout Taos Ski Basin to see if a Toyota could fly down the trails and land in the parking lot. I flew into Albuquerque, New Mexico, rented a car, and up I-25 I went. With each mile, I was in awe of the place. It seemed magical. The light hit the mountains and spread a joyous purple color. I felt a connection that I could not explain. I have spoken with my friend, Shirley MacLaine, and she felt the same way when she first drove through New Mexico.

I remember telling my father about New Mexico, and he came up with his one and only WWII story. According to him, he escorted some captured Germans to a plane that would take these scientists to New Mexico, presumably to Los Alamos, to work on the Manhattan Project. I have seen his Army records, and this could well be true. In any case, it was nice to feel he wanted to connect with me about the land I had fallen in love with. The colors, the smells, how vast and unoccupied it seemed. It just soothed my soul.

From then on, any time a job came up that went to New Mexico, I made myself available. While scouting for an Amtrak commercial near Lamy, New Mexico, two state troopers came to me with an urgency that frightened me. There had been a prison break, and the criminals were spotted near where I was scouting the train tracks. They waited until I got into my car and left. It occurred to me that I was often alone somewhere in the world, and no one knew where I was. This was before we were all connected by our cell phones. I sometimes miss that solitude.

Nineteen

I'M AN ASSISTANT DIRECTOR

In 1978 the Screen Actors Guild called a strike against commercial producers. Commercials were my bread and butter, and now I was out of work. It went on for what seemed like an eternity. I could not afford to stay in LA any longer. I packed up and headed back to NYC. As the plane was landing over Queens on a dark winter day, I knew I had given up too soon. I had to get back to my adopted home and back to work.

The first place I visited was Griner/Cuesta, the company where I had worked in the accounting office. Everyone welcomed me home, and I got to spend time with my friend Carole Pfeffer, who was still their casting director. The actors strike had finally ended, and one of the producers there said she had a job for me.

"I'm sorry you've moved back to NYC. I have a great job for you out in LA."

I didn't even have to think about it. "When do you need me there?"

"You'd go back?"

"Watch me." I canceled the company that would bring my car back to NYC and purchased a one-way ticket to LA to start over again. I was going home, but not before the most unexpected gift came.

To become a director, you just needed to be hired by a company that is a signatory to the DGA contract. To become a production manager, assistant director, or stage manager, you must either come through the DGA trainee program or be in the right place at the right time. It appeared that those who served under the director needed to know more about filming than the directors themselves.

Ever since I met Pat Curtis and realized there was at least one female DGA member, I applied continually to the DGA. Each time I got a letter stating I was eligible to apply for their trainee program. I knew I would not ultimately be accepted to the training program because I had no college degree. More important to me was that at that time, there wasn't enough DGA work in NYC, and some in the training program had already spent five years without graduating to full AD status. As it was, I was making more money per day than the trainee rate. Then my miracle letter arrived.

The DGA is divided into West and East Coast branches. It seemed someone had sued the West Coast DGA for being denied membership even though he could provide enough work credentials to gain membership. He had prevailed, and the West Coast admitted him into the DGA.

Now, the East Coast became worried. They had their lawyers review the last five years of applicants to determine who might have a similar lawsuit. Thirty-three applicants were selected as eligible to join the DGA, and I was one of them.

All I needed to do was fill out my application, and the next time I worked in the capacity I was applying for, I was to bring the paperwork down to their office. I started to fill out the application as a 2nd AD when a friend walked by and said, "Don't do that. Go for 1st AD." I changed it. My application was in, and now I just had to get a job that a DGA contract would cover.

Enter Leslie McNeil's prophesy of the future. When we first met we shared our dreams; mine was to live in LA—that was true now—and her dream was to have a baby. Now Leslie was pregnant, and her boss Lear had a job in Northern California. Did I want to take her place? I was both delighted and concerned. As much as I thought I could handle it, I had never done the job as a 1st AD. Enter all the contacts I had made in both LA and NYC. The plan was to hire a 1st AD to do the job while I would be credited with the work.

Lear was such a proponent and champion for women that he agreed to the proposition. I will always be grateful to 1st AD Carolyn Judd for agreeing to do that for me. We went off to Northern California, and it all went smoothly.

After the 2nd day shooting Lear called us all to his motel room to talk to Leslie and hear her new baby in the background. There were tears and smiles as Leslie filled us in on the birth. Then we got to hear her new daughter, Lily, whimper for her mom. I was happy for Leslie, but convinced that path would not be one for me to take. Now, I had legally worked as a 1st AD, even though it was a little shady, and Leslie had a lovely baby girl.

I flew back to NYC with Lear. The head of the East Coast DGA, Stanley Ackerman, had scheduled an appointment at his office—an appointment I knew I needed to keep. I kept my apartment on the Upper West Side. It was too good to give up. I didn't unpack this time as I knew I would be headed back to LA as soon as possible.

I met Stanley in his cubbyhole office on West 57th Street. We chatted for a short time then he rifled through his desk drawer and pulled out what looked like a business card. "I suppose you'll be wanting this." There in his hand was my Directors Guild of America union card with my name on it. As he held it out to me, he suddenly pulled it back. "You're going to LA, aren't you?"

"No," I replied, "I'm a New Yorker; I'm staying here."

He gave me my membership card, and I was on a plane back to LA the next day.

I called Blair Gilbert, who was still the production manager on *Hart to Hart.* Blair was the "fucking woman" I had hired for the commercial that my then-director went nuts over almost killing us pulling full speed off the 101 demanding to know why I had hired a woman AD for him. That shoot was miserable for everyone. But Blair and I now had a solid bond. We were both "fucking women."

I went to work as an additional 2nd AD on *Hart to Hart* within days of arriving back in LA. I found a new apartment, and my little Sam and I settled in for our new life. But back in NYC, things were not entirely settled. Many East Coast members were unhappy about allowing 33 new members in—too much competition. This group counter-sued the East Coast DGA, and all 33 of us had our memberships put on hold.

I found this out when I received a phone call from the head of the West Coast DGA; there was a problem with my membership. I was only a provisional member and could not work as a DGA member until things were settled back East.

"We have a problem," the lawyer for the West Coast DGA tells me. "You have been working for Spelling Goldberg on *Hart to Hart,* and now we find you are not a full DGA member. This is an embarrassment for us."

However, they had a solution, if applicable. Currently, there was in place a ninety-day open period for production managers to join the West Coast DGA. Would I be able to prove that I had worked in Los Angeles for ninety days during the last two years in that capacity?

All those wonderful people I had hired now came into play. With the help of my friends, I easily proved my days and was accepted into the West Coast DGA in the production manager category.

That category allowed me to work in any capacity except director. It took the other 32 provisional members in New York years to clear up their membership status. Indeed, this was a miracle of unforeseen events colliding to push me forward.

I continued working as an additional 2nd AD on *Hart to Hart* on days when they had many background actors working on the set. It's here that I ran into the first of many directors of photography who felt they owned the set.

Duke Callaghan was a contemporary of John Wayne. I don't know who had the nickname of Duke first. I doubt that either of them had never worked with a female AD before. I ran into this everywhere. On my first day working with Duke Callaghan, the 1st AD left me in charge of the set during a lighting setup. Duke finished the lighting and leaned over my head to tell his gaffer, "Tell the girlie I'm ready."

I could not believe what I was hearing. I had come this far and was now a "girlie." I think his gaffer, who was a good deal younger than Duke, was embarrassed and just gave me a pained look. I nodded and went to find the director to let him know we were ready. I knew I could not tell Blair, the production manager, so I filed it away.

I vowed the next person who belittled me would experience the wrath of God—Janet's god. However, in some ways, I should be grateful to Duke. Working with female ADs was new for many of the directors and crews. I'm sure many men who worked with me were working with a female for the first time. Maybe they also thought I was a "girlie" but never said it aloud.

A near accident made me realize how important my job was. We were doing a stunt; a car was to fly full speed down the pier and then go off into the Pacific. We rehearsed it repeatedly, just to the point of going into the water.

The 1st AD, stationed by the camera a good distance away up the hill, was to let us know over the walkie-talkie when the stunt was ready and the camera was to roll. We then would alert everyone on the pier and radio back that the pier was clear of civilians and the background actors were in place.

Suddenly, the car headed our way without any warning. Another AD and I ran like crazy warning the people on the pier. Fortunately, the stunt driver was alert and realized by us running around like madmen that the pier was not cleared. He stopped just before entering the ocean.

To say everyone was furious would be an understatement. This is how mistakes are made in filmmaking, and lives are sometimes lost. This incident on *Hart to Hart* was another wake-up call to the responsibility I would have for the safety of the crews as I continued with my career as a 1st AD.

Blair continued to hire me as much as she could. I was beginning to be accepted as part of the family. Robert Wagner was the star of *Hart to Hart,* and one day in his trailer, I met his wife, Natalie Wood. She was luminous, with a smile and a sincerely kind way about her. I was so impressed that I forgot we had a mutual friend.

Beverly Long had been our casting agent for all the LA jobs Mason/Stearns did. Before her work in casting, Beverly was an actor. Among her roles, she played Natalie's friend in *Rebel Without a Cause.* I didn't mention to Natalie that I had played Maria in *West Side Story.* All this left my brain as I stood in awe of this lovely person.

Natalie politely asked me some questions about being an assistant director. This was a genuine star, and she was interested in me and that I was a female AD on her husbands' show. I should have realized that she was an advocate for women in the film industry since her friend and mine—Beverly Long—was a true feminist.

Meeting Natalie wasn't the only perk I enjoyed on *Hart to Hart*. One weekend the transportation captain loaned me the yellow Mercedes convertible they used on the show. Breezing down Hwy 1 top down, radio blaring, I was in heaven. I thought about how my father would have enjoyed driving this spiffy convertible. It was pure bliss, with the ocean crashing on one side and the road clear before me. There was no going back to New York, going back to being a PA, waiting tables, or being an usher, and certainly no going back to being an actress. But *Hart to Hart* was on hiatus for the summer. And a new job had to be found. But I chose this life, the job-to-job freelance worker, always one paycheck away from unemployment.

Twenty

CADDYSHACK

Mel Howard was a DGA production manager I had worked with back in commercials. He had a job and wanted to know if I was interested in working with him on a Warner Bros. comedy. This film was already in the can-or finished in English-but when Warner showed it to select audiences (focus groups), it didn't play as well as they thought it should. To recoup the investment, they would reshoot some scenes. I signed on with Mel to do reshoots on *Caddyshack*.

Mel and I sat in a private screening room watching the film. When the lights came up, I looked at Mel, and he had a similar expression. Turning to him, I said, "Duh, what was that?"

We were alone in the room, so he spoke candidly. "That is the stupidest thing I've ever seen."

The film, as I recall, had eight slugs, or blank markers, that showed where there was a need for new footage. Principal photography was done in Florida; Mel and I had the assignment to fill in the blanks. So, I would have to find locations in Los Angeles that would blend in with the previously shot footage. Some were easy to find as they were on golf courses. Some were tricky to find, like a doorway to a house that had to match the interior that was shot already.

I was in my element, finding these matching doorways, and getting golf courses to allow us to blow them up and let us stay all night filming. I love these kinds of challenges. We worked for a week getting everything set for filming. Mel and I had scouted with the producer, writer, and director. All good. Except we never really knew what we were shooting. We knew where, but what exactly was elusive.

Writer/producer Doug Kenney and the star, Chevy Chase, had an interesting way of co-writing. As I understood it, at night, they would sit in a room across each other and write the scene we were to shoot the next day. Then they would toss the pages across to each other to see who would laugh the loudest. It was well documented that a good number of drugs flowed during this production, so their laughing at the pages they wrote did not necessarily mean they were hitting the mark. We didn't get those pages until the next day, so "fly by the seat of our pants" was our motto.

During our location scouting trips, I became very fond of Doug Kenney. He was so funny; he was also kind. He came to me to confide that Chevy could be harsh on women, and if I found him that way, I was to go to Doug for support. History tells us that Doug was unhappy about how the film turned out, but during our filming he kept that to himself—or at least the film crew never heard about this. One day while waiting outside the home he shared with Kathryn Walker, she came outside to chat and tell us he was going to be late. She brushed off his lateness with a smile, but she seemed a bit concerned to me. Doug finally joined us, and the day continued in a jolly way.

After all the locations were in place, the first shoot day finally arrived. The set was ready, and the first scene was with Michael O'Keefe at the golf course. I certainly knew what Michael looked like; I had seen the cut footage repeatedly. But I could not find him anywhere. I went to Harold Ramis, the director, and explained that I could not find Michael. Harold looked at me as if I were from outer space, "He's right in front of you."

Yes, I saw a handsome young blond haired man, but he didn't look like the Michael I had been watching in the screening room. The young man in front of me seemed, frankly, dull and uninteresting. Then they rolled the camera, and there he was— the bright, charming guy I had seen on screen.

As a past actress, I was fascinated by this. What was that all about? Shortly after *Caddyshack,* I did an Afterschool Special (a full-length film for TV for school-age children). Corey Allen was directing. After his star turn in *A Rebel Without a Cause,* he turned to directing and also became a well-respected acting coach. I told Corey my Michael O'Keefe story and asked his opinion.

He gave me this explanation. "Sudden permission. The camera rolls, and with the 'action' command, the actor drops his persona and is given permission to be someone else."

Some actors dissolve into their characters well before "action" and stay in character throughout the shoot. You can find them eating lunch as they perceive their character would eat. Other actors are cast so close to their own personality that they never have to step into another soul. They just play themselves. And yet again, some never find that character they were hired to play. That is a painful memory from my days at The American Academy when I was too young to find my character in our final production.

All actors have a different process. This sometimes makes the relationship between actor and crew a difficult one. Crews that have to tiptoe around an actor can become very grumpy. They remind me of my usherettes telling Diane Keaton to leave their ladies' room. They wanted their space and didn't want to tiptoe around Diane. I know many crew members who wanted to give an actor a piece of their mind, but they are not in a position to do that. Except, of course, they can complain to the AD, and they do. Everyone on the set and in the production offices somehow feels free to complain about everything to the AD. I have been the recipient of many of these tirades.

After we finished the scene with Michael, next up was a scene with Chevy. I went to his trailer to fetch him to set. Once inside, I politely said, "We are ready for you, Mr. Chase."

He mumbled a wisecrack and said, "Well, I'm not coming. I'm not ready to go."

I sighed, remembering Doug's warning. I knew I was being tested. Opening the trailer door, I saw Doug standing outside, looking very concerned. Half bravado, half wanting to do my job, but mainly knowing that Doug had told me this sort of thing might happen, I turned back to Chevy and said in a firm voice, "I don't personally give a fuck, but we are ready."

Who was I!!! Doug had this massive grin as he had been listening intently. Believe me, I've never done anything like that again, although I've thought about it often. But I would need a protector like Doug Kenny watching over me if I ever even thought of talking to an actor like that again.

If I'm painting Chevy Chase in an unflattering tone, it's because this was the person presented to me at that time. I'm told he became a different person later in life. Perhaps the loss of his dear friend changed him. Doug died in an accident (or suicide). I'm sure Doug's death was brutal for Chevy; it was for all of Doug's friends. Upon hearing of his passing, in 1980, I cried for this loss. Who knows what pushes someone to the end?

Other incidents during our brief filming presented Chevy in that same unflattering light. One night it was getting very late, and we were all tired. Chevy was hitting a golf ball and improvising some hilarious lines. The few of us still standing were having a good laugh at the hijinks. However, as time wore on, so did the humor. Chevy's demeanor was changing, and Harold Ramis understood what was happening. Chevy was a standup comedian, so he needed an audience. Harold turned to us, "If you don't continue to laugh, we will be here all night." We all became actors that night. Or an audience for Chevy's standup act.

Mel and I finished our assignment then Warner's called us back to shoot more footage. They were pleased with the work we had been doing, so why not commission more? Once again, we watched the film with the slugs in it, and once again, we set out to fill them.

I haven't mentioned Jon Peters yet, as I tried to avoid him from day one of the project. There was a very unpleasant event on our first day at the offices involving the female star of *Caddyshack*. I have omitted this incident for both legal and moral reasons. This was her first movie, and she was practically destroyed by it. The Me Too movement came too late to help her situation.

One day during our shooting, Jon called us all in for a meeting. I stood with Mel, Howard Ramis, Trevor Albert (Harold's assistant), Stanley Gilbert (our Director of Photography), Rusty Lemorande (one of the producers), and others. Like children, we were lined up to be yelled at. Jon was splayed out on his sofa, brushing his beard. He demanded to know who had told us to shoot whatever shot peeved him.

In my mind all I could see was my old boss Vidal Sassoon yelling at anyone within 50 feet, waving his cane around as a weapon. Or that DP who called me "girlie," then that director calling the AD I hired "that fucking woman." Even though Jon was yelling indiscriminately, I felt the arrows were all toward me.

I stupidly spoke up: "Jon, you told us to shoot that."

I quickly realized what a mistake I had made. All eyes were on me. You could hear a pin drop as everyone waited for Jon's response. Everyone was surprised and relieved as Jon didn't seem to care and dismissed us. My big NYC mouth would many times put my career at risk. I was beginning to see a fundamental difference between the coasts. In NYC, they told you to your face if they didn't like you. In LA, well, don't let the smile on one's face let you believe they liked you.

I think this is a good place for a quote from Bill Maher. He refers to Hollywood as filled with "egomaniacs looking to fill the hole from their childhood with applause." And although this doesn't apply to everyone, it is true for many. I include myself here.

At the final screening of *Caddyshack,* Mel and I realized how many little pieces of the film we shot ended up in the final version. We were summoned into a meeting at Orion/Warner to chat with the heads of production, Mark Canton and Mike Medavoy. They were so sincere, caring, and excited about our work. (Remember I said not to let the smiles fool you.) However, they already had two second unit film crews from the Florida shot. They explained that they couldn't give a third film crew end credit in the titles. Would we help them and not go through our union, the DGA, but take a "thank you" credit at the film's end?

Neither Mel nor I could see a future for *Caddyshack,* but we could see a future at Warner's, so we agreed. Other than the daily salary, I have never seen a penny of union residuals from Caddyshack that would have come my way had we gone through the correct process. But if you stay until the end of the movie you will see my "Thank you" credit. It's too bad we didn't have a crystal ball or simply the guts to insist on what was owed us financially and get the film credit we deserved as an additional unit.

175

Twenty-one

FEMALES NEED NOT APPLY

Everybody in the film industry has some sort of story of having been cheated out of well-earned money. We all have that in common. Most film workers are freelancers, and we go from one show to another. While waiting for one's next assignment, you must be prepared that it might not come right away, or the call might arrive, and the timing is off. When I got to Hollywood in the late 70s, everyone who shared their stories with me agreed that it took at least two years to get a chance at a solid career. Hollywood was a lover who wanted to know how much you loved it before committing to you—bringing you to the brink of bankruptcy, both physically and mentally, before those golden doors opened. But it soon became obvious that men who started simultaneously with me were getting jobs while I sat waiting. It was not a matter of talent; it was gender. After all, I was a "girlie." I hoped I would not become "that fucking woman."

It seemed at times that I had made a mistake coming West, as NYC commercial production was much more female-friendly. In 1979 I got a notice from the West Coast DGA that they were forming something called the Women's Steering Committee. This committee would look into the hiring of women in DGA categories. Or lack of hiring!

I not only joined but became the first co-chair with Nancy Heydorn of the new committee. It seems I was not alone in not finding work in the well-established white male-dominated film world. I met so many new faces at this meeting. Some women had terrific resumes, and some had even fewer things to brag about than I did. But we were equally out of work. What were we going to do about it? I don't think the DGA knew what this small group of women was planning. They were going to sue the industry.

Not enough has been written about six brave women who concocted a lawsuit and presented it to the male leadership at the DGA. Joelle Doborow, Lynne Littman, Victoria Hochberg, Susan Bay, Nell Cox, and Dolores Ferraro holed up in their living rooms putting together grievances accumulated over the years of being shut out of work they were more than qualified for.

To the credit of the DGA, they took on this challenge. But the case was not brought to the California Supreme Court until 1983. And before the DGA agreed to support us, they insisted that the newly formed Minority Steering Committee be included. Together, we set off to change the world—at least our Hollywood world.

An excellent documentary, *This Changes Everything* by director Tom Donahue is worth seeing. It explains so much of what we went through. Not much has been written about pioneer women in the film industry. In fact, one of the first film directors ever was a French woman, Alice Guy-Blaché. In 1896 she directed the first narrative short film, *The Fairy of the Cabbages*. She had a fascinating story, and it is well worth your time to look into it.

The DGA persuaded over 32 high-powered Hollywood executives to meet with us. Except for Joelle, The Original Six (the term history has given these women) were all directors, classified as above-the-line. The line refers to the budget and where each job is located in that budget. Nancy Heydorn and I were below-the-line members-below-the-line means assistant directors, production managers, stage managers, etc. We are all part of the directing team.

One of our scheduled meetings was with the studio heads whose job was to hire ADs. I have never been able to hold back when I feel I have something to say. Maybe this goes back to being a chatterbox in the 1st grade. That got me in trouble then, and it would now, also. At this meeting with the very executives I would need to call for work, I asked our lawyers and the others on our committee to please speak up. I feared retaliation from these executives.

"What's the problem with hiring ADs?" This came from the producers' side of the room. I had prepared everyone on our team for the exact hiring problems, yet no one spoke up.

"OK. Well, this meeting is over. There seems to be no problem here," said one of the suits. This was our chance, and I wouldn't let it go.

My inner five-year-old shot her hand up: "I'll tell you what the problem is."

If you see a pattern forming here, you are so right—dead silence on both sides of the table. There and then, I felt once again I was ruining my career, which had not even started yet. But I carried on. When I traveled the country as Snow White, I saw first-hand all the discrimination the Black community endured. Still, until I got to Hollywood, I never realized that as a woman, I was also marginalized and discriminated against. All the small—and not so small— jabs I had heard for years bounced around in my belly. The DP who called me a "girlie," the director stopping the car and demanding I fire the "fucking woman" I had hired for the job, things some crew members yelled at me like; "What are you on the rag?"

So many arrows came my way, some hitting the target and some so random they flew over my head. Here in this meeting room with these well-heeled executives eager to get to lunch, it got to me, and there was no holding me back. I think even the others on the committee were taken aback.

"How many female ADs, either 1st, 2nd, or even trainees, are employed on one of your shows?" Dead silence, "None, not a one." They were uncomfortable.

One cleared his throat, "Well, you're not experienced enough to get some of these jobs."

I blew it. "Really, I know men some of you have met on the golf course who now have DGA jobs on your shows. How are they experienced enough?"

My peers jumped in to save me with exact statistics. And the producers started shuffling papers and gathering their belongings. One spoke up. "Well, we will look into this."

After the meeting, I think I broke down in tears. What had I done?

Within days of the meeting, five of the execs who had sat across from us arranged for me to interview at their studios. I have always speculated that they either saw the handwriting on the wall and knew sooner or later, they would have to make a move to hire at least one of us. Or perhaps they saw in me someone who could handle the job. My money is on the theory they saw a troublemaker, and it would be better to shut me up by playing into my hand and sending me on interviews. In any case, I took all the meetings in good faith.

And here's the hopeful part: some of these men actually wanted to see if a woman could do the job. These were my saviors. One of these was Bob Haynes from Universal. His belief in me got me started as an additional 2nd AD on a few movies and TV shows.

One of the interviews I had was at Twentieth Century Fox. This studio is on the "other side" of the hill. I lived in the Valley, and the studio was in Los Angeles; without traffic it was ten minutes away. If there was traffic—and there always is—it takes over an hour. The production manager had been told to interview me, and he was not happy. After what seemed like an eternity, he looked up from my resume and said, "I see you live in the Valley." I affirmed that. "Wouldn't you rather work in the Valley?" Did he mean *Valley of the Dolls?*

The suit continued for years until it was finally rejected in 1985 by the California Supreme Court, but not because it had no basis. It did. However, the court found that the DGA was just as culpable as the producers we were suing. DGA directors hired assistant directors, and so on. The court suggested that the union clean up its own house first. Because of that legal action and the support of Bob Haynes, Abby Singer, and Bob Butler, by the time the DGA suit was rejected, I was a working member of the studio system.

As true with most whistle-blowers, the six women who came forth and stood up to the injustice in Hollywood didn't necessarily reap any rewards. That lawsuit may not have helped the women who got it all started. While they'd continue to work in Hollywood, they never climbed the mountain as high as they should have. However, Nancy Heydorn and I were below-the-line; we fared better.

Twenty-two

RUSH WEEK, WHAT'S THAT?

I got a call from one of the women I met at the DGA Steering Committee. Was I free to go to the Midwest to work on a documentary about rush week? Now, I had no idea what a "rush week" was. Soon we were in Indiana, planning our filming on how sororities selected their recruits. It didn't take long before the university realized the film would have a negative bias against this practice of selecting new sorority sisters. They ordered us to leave.

The director wanted to continue, so another campus was found. We flew down to Oxford, Mississippi. It would never have occurred to the University of Mississippi—Ole Miss— that we were out to do a hatchet job on their beloved rush week.

The campus and the town looked like a movie set to me. Spanish moss slid off the limbs of trees, quaint brick buildings, and small shops lined clean streets. And it was white, so white. Our crew of 6 was invited to all the events. We fit in, at least color-wise.

One of the most incredible things about making a film is the variety of life and lifestyles I could inhabit. Here, I got to understand the social side of college life. We sat in the ante-bellum-decorated living room of one sorority and watched a slide show of the gals they wanted—and the ones they didn't want—to join them for the coming college year. The "sisters" were coached in how to approach each pledge so they wouldn't offend them, at least not to their faces. They went so far as to have hand signals they'd pass on to each other, letting them in on some secret knowledge they had gained about the recruit they were interviewing.

One young sorority sister went ballistic over one pledge who had committed the cardinal sin of dating a different sorority sister's ex-boyfriend. Yikes, how did they keep it all straight? They were evil to this gal. They made her think she was accepted into their group. She believed them and stopped pledging to other sororities. In my opinion, this was deliberate and nasty. Now this young girl was left out of all the sororities and was heartbroken. And when the fraternity guys got in on the action, it was crazier. They drove up and down the streets, yelling, honking horns, and ogling the pledges. And who knows what else happened behind locked doors? There was certainly a lot of drinking involved.

One of my tasks was to interview the residents about how they felt about Ole Miss, particularly how they felt about rush week. Stopping an ancient Black man, I asked him, "Sir, what do you think of all this commotion over rush week?"

He half chuckled, "Well, it *ant's* nothing to me."

I pressed, "Do you feel it's a waste of time?"

"It's their time, not mine. But it gets a bit crazy, what with all the drinking and stuff. *I'ze* don't drink. Bad stuff, that is. Causes bad things to happen."

After the interviews, I had to get a picture release from whomever we spoke with. "Do you mind if I take a picture of you?"

He asked me, "What's *yas* need that for?"

"Just our records, It's fine. No one will see it."

This kind soul didn't need my interfering in his life, but I had to go on. "And would you mind signing this? It's a release so that we can use your words." I was following orders but really why did we need any of this?

He was embarrassed as he signed his personal X on the dotted line. He was not the only X I got that day. I began to wonder how anyone could tell one signed X from another. Was their identity boiled down to an X? Thinking back to all the kids I performed for as Snow White, I realized these men and women were their grandparents. How many more generations would it take for full equality? If I continued thinking about these things, depression would surely overwhelm me, and I would be useless at my job. I thanked him and went back to the motel.

We were set up to film in the auditorium the night when all the gals got their notices of what house they had been accepted to. In such a public setting, everyone would know the failures and successes of each pledge. Screams would go out, and then sobs. We were done filming, and a few of us retreated to the ladies room. There we found a young gal about to kill herself—she didn't get the sorority house she wanted. Our director and camerawoman stepped up, and we stayed with this poor young woman until we were sure she would not go through with it. We had also called for help from the university. We left when someone in charge showed up.

It seemed wrong to care that much about being accepted into a sorority. In hindsight, is this any worse than my toying with suicide when I failed an audition? Or being brokenhearted in love? Being young, it's just all so dramatic.

Back to LA and back to the job search. This is precisely when Bob Haynes entered my life and gave me my start. He was at Universal Studios, and yes, it's in the Valley. Bob was in charge of staffing the crew, specifically additional ADs. There are so many men and women who will tell you that Bob gave them their first shot. He genuinely wanted to see people thrive. Being good at your job—that was all he asked of you. Since I had already worked on *Hart to Hart,* a Universal TV show, I was a somewhat safe bet for him. He immediately sent me off to downtown LA to work on *The Sting II,* a sequel to the popular original film.

The LA Convention Center had been turned into a boxing arena. There were 800 extras, all in period dress, filling the seats around the boxing ring. I had never worked with this many extras before; it was daunting. In addition to the regular AD team, they hired three additional 2nd ADs. I was the newest in the group. Right off the bat, I realized there seemed to be chaos everywhere.

I was stationed high in the nosebleed section, and communication with the rest of the AD team was relatively weak. I had little warning about where the camera would focus and even less about what was next. The first time I realized I was caught on camera was the last. I went to the wardrobe department and got a period coat and hat to fit in with the extras. This way, I was just one of the crowd if I was caught on camera.

Then, without warning, it was announced over the PA system that for shooting tomorrow, only 300 of the nearly 800 extras would be called back. The director, Jeremy Kagan, was to go among the extras selecting the ones to return the next day. I asked the key 2nd AD what the plan was. There was none.

I took it upon myself to find a prop person and ask if they had paper tickets. Of course, they did. I then went to Jeremy and said I would follow him around, giving tickets to the extras he chose to ensure the right ones would return the next day. These people were so desperate for work that they would cling to his pant legs, begging him for a ticket. It was very sad. If I had not done this, 800 extras would have shown up the next day, swearing they had been chosen. It baffled me why the newest person on the team should have thought of this—the only woman on their team.

Suddenly, another announcement came over the PA system that they were wrapping for the day, and the buses would be outside—another thing I had no warning of. I looked across at another AD nearby, and he read the panic in my eyes. We both understood what was about to happen. It was a stampede for the exit doors. We both charged outside where the buses were to pick up the extras. They had to be transported back to the holding area miles away to get their street clothes back and sign the vouchers to be paid. They just wanted to be paid and get home. So, each of the 800 men and women wanted to be on that first bus.

I reached the first bus just as some extras began fighting to get on, even throwing each other off the waiting line and dangerously close to the bus's wheels. I ordered the driver to close the doors and gave him a new meeting place. The other AD did the same for the next bus. When some extras realized we changed the meeting area for the buses, they began to orderly turn and get in line down the street. Others were in a full-blown panic. I tried my best to calm the situation, but many were so frightened they'd be left downtown without being paid for their work. I've never had to physically restrain grown men (other than Dean Martin at LAX), but I did what was necessary that day.

It was left to the other new AD and me to return to Universal offices that night to do the paperwork. We were both exhausted. By now, we were in our 16th hour of working that day. Looking over the time cards to approve all 800, we realized many of these extras did not speak English. We found out they had been recruited from various unemployment offices and shelters. We heard the next day that many did not return their period costumes; I think these outfits might have been better than their own street clothes. Going over the day's events, I swore I would remember the mistakes made that day as I moved up in my career.

I don't think the general public realizes filming can be dangerous work. There have been horrible accidents where crew and actors have lost their lives during production. Everyone working on a film set has to stay awake and aware. That is complicated by the horrible hours we were being asked to work.

For some shows I worked on, a fourteen-hour day was a blessing. Your rest hours depend on what is called "turnaround." The time the union says is the least amount a crew can have between leaving the set and returning the next day. The union contracts vary, but generally, the time between leaving the location and returning was 9 hours. TMZ is not just the name of a gossip show. In the film world, it meant the thirty-mile zone one could work in without being paid drive time. With traffic, as it was in Los Angeles, that left very little sleep time. Oh, yes, it's a glamorous business.

These complaints and many others led the DGA to the brink of a strike. The history books say the DGA was only on strike once and only for forty minutes. That strike was in 1987, but in 1982 we were unofficially on strike for fifteen minutes. I know. I was there.

As contract talks progressed the DGA formed two separate committees to move the strike forward in case the negotiations failed. The Negotiating Committee was to hammer out the details of what the DGA wanted from the producers. The Strike Committee would prepare for the walkout. As Nancy Heydorn and I were still co-chairs of the Women's Steering Committee, we were assigned to the Strike Committee. This was up our alley as we both were so good at organization.

The chair of The Strike Committee was Clint Eastwood. As chair, he invited some of his friends and colleagues to join the committee. Don Siegel, who directed Clint in many of the *Dirty Harry* series, was one of Clint's friends. Each morning, we gathered in one of the board rooms and sat around the board table with Clint at the head. Don sat directly behind me, and I could feel his rebuff at a woman having a seat at the table while he was on the sidelines. Everyone knew about his fight with Bette Midler in their film *The Jinxed*. I got the feeling that any strong woman would not be a fan of Don's. Likewise I could not see Don being a fan of any strong woman. The days dragged on, and Clint and his studio stories entertained us, but the actual strike plans were going nowhere.

Robert Butler, who had enormous success with the TV show *Hill Street Blues,* was also on the committee. I saw in Bob a practical TV director and knew he would listen to Nancy and me and our concerns regarding the committee.

"Bob, can we chat?" Nancy and I took him outside the room. "We are going nowhere. The DGA will look foolish if we go on strike." Bob sighed. I continued, "We have no picket signs, no picket area, no permits, and nothing we need to carry out a successful strike. As the union in charge of planning films, we will fall on our faces."

Bob was reluctant to take on Clint, and he assured us that, given some time, Clint would figure out we needed these things. "Well, let's just see how things go."

We returned to the room, and in less than an hour, Bob stood up. "Clint, I'd like to take a few of us to another room and do some planning." My ears picked up. Bob continued, "We need you to stay with this committee in the board room for the larger problems. We'll just go off and do the day-to-day stuff."

I didn't look toward Clint to see his reaction; I just kept my eyes on Bob. "I'll take Janet, Nancy, and Rick, and we'll just meet in another room."

Clint thought well of the idea. "Bob, that's a good idea. Take the other board room for your planning committee."

Plan we did; we were so organized with signs, banners, buses, permits—everything needed to do a scene in a film about a strike. The negotiations were getting tight, and it looked as though we would be on strike. With no contract, we put together the first picket lines at Universal's back entrance. D-day arrived, and I was up around 4 a. m. waiting for the call to go or not go.

The call came. "Go." We met at the DGA offices and boarded our buses. I was captain, and everyone knew to follow my lead. We got to the back entrance of Universal and dispersed to the street; it was now 5:55 a. m., and there was no contract. Just after 6 a. m., a police car came up the road with the speaker blaring my name. "Janet Davidson, we need to speak with Janet Davidson."

Wow! I walked over to the police car. Two seasoned officers asked me as if I was being interrogated, "Are you Janet Davidson?"

"Yes."

"Get in. We will take you to a phone. You have to call the president of the DGA."

You have to understand cell phones were still not a commonality. Now they are a life link and have generally made life easier and significantly more manageable in the film world. You can't imagine what location shooting was like before cell phones.

They drove me to a payphone, and I called the DGA with the number the officers gave me.

"This is Janet Davidson calling for Gil Cates," who was our president at that time. A second person got on the phone, asking me again for my identity; it was very dramatic.

Gil got on the phone. "Is this Janet Davidson?" Again already. "Janet, call off the strike. We won." The officers drove me back to the buses, and I got on my bullhorn.

"Go home. I just spoke with Gil, and we won! The strike is over." Now everyone is cheering—a brief moment of fame.

That is an excellent ending to this story, but there is an even better one. Robert Butler was very pleased with the work that Rick Wallace, Nancy Heydorn, and I had done. "I'd take you anywhere. You guys did a great job." Now, promises are always made in Hollywood, but he was the real thing. Rick went to work on *Hill Street Blues,* Nancy had a job already, and I got a call from Abby Singer at MTM. The studio is named after the long-running Mary Tyler Moore show that was shot there.

Twenty-three

REMINGTON STEELE

Besides his hit series *Hill Street Blues,* Robert Butler had a new show, *Remington Steele.* He had shot the pilot, and now they had an order for twenty-two episodes. I sat across from the world-famous Abby Singer at his office on the MTM Studio lot. Abby started out as an AD, moved up to production manager, and now was an executive. Although his office was small it was comfortable. Abby was in charge of production at MTM Studios, and Remington Steele was one of their shows. I was both nervous and excited at the same moment. After the usual hello's and "how are you's, "Abby offered me a seat across from his desk. A large desk so covered with paperwork that there was not an ounce of visible wood surface.

"Bob tells me how much he liked working with you on the Strike Committee. He thinks you'd fit in perfectly here at MTM. One of the 1st assistant directors slots is open on *Remington Steele*, and Bob would like you aboard."

I had no idea what *Remington Steele* was about, nor did I know who would be in it. Abby gave a brief description. "It's our new detective show, sort of comedy and drama combined. Stephanie Zimbalist is staring and a new Irish guy, Pierce Brosnan."

Now I digress for a bit. Abby was famous on all film sets, even in foreign countries. The last shot of the day is called the "martini." This tells the crew to start packing up; the workday is ending. The second to last became the "Abby Singer," or the "Abby." There are many stories of why this second-to-last shot got his name attached to it. Abby said he used it to trick the guys upstairs (producers) when they demanded the show wrap on the next shot. Abby would make a show of it and announce the very next shot was the last shot, but he'd call it the Abby, not the martini, which the crew knew was code that it was not, in fact, the last shot. Soon it became a helpful tool to prepare the crew for the end of the day.

Abby's wife told me they were on vacation in Israel and stumbled upon a film crew. Suddenly the AD called out the "Abby Singer." She went to him and said, "That is my husband, Abby Singer." The Israeli AD laughed and was amazed that Abby was a real-life person.

So, the famous Abby Singer offered me one of the two 1st AD slots. On a film series like *Remington*, you alternated directors and 1st AD. This is so there is no time lag in production. While one team, director and AD, preps the next show, a different team of director and AD shoot the current show. It ends up that each AD shoots eleven episodes a season.

Now, I had never held the position of 1st AD on anything but commercials. The look on my petrified face gave me away. I don't think I know of any man who would have questioned taking the job, even if they weren't qualified.

Abby, being so wise, saw fear on my face. "Would you rather be the 2nd AD?"

I had butterflies in my stomach. I wanted to move up the ranks but also knew, as a woman I'd have doubters waiting to knock me down. "Yes, I think that would be better."

The production staff of *Remington Steele* shared a building with both *Hill Street Blues* and *St. Elsewhere.* The 1st AD on St. *Elsewhere,* Pamela Grant, became one of my best friends. She was only a few years younger than I and also an ex-New Yorker. We had both started out in commercials and had actually worked together, even though we never met. I did my part on the East Coast as she carried out the West Coast portion of the shoot. We worked well together.

Now sharing office space we got to know each other so well that we'd compare notes and paychecks. Her show was easier to shoot as it was most always interior scenes shot on their stages, unlike *Remington,* which was shot half the time out on location and had stunts and special effects. Yet, we were paid the same. Until the overtime kicked in, which I had plenty of.

These three shows became TV history. It was a thrill to drive onto the MTM lot each day. I had my own parking space with my name on it. It tickled me every time I drove past the gates. This studio, nestled on a quiet street in Studio City, had been the home of the Mary Tyler Moore Show, and the studio bore her name. Many times I felt like throwing my hat into the air as she did at the opening of her iconic TV show. Even more exciting, it introduced a new star to America—Pierce Brosnan. To this day, when anyone asks me who my favorite star was, I'll say Pierce.

If you look up *Remington Steele* on various internet film sites, it is often referred to as "ground-breaking." I knew it was a very different show even as we filmed it, and it was sometimes challenging to shoot. We had stunts and special effects that no other TV series was doing in those days. It was a learning curve for all of us. Indeed, working full-time on a series was a challenge for me. Becoming a star was its own challenge for Pierce.

I have to confess that, at times, Pierce's handsome face would distract even me. I wrote earlier of our encounter with the grade school kids and how Pierce realized that stardom was changing his public and personal life. With each passing day, his fame grew. But he stayed the same kind person I first met.

In my career, I have only gotten two autographs. Both were not for me but for my father. I think I was trying to prove to my father that I was successful. We worked with Buzz Aldrin in the mid '70's doing a commercial for I don't know what. He had just written a book, *First on the Moon,* and he insisted he sign a book for me.

I thought, great; I'll give it to my father. When I gave it to him, he had a fit. "Did he touch you?" Huh? What? Where did this attitude come from? Perhaps he knew more about men than I gave him credit for.

The next autograph I asked for was from Pierce. My father had a different reaction to this one. He proudly hung Pierce's autographed face on the wall of the liquor store he worked at. The liquor was of no interest to him but he could gamble as they sold off-track betting tickets there. That must have felt like home to him. I never spent too much time on why he had such wildly different reactions to these men. Really, I never spent any time trying to understand him. I'm sorry for this.

It was clear to everyone that one of the 1st ADs working on the show was just not into the show. He'd disappear for what seemed like hours at a time. I liked this man, but he was very cavalier about the work. That was to my benefit as I took over the set as the 1st AD quite often. It was indeed on-the-job training. The directors began to rely on me more and more. My confidence grew with each episode. After five episodes, that AD left the show, and I was asked to move up to 1st AD. This was amazing. So few females were working in this category, and I would take on one of the most challenging shows produced at that time. I would not fail.

Soon after I took the reins of 1st AD, Pierce had to do a scene in the shower. He took his robe off, and there he was in his little black briefs. As he stepped into the water, he looked at me, the only woman on the set; "Ah, Janet, this is what you've been waiting for." He has a great sense of humor.

A year before, I was hired on an American Film Institute student project. Jeff Goldblum was our male lead. There was a scene where he and the female lead were in bed together. Jeff looked around at the all-female crew and confessed, "This is making me nervous, having all of you women look at me."

Our female star sat straight up, "How do you think women have felt all these years with all male crews?"

Jeff nodded; he got it.

There have been many reports of the discord between our *Remington* stars. Stephanie Zimbalist could not have been more different in upbringing and social commitment than Pierce. Her father, Efrem Zimbalist Jr., had two long-running TV shows, *77 Sunset Strip* and *The FBI*. Stephanie grew up in the Hollywood system. Pierce's Irish background was far from the Hollywood world. He was happily married with two children and another one on the way. Stephanie was single and devoted to her Bible studies. But on camera, they worked, which is all that is important in TV land.

For those of us in production, there were certain lines we could not cross. One of our producers, Gareth Davies, learned I had spent a Christmas with Pierce and his family. He was furious and called me into his office. He was concerned Stephanie would find out, and he had enough trouble trying to calm her fears that production was paying more attention to Pierce. She seemed concerned that the crew "liked Pierce better than me." So, I was warned not to take sides and become too friendly with Pierce. Or perhaps Gareth was just upset he hadn't been invited to the Christmas gathering.

I had an assistant who would sit with Stephanie and read the Bible during breaks, and that went very far in calming her.

In retrospect, I realize how hard it must have been for her. She had a recognizable name, and I'm sure was hired well before Pierce. It was supposed to be the Laura Holt (her character's name) show, but it became Pierce Brosnan's show instead. I'd love to put a virtual arm around her now and give her a good hug. Years later, I did go to see Stephanie in her theatrical run of Sylvia. She was terrific in the role. She seemed happy to be away from the grind of TV.

There was a wonderful character I met during *Remington*—Lois Thurman. She was a script supervisor a few months short on her retirement plan. She needed a job that would only last long enough to give her the required days to retire with full benefits. She also needed a place to live as she had already moved away from Hollywood. So, she came to live with me. Lois had been one of Alfred Hitchcock's script supervisors: *Marnie, The Birds, Torn Curtain,* and *Family Plot,* and with a few drinks in my kitchen, I could get her to tell me Hitch stories.

How she became his script supervisor is in itself a pure studio tale. Like all the jobs in Hollywood in the 50s, script supervisors were also males. Hitchcock needed a new script person, and Universal sent another man his way. As Lois told it, Hitchcock was furious that the studio should pick someone for him and not allow him to choose for himself. So, he demanded that all the secretaries on the lot be lined up for him to choose from. And, of course, they were all females. Lois said she was the tallest and the blondest, and she was selected. She knew nothing of being a script supervisor, but she knew how to be a good secretary, and that's what Hitch needed.

Lois never let on to our directors on *Remington* who her previous director had been. Had some of them known that Lois had worked with Hitchcock, they would have been intimidated, and rightfully so. Some of the newer directors could have learned a lot from Lois. I know I did. She never bragged about her life and her life experiences. A few years ago, I got a letter from a lawyer in Tucson. To my surprise, Lois had left funds for me in her will. After all those years, I realized how we cherished that short friendship.

Lois kept such a low profile that I'm sure no one ever referred to her as a "fucking woman." But that phrase appeared in my life once again. Were all strong women to have that moniker? One of the better consequences of the earlier lawsuit and our strike was that producers realized they had to hire some female directors for their shows. *Remington* had a female director for the first time, and I was her AD. One of the AD's jobs is to keep the office informed of how the shoot crew is doing. As I moved on in the business, I could predict, sometimes within minutes, where we should be in the day's lineup.

Since we still didn't have cell phones, calling the office was always a chore. Sometimes I'd have to get a driver to take me to a phone. This took me away from the shoot and always annoyed me. We were shooting at a home in the Los Feliz section of LA this day, and I could use the house phone to check-in. I got word that Gareth Davies, our producer, wanted me to call immediately. I was on the downstairs phone with him, and he was angry at how far behind we were. At the time, *Remington* was known for having long hours and tough shooting conditions. Except for maybe two well-seasoned directors that could keep up with the show's pace, we were always behind schedule. There were never enough hours in the day for all we had to accomplish.

As I called in to tell Gareth where we were time wise, his first response was, "What is the fucking woman doing?" How do you answer this? I tried to calm him down and assure him we were okay and that we'd pick up the pace. I actually didn't believe this; she was far behind. After he slammed the phone down, I heard a second click; our director was listening in on the extension upstairs. Now I had a furious producer and an enraged and hurt director to handle. It was a while before we had another female director. It is the case that one male director can seem to "fuck up" many times, and it's forgiven. But if one woman is less than perfect, all women are to blame.

The incidents of what we might call my sixth sense are numerous. At work, I would know things were going to happen and was able to schedule the shoot around them. Abby Singer asked me once why I was changing the schedule for the next day's shoot. We had a rain forecast, and he wanted to switch locations from the beach house we were scheduled to shoot to our stages. Somehow, I assured him the rain would hold off.

"On what do you base this knowledge?"

I answered, "I just know."

He had grown to trust this sixth sense of mine, and he agreed to go ahead and shoot at the beach. We finished filming that day just as the rain started. The set dressers could not even strike the furniture because the rain was so intense. Malibu was flooded for four days, but we finished our shooting day and were on schedule. Abby never questioned my sixth sense again.

At the end of our second season, one of our directors, Jeff Bleckner, asked me to be his 1st AD on a movie of the week he was hired for. I had only one episode left for the season at *Remington*, and the director of that episode was Don Weis. He was a seasoned pro who had been directing since the early '50s and could have done every job on the set by himself. I spoke with Don, and he gave me his blessing to leave early. Then I went to Gareth to seek permission to leave, take this opportunity to move up in my career, and put a movie on my resume. In his best, calmest English accent, Gareth told me I could not leave the series early, no matter who the director was. They just could not afford to lose me. Very flattering, but not true. I stayed and finished the last *Remington* of the season.

Episodic TV in those days had a season or a run. Production would end around March, and then wait to see if they were "picked up" for another season. At that time, a full season was 22 episodes. You were lucky if you were on a show that got their pickup before the show wrapped the current season. This was the best of all worlds. You knew you had a job to return to when filming resumed so that you could afford to take three months off. If your pickup had not come during filming, you had to nervously wait until the networks announced the new fall lineup. We were a hit and had already been picked up (renewed), so we knew we were returning to *Remington* for a third season.

Then the phone rang, and it was Gareth. A show had been canceled, and Gareth's friend was the 1st AD on that series. Gareth was sorry, but they were replacing me with this guy. I was furious, devastated and frightened all at the same time. I had just bought my first house and had a mortgage to pay. *Remington* had become my family, and I would not see them again. It's common to bond with your fellow workers in this familiar way. Love or hate them, you are locked together for hours, days, and weeks of hard work.

I looked back on Gareth's telling me I was too important to the show to leave early for another production—and only a month or so later, I was fired! In one of the subsequent DGA contracts, this firing without cause became illegal, and I would have gotten a good amount of money for Gareth's choice. However, producers can always find a reason, something to justify their actions. My thought process of not being good enough began to take hold, and I had to have a stern talk with myself. I consoled myself by thinking they would have brought someone else in after that first season if I were not up to the job.

In the early days, when I was still the 2nd AD, Gareth had proved to be an ally. After I yelled for quiet one day, a crew person yelled back, "Are you on the rag?" Meaning was I having my period, and this demeaning comment was meant to send me into a fit of tears. Instead, it got him fired as Gareth was standing near me and heard him. I don't think he ever considered me as one of those "fucking women." He was just one of many men who felt a man had a family and needed the work.

I needed to keep working as much for the money as for my sanity. So, I took the 2nd AD job on the same movie that I had been offered the job of 1st on. This was not a great move. It was called *When Your Lover Leaves*. Since work was my love, it rang a bell with me.

The best part of this film was shooting on the beach in Santa Cruz, California, and my best friend, Libby (Cinderella), was working on the show also. She had moved to LA and was now a costume designer.

This was a Ron Howard/Henry Winkler production. I must have missed the day they were on set, or more likely; I was redoing paperwork the 1st AD relegated me to. It was very frustrating for me to go backward and take orders again. He and I had very different working styles, which made matters worse. On top of all this, the lead actress, Valerie Perrine, had something physically or mentally amiss. Each day we fell farther and farther behind. She had a terrible time remembering the simplest of dialogue.

My relief from this insanity was to ride the roller-coaster at the end of the day. The guys running the ride got to know me. When one turn around the hills and valleys of the ride stopped, I would not get out of my seat, and they'd say, "Going again, miss?"

"Yep." Once out of earshot I'd yell, scream, and cry all at the same time. Tears would shoot out sideways as the wind carried them along.

One night instead of riding the roller-coaster, a crew member and I went out drinking. It was unusual for me to drink, let alone during a show. I stumbled back to the hotel, and, fortunately, Libby got to me and threw me into a cold bathtub. I hated being a 2nd AD and didn't want to return to that. By now, Gareth's phone call had set in, and I faced the reality of my looming unemployment. Making phone calls to producers and directors for me was like auditioning for the part. It was a different version of my eight bars and "thank you, bye-bye." I loved doing *Remington Steele* and cried many nights at not being back there.

The film fell horribly behind schedule, and on the last day, we had to make up an impossible number of pages—26 to be exact. The average day would cover maybe 5 or 10 pages at most. It was too much work to ask anyone to do in one day, and our star was definitely not up to it. We made cue cards and placed them from one location on the set to another so she could follow her blocking that way. Then I would walk from one cue card to the next, and she would watch and follow me. We put them inside cupboards and drawers with tiny arrows pointing to where the camera would be next.

Somehow we finished that show all in one piece. Then back home to LA. Back to making phone calls for work.

After my time on *Remington,* I did see Pierce on a few more occasions. I visited him on the set of a film he was doing after his wife Cassie passed away. We sat and chatted about life. He had been offered the new James Bond film, but NBC would not let him out of his *Remington* contract. In a way, I saw this as a gift. Remembering how mobbed he was at the grade school, becoming

James Bond would have left him no privacy. I could never forget how when I was a student and how crazy wild the Beatles fans were. From that day forward, the magnitude of their fame never left them off the pages of the tabloids. This would have been miserable for Pierce. And not allowed him his time to grieve his loss.

"Pierce, that ended up being for the best. You got to spend the time you had left with Cassie without the paparazzi hanging around." He agreed, and I think he knew his time to be Bond would come around again.

The last time I saw him was while living in Santa Fe. He was doing a film there, and they had a second unit for which they needed an AD. I was already directing and hadn't done AD work for a while, but it was Pierce. The reunion was sweet. He was working underwater in a pool; I was doing the usual AD work on the sidelines. The producer, director, and DP huddled to chat when the shot was done. I was on the outside of their private huddle. After all, I was only the AD. Hollywood has a pecking order, and almost everyone knows their place. As Pierce got out of the pool, I went to walk him to his trailer. He noticed the executive group huddled and asked if I had met the producer.

"No, it's OK."

He grabbed my hand and led me into the middle of the group. "This is a dear old friend of mine. I want you to meet Janet Davidson, who is a director and a great person." Then he winked and walked away.

I was now on equal footing with the executives in the huddle. Pierce knew the game and wasn't having someone he cared for left out. Except on the big screen as James Bond and in many other wonderful roles, that was the last time I saw Pierce Brosnan, the handsomest man in the world.

Twenty-four

THIS IS MURDER, SHE WROTE

I now had two mortgages to pay. My dear friend, Leslie McNeil and I decided to enter into a business arrangement and purchase a vacation house in Lake Arrowhead, CA. I was only in my house in Van Nuys a few months before Gareth handed me my severance check. I needed income, but my ego needed to get to work even more. I knew how much I'd miss my *Remington* family. I had to dry my tears, rage against the business, and then get on the phone to look for my next job. The first person I called was Bob Haynes at Universal. "Bob, I'm not returning to *Remington Steele*. Do you have anything for me?"

"Sorry for their loss, but I have two new shows we could use you on."

I chose *Murder, She Wrote,* and they accepted me.

Knowing I had employment ahead, I decided to consult a Beverly Hills plastic surgeon to see what he would do about my face. He prescribed a face lift. So, at 35, I had my first face lift. The theory is that if you pull the skin back, the surface is smoother, and the pockmarks aren't as visible. It worked, and I was so high on the results that I could not wait to show myself off.

Murder was a throwback to the old way of doing TV. Its star, Angela Lansbury, was a Broadway fixture. I never did mention to her that I had been an usher at her show, *Mame.* It was a family affair for Angela. Her husband, Peter Shaw, was an executive producer, and her son, Anthony Shaw, was her assistant. Anthony learned quickly and went on to direct over 60 episodes. Angela brought on many of her friends from Broadway, which was a gas for me. I could sing all the songs from the shows I had seen them in.

After the fast pace of *Remington,* I was a bit out of step with *Murder.* The production office was headed by a man who was a fixture at Universal—Robert O'Neill. He was very set in his ways, and I think I was the first female AD he had worked with. It was tough for me to keep quiet about some of the decisions that were just not top-notch ways of doing current TV. But I knew who had the real power—Angela. She was a force to be reckoned with. She and her family escaped the blitz in London and arrived in America in 1940. She had more energy and spunk than anyone I've ever worked with.

I would watch her carefully; she could shed her loving and warm smile on a crew member, and then they were gone the next day. Angela would feel quite sorry for them when they would come to her in tears, complaining that her husband had fired them. But I knew it was all Angela. Peter only followed her instructions. And why not? Her name was up there, and her tireless work ethic at her age kept the show going.

One night while on location in Mendocino, California— which doubled as a coastal Maine town—we were having a lovely crew dinner when the production manager, Mack Bing, got into a fight with Robert O'Neill over the . . . Crusades! Angela was at the far end of the table and deep in a conversation with Peter.

Now, Robert was a devoted Catholic, and Mack was a Jew. Mack held the position that Catholics had killed Jews during the aforementioned Crusades. Robert was in complete and utter denial of this historical fact. I could see Mack was sort of teasing Robert, but Robert was dead serious. Since I was sitting next to Mack, I nudged him to stop. He didn't get it, so I leaned close to whisper. "Mack, Robert is serious."

"It's the Crusades, for God's sake. He can't be serious."

I gently kicked Mack under the table and whispered again. "Mack, I'm telling you to stop this argument now."

Instead of stopping, the argument escalated. Misreading people and taking the wrong turn in the relationship is easy.

Mack was fired the next day. You just never know in the world of filmmaking what is going to end your career. As Tyne Daly said to me once, "It's never what they tell you it is." In Mack's case, the Crusades took him out.

One winter day, I got a phone call from my father's neighbor in Queens. This woman had gotten my number from him as the ambulance was taking him away to the VA Hospital. I was in prep on another *Murder* episode, so I could take a Friday off and fly to New York. I arrived at the hospital decked out in my new fur coat. It was cold in New York, but I was showing off. As I walked down the hallway where his room was, I passed a man lying flat in the bed with long hair and a beard, and his skin turned black from his chin to chest. I walked by with pity, but I caught the name Davidson out of the corner of my eye.

It took a minute as I stood there staring at the printed sign, then I backed up and went into his room. This 6'2' man could not have weighed more than 140 pounds, and the black skin was from pernicious anemia. His teeth were missing, his nails long and yellow. He was weak and had trouble speaking, but he seemed grateful I was there. I think he asked me how I was, but his real interest was in his money. "They stole all my money."

I asked him who he was talking about.

"The guys who brought me here. Those ambulance guys. I saw them take it."

"I'll go to admittance and ask about your money." This made

him feel better, but I knew there was probably no money in his pockets. He didn't seem concerned about his health, only his supposed money.

I could see the nurses had formed an opinion of me. Hollywood daughter arrives in a fur coat to her neglected father. The coat was a mistake. They told me to go to admitting and ask to see his belongings. When I arrived and gave his name, they gave me gloves. The clerk had a mask and gloves on himself. The minute the clothes came out of the bag, I understood why. The smell gagged me. The sight of his tattered pants brought tears to my eyes. I started to go through the pockets and knew there was nothing to be found. I just waved my hands and told them to discard everything.

I returned to his room empty-handed. "There was no money."

He then suggested I go to his apartment in Queens. I didn't want to do this, but it seemed important to him. I had rented a car at the airport and now drove from Brooklyn VA Hospital to my father's apartment in Queens. Opening the door to the small studio apartment I had only seen briefly once before, it seemed at first glance tidy. His bed was a sleeper sofa, and next to it was a table with some coins on it. I went to gather them up. They were stuck in dried juice from the popsicles he was living on. Next to the change were the OTB (off-track betting) tickets. Eviction notices were there also. I had been sending him money for his rent, but the landlord never got it. The ponies still won all his attention.

Looking in closets, I saw the china and silverware from my childhood home. In his drawers, next to some family pictures, were a few "girlie" magazines. All the postcards I had sent him from my trip to Europe were tied with a rubber band. They were covered in mice feces and roach dropping. I thought the rug, with a black border around it, was so unusual–until the border moved. I now realize the room was crawling with roaches. I don't know why I didn't see them right away. Then I realized there were roach eggs on all the china, silverware, and any family pictures he had.

I called Goodwill and told them to take everything in the apartment. I knew he was not ever coming back there. It was sad to leave behind the few treasures my mother had collected, but I had moved beyond these also. I could not wait to get back to LA. I took my rental car to the airport and flew home to the comfort of sunny California, and back to working on *Murder.*

Angela wanted to know how my trip to see my dad went. What could I say? Tell her the truth; my father was living as a homeless vagrant, he was still gambling even though he was confined to his house. No, I just waved the question off. I didn't want to drag my father's life into my comfortable situation with Angela. However, she would never have been judgmental about the situation. I felt at home with her and we got along so well that she invited me to stay with her and her team in her trailer during lighting setups. When Angela was a child, she and her parents lived with Ernest Holmes, who wrote *The Science of Mind,* which was similar to Christian Science. We'd have prayer sessions and read remarkable passages from his books. I cared for Angela and believed she cared about me.

I returned to New York the following month without the fur coat. The same nurses came to me. Now there were no sideways glances, and it wasn't just the absence of the fur coat. "We understand now." "Wow, your dad is something." "He doesn't want any help." "How stubborn, and what a temper." These were an assortment of comments the nurses had about my father. Part of me felt my feelings towards him were validated, but there was a small part that wanted to say, "Don't talk about my dad that way."

They had lived with an impossible man for only a month and now understood why I had given up on him. He was in a single room and I sat next to his bed. He teeth were missing, but I was so used to him without his teeth I barely remembered him with teeth. He seemed to want to chat. My visit coincided with a Women's Rights March in Manhattan; my father asked me if I had gone. I told him I had. "Oh, I always believed in that."

What was I hearing? I started to tell him I'd become a Democrat; I expected a blowout. Instead, he tells me, "I always voted Democrat. I only wanted to keep the peace with your mother's family, so I let them think I voted Republican."

I know this is not totally true. I went to school with "I Like Ike" plastered on my notebooks. Yet, I never knew what to believe about him or what came out of his mouth. His mind and inner thoughts were for him alone. I think he was trying to find common ground after all the years of our separation. I doubted he ever voted anything but the Republican party line. Then he really surprised me by opening up about his relationship with my mother.

"Your mother and I, well, I can count the times on one hand when we had sex."

Oh, cover my ears. Who wants to hear this stuff, and why is he telling me this?

"I had a lady friend, and she and I had more sex in our short time together. She played tennis with me."

Did he want me to confess my sexual life? I just wanted to change the subject. I ventured into a different avenue. A road I had never ventured down before.

"Why didn't your support my wanting to act?"

He seemed genuinely hurt by my asking him this. "What? I always supported you."

"No, you always told me so-in-so was better than I—better

singer, actor, and better at everything. I couldn't even play tennis the way you thought I should. Why did you do that?"

"I did that to make you stronger. I knew how hard that business you wanted to be in was. Your mother made you soft. I needed to make you stronger."

What BS, that's all I could think. Who was this man? In retrospect, I should have asked him more questions about his life, his childhood. I suspected that he wanted to perform. All the poetry recitals and stories he'd go into whenever he'd get the chance. Had he wanted the same fame I had sought? If I'd asked him then and there, would his answers have helped me move on? But I was not ready for this. I needed to get home and back to my life.

On the plane, my mind wandered to what ifs. Who would I be if I had a father who chose another way to support me? A hug, a smile, a proud father. What were his wounds? Were they so deep that he had to wound me also? I grew weary of my inner thoughts and promised myself I'd sort it out at some future time when I could rationally dissect all the years of hating him. When I could, I'd try to learn more about my parents.

That time visiting him at the hospital would be the last time I saw him.

Occasionally, he would call me desperate to leave the VA Hospital. He swore he was being used as a teaching tool. I had no experience with hospitals and could not believe him. I wish I had understood the system better; to them, he was a pincushion, a nobody who had no advocate to help him.

I went back to work on *Murder, She Wrote*. Angela was always steady, but you could see she would get tired. How she did all those years on that show amazes me. I only worked on that show for one year. I had so many run-ins with Robert O'Neill that I knew I wouldn't last, no matter how much

THIS IS MURDER, SHE WROTE

Angela liked me, and I respected her. I used the excuse that walking over so many dead bodies each episode was getting to me. Frankly, I thought I was better than that show.

Murder, She Wrote was on the air for 12 years. That would have amounted to a lifetime job in TV. Maybe I was wrong, and perhaps I could have stayed on *Murder*. I'm not sure why but being on a show for a long time, or being in a relationship for some time, did not sit well with me. Would there be something better around the corner, new and more exciting? I needed new things, places, and people, even if that was sometimes lonely and scary.

I am such a contradiction. On the one hand, I need the stability of my own home. On the other, I can't wait to pack my bags and leave. I find this need to move on strange, as I was always afraid of being penniless and homeless. I'd term it my shopping cart future. Me, a shopping cart filled with whatever and any small dog I would have at that time. Thankfully so far, that hasn't come true.

My father would have been on the streets had he not served in WWII. We had things in common: we loved the smell of jet fuel, baseball, and cars. He loved to drive. We'd go to car showrooms and be window shoppers. If I've misspent money in my life, it was on cars. I love them and the freedom they represent.

Perhaps his love of cars is why our family car always returned without a scratch when he'd act out and drive away from the house like a man possessed. The car might have been his place of peace. Maybe the movement tricked him into thinking he was going somewhere. Perhaps he and I had much more in common than I thought.

When the chance to see the USA on a bus came along, I took it.

Twenty-five

ME & TEN GUYS TRAVEL THE U.S.

In 1986, ABC had a huge hit with their series *Moonlighting*. The network was riding high in the ratings, so they had advertising money to spare. They created a campaign to highlight their new fall TV series. There were nine of us on the bus and two in the equipment truck following us. I was the only female. We left Los Angeles with a schedule to hit all the perimeter states and then, on occasion, take side trips-driving or flying-into the interior of the US. Circling the country, we would end up back in LA a month later.

On the bus was the director, producer, director of photography, camera operator, camera assistant, soundman, a PA, me—as the 1st AD—and the bus driver. There were two grips in the equipment truck. An advance group also set up our arrival in the next city we were to visit. The theme was "Something's Happening." Of course, that something was on ABC. We'd set up the camera and give fifteen seconds of fame to whoever wanted it. They could say something, sing, dance, or do anything they wanted. Back in LA, the editor would decide who made the final cut.

It was quick and dirty filmmaking and sometimes hysterical to boot. People do and say the strangest things. They would show up in costumes, sometimes with prepared speeches, and sometimes with improvised things that ranged from clever to insanely stupid. I don't think that same trip would be advisable in today's political atmosphere.

This was early TikTok. What people will do to be seen and heard for that brief moment of fame amazes me. We'd pull up to the designated area, and the people waiting for us resembled an audience of *The Price is Right*. The crazier you looked and sounded, the more likely you would be used in the commercial. It was an interesting cultural experiment. The folks in the South expressed themselves more vividly than when we got to Northern cities. They were more reserved in their approach to fame.

Living with all these guys did get to me at times—how they eased their boredom with crude jests and humor. These same guys would act differently if we were working on a set. But on the road, it was freedom from any supervision. It was a boys' club, and I became invisible to them. I don't know how many times the guys in the equipment truck passed the bus and mooned us. Something they would have been fired for back home on a proper film set. After a while, I longed just to chat with another woman. I could not believe how many fart jokes grown men can make. However, all the guys treated me just great.

I had a wonderful surprise birthday celebration in Biloxi and a second celebration at Disney World. We got there very early, and we had the park to ourselves. All the Disney characters were there for us to film. It was joyous. I got to kiss Jiminy Cricket.

The saddest and ugliest part of the trip was in South Carolina while filming at The Citadel Military College. I wasn't allowed on campus; there were no female cadets allowed as yet. Our Black bus driver and I sat on the bus, while the crew filmed inside the Citadel. I was furious.

The guys came back in a very high mood. I guess being with that many cheering men taps into some sort of bonding. They were not the least bit embarrassed that the two of us were just sitting here on the hot bus waiting for them. It's not that they were unkind, it just didn't occur to them that the situation was unfair. It would be 1995—eight more years—before women were allowed to enter and study at the Citadel.

The states whizzed by. Many of our stops I'll never forget. One morning in Washington, DC, the National Park Service stood by as we filmed at the Lincoln Memorial, then moved on to the Capitol grounds. Moving north, we debated skipping NYC as the advance group warned us that no one seemed interested in meeting our bus. I guess they felt too sophisticated to be a joke on TV. Time won out, and we zipped past my home town. Up the coast, we went with Maine lobster fishermen. On to my first time in Chicago, but it would not be my last.

In Michigan, we filmed at the GM plant. Whereas the guys were fascinated by the cars, I was interested in the women on the assembly line. They told me they had been secretaries, and during one of the largest strikes, the management had put them on the assembly line. Once the strike ended, they were offered their secretarial jobs back, and no one accepted. They stayed on the assembly line. One told me it was hard work, but it was freeing not to be at someone's beck and call. They felt here, on the assembly line, they were actually doing something, making something other than coffee for their bosses. Wow, I could understand that logic.

We hit Northern California for the last part of the shoot. The plan was to have a huge circle of people, and the bodies in the center would line up to spell the ABC logo. We had around 100 extras that day. A helicopter would then come in and film when the circle was complete. Today that would be done by a drone, and it would have been so much easier.

First, I placed the extras in the middle of the field and had them form A, B, and C. This was no small feat. Then my PA and I made the best and biggest circle we could make around the letters in the center. Our director was in the helicopter and would radio me where the holes were, and I'd try to fix them. I stayed in the circle as the helicopter twirled around us, filming. Thankfully this time, there were no sand dunes to harm me.

We traveled through 32 states in one month. I can say in the end: this job was great fun. Sort of a paid vacation, complete with fart jokes.

Twenty-six

NATIVE SON: CRAZIEST JOB EVER

There isn't a filmmaker alive who doesn't have incredible "war stories" from the films they've worked on. A few are actually from war-torn countries. Some tales revolve around a difficult celebrity, or a city, state, or country, they worked in. Like other filmmakers, I have mine. I think the craziest one is from my time working on filming *Native Son.*

It was 1986, and I got a call from a producer named Diane Silver who wanted to meet with me. She'd acquired the rights to Richard Wright's brilliant novel, *Native Son.* Set in 1930s Chicago, a devastating tale of a young Black man—Bigger—a product of American culture and the violence and racism that suffuses it. Diane assembled a fantastic cast that included Geraldine Page, Matt Dillon, Elizabeth McGovern, Oprah Winfrey, and many more great actors. They all wanted to be part of history by working on this picture. To produce the film, Diane enlisted the producers of *American Playhouse,* a Public Broadcasting System series that prided itself on bringing masterpieces to American audiences. Lindsay Law, a genuinely respected producer, was to be our producer and connection to *American Playhouse.*

At our meeting, Diane explained that she had just fired the show's production manager and was looking to replace him. She said he didn't "get it" and felt she'd be better off working with a woman. I was excited by this project; however, I should have done my research and asked more questions like what "get it" meant. The chance to work with a female producer matched my philosophy to support women in the film industry. She assured me that everything had pretty much been put in place by the former production manager. (That should have been a red flag. If he did a good job, why did she fire him?) Director Jerrold Freedman, the cast, the crew, locations—all ready to go. Would I take the job? I had been a production manager on a few small movies and, before that, commercials, but never a full big-time movie. My ego took over, and I convinced myself I could do this.

Who wouldn't have taken that job? What an opportunity! That was before I learned I was not the second production manager, but the fifth Diane had given the job to.

We were to film in Chicago and Los Angeles. I was certainly familiar with LA, but not Chi-town. I knew a few of the actors already, though not the crew or director. Lindsay Law was the producer from *American Playhouse,* and I felt I could rely on him and trust his judgment. We all converged at our Chicago lakefront hotel on a bitter, cold, late February day. Our production offices took up many rooms on the hotel's second floor.

As production manager, I should have had all the contracts for the crew, talent, and location but had received none. I enlisted the support of Lindsay, and we met with Diane, who was very secretive and suspicious of Lindsay and me. We asked for all her paperwork, and she ignored us. We had the first of countless blowouts at that meeting, this one over hiring local carpenters to build sets. After much arguing, Lindsay and I got Diane to sign for a carpenter. One man! How was one person supposed to build a set? I got up from my chair to show her how impossible it was to hammer nails in a set wall, which isn't attached to anything if someone else wasn't there to help hold it up. But it was useless; she did not want to sign for a second carpenter. Then she wanted the same lone carpenter to paint the set also. They're not even in the same union category. It was clear that Diane had little real-life experience in filmmaking. Her talent was as a deal-maker.

What had I gotten myself into? Could I get right back on the plane to LA? Lindsay threw a union contract at Diane for the second carpenter and said, "Sign it, now." With a dramatic show of disgust, she did. This was a small victory, but we had much more crew to hire to get the show on the road. I realized that Lindsay and I were on the same page. We wanted to get the show done and done well. It would be up to us to get the nuts and bolts of the production accomplished. Diane seemed to take this incident as a declaration of war in which Lindsay and I were her enemies. Perhaps if Lindsay or I were under less pressure, we could have taken more time with Diane to assure her we were on her side. But I doubt it.

I soon found out she had not made any agreements with a local bank, no checking accounts set up for the show. Without this banking support, we had to get cash FedExed weekly to make our payments. Most of the LA crew and the actors were paid out of an LA payroll service. But per contract their weekly per diem (money paid for living expenses out of town) was to be in cash. All the extras and locations fees were also paid in cash, and I would be the one paying them. The extra casting agency suggested I get a bodyguard, as some locations we would be using were not in the best parts of Chicago. So, my bodyguard and I would go together to the various spots, open his car's trunk, and pay the background actors as they lined up by the vehicle.

Although unorthodox, this could have worked, except that Diane insisted that she be the only one to receive the money when the FedEx delivery came in. I would then meet her either at her hotel room or she would come down to my office with the cash for the day. So, if I knew I had to pay 50 extras that day, she would give me precisely that amount. If we suddenly had 51 extras, I would have to find her and get additional funds. This was a waste of my time, and my time was spread very thin. I admired her for her vision to put together this fantastic production, but I hated how sloppy the show was being run. Diane couldn't deal with the details; her only genuine interest was in being on set and trying to tell the director what to do, and she forgot that a producer has to "produce" the show, which means much more than sitting on the set chatting with actors. So, it was a giant, ongoing mess.

One day I got a frantic call from the set dressers who were being held at gunpoint by the owners of a barbershop we'd used earlier that day as a location. The owners had not been paid and were holding the crew as ransom. They had been promised cash, and they saw no other way of ensuring they'd get it. I could tell the set dressers were scared and furious at me. No one on the crew understood that Diane was the keeper of the cash, so of course, they would blame me for anything and everything that went wrong money-wise.

The lead set dresser was crazed, calling me every name in the book. I had no time for an explanation; I just needed to get the store owner paid and our crew released. I gathered up my bodyguard and went looking for Diane and the money. She was with the filming crew at our next location—a garage in a dicey part of town. I stormed up to her.

"Where is the money for the barbershop? The crew is being held hostage, and I must pay the owners to get them out!" I didn't care who heard us.

She swore she had paid them.

"Where is the receipt?"

She ignored me and started to walk away. I tried again. "Diane, listen to me. Our crew is being held at gunpoint. Did you pay the barbershop?" She continued to walk away. I was tempted to put my hand on her and get her attention, but I also had the whole crew watching me. I realized we were getting nowhere. Fortunately, I had some cash in the trunk of my car earmarked for the extras the following day. It would be just enough to fulfill our contract with the barbershop. My driver/bodyguard and I drove directly to the barbershop. Since the crew and the owners were furious, and I was the object of this fury, my driver went inside to pay the ransom. I sat in the car as the angry crew was set free. They all quit the show then and there. I should have too.

Another morning, Matt Dillon came to me in my hotel office a large meeting room now with desks and tables. He seemed so young to me; well, he was young. "I need to have my car keys, and where is it parked?"

"What car?" I asked.

"It's in my contract," he replied, "I get a car for my use."

He wasn't being belligerent, just wanted what was due him. Obviously he had no idea that I had never seen the contracts. Diane happened to be passing by. "Diane, I understand Matt gets a car." She would not dare to question this while he stood before us. Instead, she just stared blankly at me. She never made eye contact with Matt; she stayed focused on me.

She sort stammered then under her breath, "There, well there's…"

I got where this was going, "Okay, Diane," I said. "Give me your car keys." This was the only solution I could find.

Caught in the middle between Matt and me, she flung the car keys at me and huffed off, growling, "You really are a major fucking bitch!"

I now had a new identity. This became how the actors, good-heartedly, greeted me in the morning: "Good morning, MFB."

We were in our third week of shooting in Chicago. The LA crew informed me they would be gone by Sunday if they were not paid their per diem. I called the LA office and begged them to send the funds directly to me, not Diane. Lindsay got on the phone to back me up. The LA production office was beginning to understand the dysfunction we were working under. They agreed I'd have the funds Saturday morning.

On Thursday of that week, my assistant answered a call for me.

"It's a nursing home for you."

That could be only one thing. I took the receiver, "Hello."

"Ms. Davidson, is that you?" I confirmed it was I. "This is Mr. Mancuso from your father's nursing center. I have Officer Murphy here."

"This is Officer Murphy from the 60th Precinct. Is this Janet Davidson?" Again, I confirmed my identity. "Sorry to inform you that William Davidson, your father passed away last night."

He gave me the name of the funeral home my father would be taken to. I'm not sure why the police officer had to be the one to impart this sad news to me; I guess there is some sort of protocol. Sooner or later, I knew I'd get a call from someone. When I had visited my father at the VA Hospital, I could not ignore this massive aneurysm that protruded almost two inches from his chest. The doctors had concluded it was inoperable and would burst at some point and kill him instantly. Now it had fulfilled its mission and killed him.

Everyone in the office wanted to know who was on the phone. I simply told them what had happened. They were all very supportive, but I had to get out of the office. I just needed to be by myself. I gathered that same fur coat and walked along Lake Michigan. The temperature hovered below ten degrees, and the wind from the lake blew through me. I didn't feel it. It was like I was watching a dramatic scene in my own film. Before my mother died, she had warned me, "Be careful of your grandmother. She will outlive us all." Now Grandma Davidson was, in fact, the last one standing, besides me.

When I returned from the office, the day's shooting was over. Some of the cast liked to drop by the office at the end of the day. When Elizabeth McGovern came in, she took one look at me and asked what was wrong. I told her.

"You are not staying here a moment longer; we are going to dinner." She rounded up some of the other actors, and we headed out.

There was room in the restaurant we stopped at, but we had no reservations, and they didn't want to seat us—until Matt, who had been parking the car, came in.

"Is he with you?" A starstruck hostess ordered the seats rearranged pronto. I sat across from Matt, the only male in our group. D-I-L-L-O-N, as my father had spelled it out to me. Now it was impossible not to feel great sadness. Of all the human beings in the world, how could I be sitting across from someone with my grandfather's name, on the day my father left the earth? This name that only entered my life a few years earlier. Dillon, I should have been Janet Dillon.

I made a plane reservation for Saturday to New York to attend my father's funeral, which I had arranged long distance. That morning I sat in the office with the crew outside my door. They were all very respectful of the fact that time was going by, and I might miss my plane, but they wanted their money. At this point, they had not received their per diem for three weeks. Everyone saw the production's dysfunction and suspected they'd be left high and dry. If they weren't paid that morning, they would be on a plane headed home. I had insisted that LA send this FedEx addressed to me, only me. And yet there was no delivery.

There was no money, and I did miss my plane. I had hired a minister to be at the cremation; if I didn't make the ceremony, the minister would read to an empty house—nobody but him and my dead father. But the film would be shut down without a crew, and my work ethic took over. I called LA, and they insisted they sent the funds to be delivered to me, not Diane. So where was the money? I had little time to spare. The next plane from Chicago to NY might still get me there in time.

Suddenly, one of the electricians from the crew ran into the office. "Diane intercepted the FedEx delivery," he told me, "and she has the money upstairs!"

I was beyond furious. We marched up to her room and banged on her door. She didn't realize I knew that the money had arrived and that she had it, so she opened the door. Seeing my fury, she knew the gig was up; she ran to the bed and flung herself on the money she'd been counting spread all over her bed. I no longer cared. I threw her off the bed, collected the money, and went downstairs to pay the crew.

I got the next flight out. But I'd missed the service. I rented a car and went to my grandmother's apartment in Jamaica to tell her that her son had died. I told her as gently as possible. She wailed, screamed, and somehow blamed my mother, who had been dead for almost 15 years. In her twisted mind, my father would have somehow straightened his life out had he not married my mother. I couldn't take it and tried to leave. She came at me, grabbing my arms and clothes, pleading for me to stay with her. We were on the verge of another physical fight, one I was in no mood for. I extracted myself from her grip.

I calmed down and once again told her that she had to leave her apartment and that I would help her find a place in a safe residence. I tried one more time and gently told her she could not live alone anymore, that if she stayed there alone, the city would come and take her and everything she owned away. She threw me out; she was not leaving.

I flew back to Chicago and, at the airport, met Elizabeth McGovern, who had also been away for the weekend. She politely asked how the funeral had been, and I didn't tell her I never got to it. On our way to the waiting car, we passed a newsstand with a story about Sean Penn and Madonna on the cover. Elizabeth had been engaged to Sean. "What do Madonna and I have in common?" she wondered aloud.

Relationship-wise, I had no idea what these two women had in common. But now they were bonded by the ugly side of fame that puts your personal life on the cover of supermarket trash. She seemed sad, and I reflected that no matter how famous one is, we all carry a burden, a sorrow, a broken heart. Elizabeth was always a genuinely sensitive and kind person to me.

The nightmare of *Native Son* wasn't over. Most of the crew still had no idea what was happening behind the scenes. They saw me only occasionally as I was too busy putting out fires to visit the set. Only Lindsay Law's dedication to the film and profound honesty kept me there. I figured the worst was over; we were about to return to Los Angeles to finish shooting. I'd be home, sleeping in my bed.

Because of Chicago's reputation, we had loads of police protection while we shot there. When we scouted the South Central area of LA, the crew didn't want to leave the scout bus. They wanted to know where the police were. What was home to me felt very unsafe to them. However, the filming went off perfectly until the last week of shooting.

An independent film has to be bonded to be able to use union contracts with SAG, DGA, and IATSE, and there are specific companies that do only this. If the bond company sees irregularities, they can take a movie over. The bond company for *Native Son* was getting daily reports of the chaos. So, after we returned to LA to continue shooting, the bond company took over the film. Everything we did from then on had to be approved by them.

But they trusted Lindsay, and Lindsay trusted me, so we were left in charge. Diane was banned from the set. She was forbidden to talk to the actors, crew, or director for the remainder of the filming. Of course, she would have none of it; she plotted to take what she felt was her film back. After all, she'd gotten the rights to the book and put together a great cast. Like many producers I've known, the fatal flaw is not trusting or not hiring the right people to carry out their vision. In this case, she might have hired the right people; she just could not let go and let us do our jobs.

I first became aware of her behind-the-scenes shenanigans when one of the actors came to me, shouting how I was destroying him and spreading all over Hollywood what a bad actor he was. I was shocked, but I knew it was Diane behind it. It seemed she was calling whoever would pick up the phone to spread evil fiction about Lindsay and me. I told the actor that this was a lie, that I was too busy to even watch dailies, so I had no opinion about his ability. But that logic didn't ease his mind.

Then, things got really out of hand in the final week of shooting. I received a call from the production office that the Immigration and Naturalization Service had just left them following up on a tip they got that we had hired a crew of non-US citizens and were on their way to the set. Diane had hired a good crew, a few of whom were from New Zealand and Canada. Now, suddenly we were a target for INS. I went to the 1st AD and let him know the situation. We worked out a signal whereby the crew the INS were interested in would "take a break" somewhere off the set if I could not get the agents to leave.

Fortunately, we were shooting inside a building. A shiny black sedan pulled up. It was essential not to let on that I had been warned. I was frightened, as I knew I'd be lying to federal agents, but I mustered up my former acting talents and met them with a cheery, "Can I help you?"

The agents showed me their badges and pulled their jackets aside so I could see the guns holstered to their waists. They explained about this "tip" that our film was working with illegal aliens. I told them that inside we were shooting an intimate scene, and I could not let them in the building at that time; if they wanted to come back later, I could let them in then.

I'm sure they didn't buy this, but it was a different time, and a crew of Canadians and New Zealanders didn't bother them. I don't know how they would have reacted if the crew were Mexican nationals. I assured them I would have the workers in question at the Los Angeles Department of Immigration Monday morning.

That weekend the non-US crew made arrangements to leave the country or just hide out. Both Lindsay and I knew Diane was behind this event. She'd rather shut down the film than lose control. But her plan did not succeed. Our director, Jerry Freedman, and the crew that would be leaving put forth names and numbers of crew they knew who could fill in. By Saturday night, the new crew had been hired so the film could carry on.

For many reasons, I was left out of this plan. They met on Sunday with the newly hired crew and reviewed what had been shot, the film's look, and what was left to complete. On Sunday night, Jerry called to tell me that filming would continue as usual Monday morning. I did not know about this meeting until Sunday night because the departing crew, especially Thomas Burstyn, our director of photography, were all still under the false impression that I had called the INS. But both Jerry and Lindsay knew who had made that call.

The proof came on Monday when the bond company contacted Lindsay and me. They'd received a letter from Diane explaining why we had to shut down and stop filming. In the letter, she stated that I had hired an illegal crew and that they had been deported on Friday. Desperate to regain control, she threw six workers under the bus and threatened the film she had worked so hard to bring about.

I explained to the bond company that we had not shut down but were on schedule to finish that Friday. I called the head of Immigration in LA and explained that I was sorry I could not present the crew in question, as I had promised—that when I arrived at work, they were gone, and I didn't know where to. (I was speaking the truth; they never confided in me where they had gone to.)I invited him, or any of his agents, to the set to see for themselves. But he simply took my word for it that they were gone. I'm sure they were happy that the case was closed. I wish I had seen Diane's face when the bond company told her there was no problem and the filming continued.

My job was winding down, but there were loose ends to take care of. One of them involved Geraldine Page. This incredible actress was brilliant and totally in charge of herself in front of the camera, but childlike and a bit helpless the rest of the time. Even after the divorce, her ex-husband, Rip Torn, took special care of her. Now Rip wasn't there, and she had been calling the production office all morning in distress.

Her passage back home to New York was all booked. All she needed to do was go downstairs to the waiting limo. But this seemed impossible for her. I arrived at The Chateau Marmont, where she was staying, to find her sitting on her bed, bags packed. One day during filming I snuck away from my desk to watch her act. She was so confident and in control. Now, she was almost childlike, frightened and confused. It appeared she was panicking over two things: first, how to get to the airport, and second, the gold statue on the floor next to the bed. She had just won that Oscar for her beautiful work in *The Trip To Bountiful*. She flung her arms around, pointing toward it. "What do I do with this?"

I took a deep breath. As a young actress, after each Oscar telecast, I would go into the bathroom, hold my hairbrush to the mirror, and pretend to accept my Oscar. Every actress I knew did this. It never occurred to me that an award like that could be a burden. But now here I was, probably as close to an actual Oscar statue as I'd ever be. I suggested we pack the Oscar in her bag and go downstairs to the car. After a few minutes, she seemed to calm down, and when we got to the limo, the driver assured me he'd take good care of her. To this day, I am still amazed by the brilliance so many actors have on screen that they seem unable to bring to the rest of their lives.

Filming was over and I was recovering from what had become a horrible time for me. I briefly saw Diane at the movie's premiere. But by then, there was no recovery from the hurt and bad blood between us. Diane sued Lindsay Law and me for conspiring to take her film away. We were deposed independently for over three hours, but nothing came of this lawsuit. After the premiere, I never saw Lindsay again. I think no one wanted to be reminded of that experience.

Sometimes films that have a rough time getting made end up doing wonderfully at the box office, and all is forgiven. *Native Son* came out to fairly good reviews. The film critic Roger Ebert gave it three stars and a thumbs up. However it received a low box office turnout. I doubt a good box office take would have changed how I felt about making that movie. I did have a clear insight; I hated being in an office. I wanted, needed, to be on set with the actors and the crews. I'd never production manage again.

Physical and mental exhaustion poured over me. Like many freelancers, I was petrified that I would never work again. I felt I had the whole women's movement on my back—if I didn't make it, it just proved to the chauvinists that a woman couldn't cut it.

I needed to get away. Years earlier, my friend Libby and I had taken a trip to the new Club Med in Martinique. Club Med offered Americans a new type of vacation, and I loved it. There were no responsibilities, schedules, or pressure—just the beach, fun activities, and eating and drinking, all on one's own time. So, I took myself off to a Club Med in Mexico. For one week, I didn't care about TV, film, the women's movement, or anything. I just had fun. I had sex with a young Mexican horse wrangler. I ate and drank, swam, and slept.

Upon arrival home, I sat in my house for a week and cried. I cried for the years I had not allowed myself a break. All those years, I'd forced myself to make work calls to find a new job as soon as the last one ended. I worked even if I was sick, smiled when I wanted to scream and dragged myself forward—and to what end? With *Native Son,* I had allowed myself to stay in a situation that was both professionally and personally harmful to me. Why? I simply could not be seen as a failure.

This was burnout. I had not allowed myself time to feel my father's death and think about what it meant. I felt I could not afford that time, monetarily or emotionally; I had to return to work immediately. Part of this was true. It was still not easy for a woman to get a job. A man with my skills could make one phone call and be off to his new job. The buddy system would get the word out that so-in-so was available, and he'd have a job. The women's network was still growing, and sometimes women didn't help other women. I am so glad to see that ugly trend ending.

The fear of becoming that homeless shopping cart woman deepened. This was undoubtedly a permanent insecurity brought on by growing up in a household always on the financial edge. I lost days of job searching, letting my mind and body wander off to sad places. Finally, I had to snap out of this malaise and make my next work call. I berated myself, trying to remember how much I loved my work, knowing how many people would kill to be where I was, and telling myself that burnout was a luxury I could not afford. And then I got a phone call that changed my life.

Twenty-seven

CAGNEY & LACEY

By 1985 the groundbreaking series *Cagney & Lacey* had been on TV for four years. Production was halted mid-season for the birth of Tyne Daly's daughter Alyxandra. When Tyne felt ready to resume filming in early 1986, they started up again. I got the call to join them as one of the two 1ˢᵗ ADs. After *Native Son,* I was thrilled to go back to TV. I had been so busy working that I had never seen an episode of *C&L.* I hadn't seen many of the shows I worked on as there was no "on demand". If I wanted to see a show I'd have to put a DVD in my recorder and set it for a certain time. Then I'd have to find the time to actually watch the show. It may seem as though two women carrying a show is not that big a deal, and it shouldn't be, but *Cagney & Lacey* was the first to have two female stars. Two women carrying prime-time TV and doing it in such a ballsy way.

This would be the first time I joined a series already in production. By now, the producers understood their stars and had figured out what worked and what didn't. Well, sort of; life is not a stationary thing and changes do pop up. I had to learn the pitfalls and the joys of this show quickly. Previously, they had a female 1ˢᵗ AD, so the crew was used to a woman in charge. Having a female AD sat well with Tyne Daly and Sharon Gless; they were all for women in control. *C&L* even had female directors!

Barney Rosenzweig, the co-creator and executive producer, has written a book on the series, *Cagney & Lacey . . . and Me.* Anyone who wants the history of this amazing series would love it. In so many ways, Barney was ahead of the curve. He was determined to keep the production cost as low as possible. One way he accomplished this was they didn't use studio facilities. Instead, he rented a warehouse just outside of downtown LA. And that was our home away from home.

When you use studio facilities, the stages, prop house, wardrobe, etc., a percentage gets added to your budget. Once on *Remington* we went into our eighteenth hour, and everyone was exhausted. I called Abby Singer, the producer in charge of our show. "Abby, things aren't going well. The actors are exhausted. Please let me wrap the crew, and we can come back tomorrow and pick up the rest of the scene."

"Nope, we aren't on that stage tomorrow."

"I know, but it would be easy to walk away tonight and pick up tomorrow. It will get done three times faster when everyone is awake. Heck, Stephanie just fell asleep in the middle of Pierce's monologue. Think about the overtime you will save on."

"Nope, we aren't on that stage tomorrow. I'm not going to pay for that stage tomorrow. It's more money than overtime is."

"Abby, how can that be? We are an MTM production, and MTM owns the stages. Is there no financial break there?"

"Janet, stop arguing and get the scene finished. Tonight!"

So, I was familiar with the logic of finding a facility, probably not a conventional stage, that a production company could lease and avoid the heavy studio charges. Barney took a lease out on an unused warehouse near downtown Los Angeles, which happened to be on Lacy Street. The sets were built throughout the floors of the warehouse.

Outside the top floor of the warehouse lay the Amtrak train tracks. "The Jane" was the set that occupied that top floor. When the writers did their initial research, they realized many police precincts didn't have female restrooms; they only had "johns." So, *C&L* would have "The Jane." There was never a train schedule we could count on, so many scenes shot there were interrupted by the train whizzing by and shaking the top floor. Sometimes we could laugh it off, but other times it was impossible for Tyne and Sharon to continue. If I could feel the train coming, I'd hold off on starting the scene, especially if it was a dramatic one.

I could not, however, hold off the rain, and when it was LA's rainy season, we had to hold umbrellas above our heads to keep dry. Sometimes we'd wait for a rat to scurry across the set. Or for someone to stop walking as the floor creaked so badly. This would be the first warehouse I would work full-time in, but not the last. Taking over warehouses became a trend—conditions weren't great, but the money saved was worth it to the producers. And Barney started it all.

Tyne had already won three best actress Emmys by the time I arrived. She was the acting queen of TV. Sharon Gless was an outstanding actress also, but her role as Cagney was much less showy than Tyne's Lacey. But they were TV royalty, and as such, they had their quirks. *C&L* was a challenging show to work on. The hours were long and tiring. For me as an ex-actress, I loved watching the gals work. I began to see patterns they each had; some that worked very well together and some that could cause us trouble.

Even though they previously had a female 1st AD, there was one director they tried to keep me away from. Ray Danton had been an actor and was now directing. He was tall and dark; I mean, his whole demeanor was dark. He wore black clothes and spoke with the most resounding leading man voice. Barney liked me working for them and felt if I had to work with Ray as my director, either Ray would destroy me, or I would quit.

One day our production manager, Ralph Singleton, told me they had a schedule change, and I would be working with Ray. Could Ray be worse than the "tell the girlie I'm ready" DP I had endured on *Hart to Hart?* To say that Ray and I got on great would be an understatement.

During pre-production, the director, AD, and location manager go on a scouting trip to find the right location to shoot at. One day, Ray turned to me in the scout car. "They say I don't like working with women."

The driver and location manager stiffened up; they liked me and hoped Ray would be nice. I was on pins and needles; he continued. "I just don't like working with incompetent people, and if they happen to be women, so be it."

Then he turned directly to me. "But you, I love you; you know what you are doing."

Everyone released the tension that had built up in the car. I was shocked. I suspected he liked working with me, but until then, I had no proof of it. So I was very pleased.

Ray was not a healthy man, and he was on dialysis. His health would make some days difficult to get through. During the filming of one episode, he ended up in the hospital. From his hospital bed, he demanded that the producers let me take over the directing helm. As fate would have it, I was also in the hospital that day, having a biopsy on my breast. A different director took over for the day.

I was fine the next day, and Ray again begged them to let me direct. There is a DGA rule that whoever takes over has to continue. Now I never questioned that, and maybe they made it up not to give me an assignment. And until Ray suggested I could do the job, it wasn't in my mind. From then on, it was. It seemed a natural combination of my past acting and current production knowledge.

What a lesson for me on not judging someone by their history with other people. So many times, I had worked with an actor or director and gotten warnings from others about their good or bad behavior. My belief was to let them show themselves to me and who they are. Of course, sometimes the warnings were too true, and I should have listened to them.

We shot in Los Angeles, but the show was set in New York. I had an advantage here, having been born and raised in NYC. When something wasn't quite right, I could spot it. However, although Barney was from Los Angeles, he thought he was a New Yorker. No extra or actor could wear sunglasses in a scene. We had words over this as many people in NY wore sunglasses; they may not need them, but they wore them. Sharon, however, needed them just as I did. Our very blue eyes could not take either the sun or some of the set lighting. Before Sharon came to the set, one of us with blue eyes had to stand in for her to see if we could even open our eyes. Sometimes the little things get loads of attention in the film world.

One episode was to take place in Los Angeles. The gals had to extradite a prisoner to NY. We were shooting a hot tub scene at a home in the Hollywood Hills. The actress who had been cast for this scene did not appear. Finding out that she would never make it in time, Ralph, our production manager, came to me. "You were an actress, right?"

I replied, "Yes."

He went on, "So you still have your SAG card?"

"Yes."

"Well, you do the scene."

I did get a bit excited by the prospect of being in front of the camera again. But not in front of the crew I knew so well, who would definitely tease me about this later. I gave over my radio (every AD has a walkie-talkie on their side for communication with every crew person), and Ralph took over my duties as 1st AD. I went to hair/makeup/wardrobe and plopped into the hot tub, costumed in a swimsuit. In the scene we were to shoot, *C&L* had been tipped that the house's owner, me, had information on the whereabouts of the perpetrator they were hunting for. We did one take, and I watched Tyne and Sharon look at each other, turn away from me, and start chatting. In unison, they huddled with Ralph.

The next thing I knew, Ralph was headed my way. Oh, geez, was I that bad? Instead, he relayed the message from the gals. They felt it would be more authentic if they could not see my swimsuit. They insisted that they not see my swimsuit. Those ladies could be very mischievous. I took down the straps—so I appeared naked in the hot tub—looked them in the eye, and we all laughed.

I did learn more than one lesson that day. "Video Village" is the term used for where the director sits watching the monitor during filming. It's also where all the executives come and sit and where the actors might also be found between lighting setups. This day, as an actor, I got to sit in at video village while waiting for the crew to finish lighting. It's where above the line hangs out, not the crew.

Both Sharon and Tyne regarded me differently from that day on. ADs are usually not considered creative types. I disagree totally with this. We are the ones who take what's on the page and create a schedule so the words can be transformed into film. Sometimes things are written that just don't fit into a schedule. For instance, one short scene written to take place in a restaurant costs money and time. Why not take that scene to a park bench? ADs come up with these types of solutions all the time.

The scene was "in the can" as I got out of the hot tub, I heard Sharon tell Tyne, "She's really very funny." I could not have planned this to go any better. But this little incident went very far in both Sharon and Tyne approving me to direct one of the episodes. Acting in this scene was easy, but I realized it wasn't home anymore. I loved being behind the camera.

As an assistant director, one is responsible for the background actors. I always wanted to direct the background rather than have my 2nd AD do the work. One of my last acting jobs was on a film, and that director seemed to have little regard for the background actors. He would divide us by numbers; "group 1 cross here, group 2 laugh here." It was humiliating, and the lead actress, Diane Canyon, took him to task. "Treat them as the actors they are. Tell them why they are laughing." I always worked this way, giving the background actors a reason for doing what they were doing. This was a challenge to always come up with a new and interesting scenario for the scene. After a while, I started to run out of ideas.

I was headed to NYC for the holidays and thought I'd contact C&L's police advisor when there. He set me up with a day in the precinct. It was very cool. I ended up with many ideas for background material this way. For instance, a group of school kids were touring the precinct, and I used it. Another one I had fun with from my tour—a prisoner was brought in and put in a holding cell. He paced and paced the cell. After a few hours, an officer offered up this, "He probably is innocent. The guilty fall asleep almost right away. Nobody who is innocent can sleep in a cell." (I made a note for myself in case I ever got arrested.)

I left the ladies' room (they had one) and passed the guy they'd brought in with the one currently in the cell. The guy on the bench outside the squad room was sound asleep. I mentioned that to the officer. Before you knew it, they pulled a warrant for the sleeping beauty and arrested him. I used that in one of the episodes.

That is one of the joys of filmmaking. Unless you are directing a fantasy or something no one has ever done before, life is a pretty common experience. Observing life in all its colors is a wonderful occupation.

If I paid attention, I could usually see dark clouds rising up in the actors' eyes. Tyne and I would have run-ins now and then, but always, all was forgiven; we both realized we were just trying to make the best show possible. By now, I felt that my training as an actor and my knowledge of the technical side of filming would make me a good director. I went to Barney and asked for a slot, an episode to direct. He was very receptive. I'm sure the gals had spoken with him already. And having Ray on my side went a long way.

One night I left the stages with my name posted to start prep as a director for the next episode. I spent the night alternating between terror and complete joy. Arriving the following day, my name had been replaced with another female director. I now alternated between fury, sadness, and questioning why this had happened. Barney reassured me I would get to direct one day, but not today.

Then the same scenario occurred again, with the same director replacing me. Barney took me into his office to explain that one of the male writers wanted to direct and threatened to quit if I directed before him. Hence my directing debut would have to wait until Barney could find a slot for the male writer to direct.

To make matters worse, it was rumored that Barney did not want this writer to direct. Why was my career stuck between these two grown-ups who already had great jobs they loved and that paid them handsomely? The female director that got those two slots also got a third one. However, this time I was not her AD. That episode did not go very well, and Barney called me into his office to ask what I thought had happened.

The computer in my brain ran through a few scenarios but I went with what I was actually feeling. "She didn't have me as her AD. It's as simple as that."

This was uncharacteristic for me, as I hold that every woman that fails shuts the door for another woman to succeed. Here I was, throwing her under the bus. I liked this woman. Was I that desperate to direct? Is gaining an assignment worth being untrue to your beliefs? Or was I learning the lesson of how to get ahead in Hollywood?

I felt very confident in my work life but still had lingering insecurities about my appearance. The face lift I had improved my appearance, but I still saw the flaws. One day on *C&L,* I felt one of our regular extras staring at me. I must have been on edge for some reason; I turned and snapped at him, "What are you looking at?"

He was taken aback. "Your blue eyes, what else would I be looking at?"

I took a beat, then asked him, "You're sure you weren't looking at my skin?"

How self-absorbed and paranoid had I become? The ironic part is that my eyes are pretty impressive. But it was still hard to convince me that my eyes were more compelling than my lousy skin. My friend Pamela asked if I would trade my eyes for her good skin. That was a question I never expected to ponder. So much wasted time is spent on what is wrong with us. I thought back to when I was watching one of our cast rehearsals and heard from behind me, "Did she give you the look yet?" One of our regular crew guys was chatting with a new crew person.

"No, what's the look?"

"Oh, you will know it when you get it."

Years before, my friend Mel Howard invited me to the set where Paul Newman was directing *Shadow Box.* Mr. Newman wore his famous dark glasses, even when directing his wife, Joanne Woodward. He had finished blocking the next shot, and the crew took over the set to light it. The camera operator and I were friends from another show, so we were in the back joking around.

Suddenly, Paul Newman heard us. He turned and took only one side of the sunglasses down. One incredible blue eye shot us both a disapproving look. It almost felt as though a laser hit through us, and we were pinned down on the back wall. Now I fully understood the dark glasses. The saying "the eyes are the window to the soul" could not be more accurate when giving an actor a note. If you try to con or trick an actor, they can spot the lie in your eyes. In a sense, a good director also has to be a good actor and be able to hide one's true feelings about the performance.

I never wore dark glasses to direct, but I tried to always collect myself before going to an actor to give a note. I wish I could say that I took the same precautions in my personal life. I was often asked what I was mad at. Now, the term "resting bitch face" is pretty popular, which is what my face would contort to. Most of the time, I'm not even present but off in some corner of my brain. It's a question I've asked myself often: why do so many men seem to feel it's their job to ask women to smile?

1988 would be the last season for *C&L,* and I finally got my directing shot. We shot downtown at a, well, fleabag hotel.

When we arrived, we had to wait for the police to carry away a dead body. Great start! But I was in heaven. It went very well, and everyone seemed pleased. It felt so natural to me to be in charge. I was never tired or even stressed. I was just sailing on my own calm ocean. The only missing thing was no mother or father to call and brag to. I do believe they would have been proud.

I had offers from a few agents, and I was so filled with hope that I would not have to AD again. Not that I hated being a 1st AD, I loved it. After directing my episode, I was happy to strap on the walkie-talkie again, at least until the end of the season.

I contend that the 1st AD job is the most demanding on the set. Everyone feels they can complain about every little thing to the AD. Sometimes I'd get angry and tell whoever was in my face to go to the producer, writer, or director with their outrage. They rarely, if ever, did. The AD has a lot on her/his plate, ranging from keeping everyone safe to answering why the caterer ran out of ketchup.

Because our stages were in a warehouse district, there wasn't even a restaurant to go to. We had breakfast, lunch, and sometimes dinner from the catering truck. This constant togetherness created many a relationship. One that few if any of us saw coming. One morning, the headlines in one of the rags spelled trouble for us all. Barney had divorced his wife, the co-creator of *C&L*. He was reportedly dating Sharon. Tyne had not been told of this but read it like the rest of the crew in the gossip paper. This led to a few very unpleasant days. The eggshells we were all walking on were breaking under our feet. Barney ultimately married Sharon Gless. And in the end, Tyne and Sharon's love for each other won out.

Cagney & Lacey wrapped their last episode in 1988. We were a family. I knew it was time for the show to conclude, and I looked forward to new adventures. However, it's never easy to say goodbye to family. With my parents gone and cousins scattered all over the globe, work, my friends, and whatever dog or dogs I had were all the family I needed.

Twenty-eight

NOW I'M A DIRECTOR!

Hiatus—this can be a filmmaker's favorite word. Those three months you have off after a series wraps, and before it begins again, amount to play time. That is, as long as you know you have employment waiting for you. I had saved up enough money to last six months of no work. Enough time to scout around and get my next directing gig. The gang at *Cagney & Lacey* were impressed enough by my episode that they helped me get an agent. With their recommendation, I now had representation. I was all set; money in the bank, agent at my call, and confidence in my pocket.

None of us saw a six-month writer's strike ahead.

As things heated up, the DGA as well as all the other film unions joined in to support the WGA. We hit the picket line many times almost as a social event. My dear friend Pamela—who I shared that office space at MTM—had also moved on to other opportunities and we were both out of work now. So we decided to sneak away from the picket lines to a Club Med in Mexico, one we could drive to. Surely this would be over by the time we got back. My cousin Paul was in the hospital in San Diego; we planned to stop there along the way. He had moved from Texas to La Jolla, CA.

I knew Paul had AIDS, but at that time I didn't really understand what that meant; well, I didn't want to understand. He downplayed his condition to me, and I wanted to believe it.

When we got to the hospital, a doctor met me. "Only family can see him right now."

"I am his cousin and his only relative here on the West Coast."

"When was the last time you saw your cousin?"

I had to think, although we were close I was so busy with my career that I didn't get down to La Jolla that much anymore.

He continued, "You might be shocked by his appearance. He is frail, in and out of consciousness. I must prepare you, we expect end of life to be near."

WHAT! No, there was no way I was hearing this. The doctor ushered me into Paul's room. He was hooked up to an IV but little else was being done for him. I knew I would stay through the night with him, but Pamela was downstairs waiting in the lobby for me. I went to her.

"Pam, he's not doing well. I have to stay the night with him."

She totally understood. Since we had only one car, she was now stuck in San Diego at a motel to wait out the night. I called Paul's sister, my cousin Barbara. She knew nothing of his situation but had suspected something was amiss. She got a plane from her home in Tennessee and flew to San Diego. In what seemed only hours Barbara was there with me. Paul was in a coma, and we sat all night on either side of him. Praying. Yes, I still remembered how to pray, and it felt good.

Both Barbara and I fell asleep with our heads on the bed. When we woke up, Paul was awake and told us this: "I woke up around 1 p. M. and I remember looking at the clock. You were both here, thank you."

He was so well he wanted breakfast, a good breakfast, which I went and got for him. This request might have been for the benefit of both Barbara and I, to assure us that he felt better. Even in dire illness he was always kind. He only took one small bite. We chatted on and I told him that Pamela and I were on our way to Mexico. He wanted us to continue our trip. Since Barbara was with him now, I thought it would be a good time for them to get acquainted again. Barbara was a few years older than Paul and was already married and out of the house in Texas when her parents asked Paul to leave. Barbara and I never discussed his being gay. Whatever she felt about it, her love for him overtook those feelings.

I called Pamela and off we were to Mexico. My heart was heavy, but I knew Paul wanted me to have a happy time.

Many weeks later Paul told me that when he woke, he was ready to go—to die—but he saw us and realized we were not ready. So he stayed. I have no idea if that can be controlled, but I saw he believed it. I also wonder if it was the right thing for him to "stay." The illness ravished him, and two years later he passed; he had gone through the hell.

What must have hurt the most was his families reaction to his being gay. I remembered that conversation I had with his mother, my Aunt Ruth years before in NYC. Both sisters had very puritanical views on sex and relationships. I could not help reflecting on what my Mother would have thought about me having sex—and enjoying it. All those "sin and be sorry" Bible passages Ruth sent to me, what must Paul have gone through?

Only as an adult can I see, and understand better, the world my mother and her sisters were brought up in. How different my world was trying to be. Women all over were breaking barriers. Physical and mental walls were coming down. To some life might be simpler if you have a strict code of wrongs and rights. If there were no gray areas. My life and my cousin Paul's were speckled with grey tones. The strict beliefs I was brought up with no longer made sense to me. I was changing, and more changes were to come.

Despite all the drama back home, Pamela and I had another great time in Mexico. When the week was over we returned to the ongoing strike. There were no signs of an agreement. The WGA strike went from three months to four months and no sign of a settlement. Now everyone was beginning to panic. I had always lived in fear of losing everything I had in life. Seeing how my father and grandmother lived confirmed for me that my heritage of poverty was always around the corner.

Finally, after six long months, the strike was over. The first call I received was from the production manager of *China Beach,* an episodic show I actually enjoyed. He was offering me a slot as one of the 1st ADs. This was not my plan to go back to AD work, but the bank was empty. I had to go meet with the producer, John Sacret Young.

I could hear John yelling at the top of his lungs as I waited outside his office. When I walked inside, it looked like a war zone. Scripts, books, furniture overturned. He righted a chair for me to sit down, and then in the gruffest voice asked me, "Why are you here? Do you want to be an AD or a director? Cause I have your directing tape right here."

He's now rummaging through a series of tapes to find mine. Oh, God, how do I respond?

I stammer, "Well, John, I really want to direct, but of course I love your show and would accept an AD slot." I knew as I left the office that I would get neither job. I don't know how I could have handled that any differently.

I called my agent and told him what had happened. "Oh, didn't I tell you I sent your directing tape to John?"

Nope you did not.

Sometime during that year, a messenger came to my door. He was sent by Warner Bros, who produced *China Beach;* he handed me a package containing a DVD of my *Cagney &*

Lacey directorial debut. It seemed that producer, John Sacret Young, had one of his top directors, Rod Holcomb, look over all the new directors' tapes. The note that Rod sent to John was attached.

"This is the best of the new directors' tapes. Lovely work. She will fit in fine at *China Beach*."

I sat and cried. Clearly, my agent was a bit at fault for not telling me he had sent my tape to them. But I also blamed myself; if I had not spent so much money during the strike, if I didn't have a new car, if I could have known more about John Sacret Young and how to handle him. If this, if that—they are the headaches of life. We "if" ourselves to death. But, in the end, would it have turned out differently? I doubt it.

A year or so afterward, Mimi Leder (producer/director) called me to see if I was interested in shadowing on *China Beach?* Shadowing means following the various directors and learning from them. It is a concept the DGA put in place especially for women and minorities to get familiar with the workings of a particular show and, hopefully, get a directing assignment on said show. Shadowing usually took around three months with no paycheck, just faith that the time spent would result in a paying job.

I had taken an AD job on what turned out to be a difficult movie that we shot in North Carolina and was exhausted, so much so that I could barely pick up the phone. After pleasantries I simply said to Mimi, "No thank you." That might have been a more truthful response than I'd like to admit. My soul was beginning to be tired of the fight. Or did I think I was too good to shadow another director? As an AD, hadn't I been doing that for years? A few days passed, and I was up and about; I began to vaguely remember the phone call. I just hoped I had not been rude to Mimi—I respected her greatly.

I continued taking assignments as 1st AD. This one was a new series, *Life Goes On.* All the producers knew I wanted to direct, and they seemed okay with it. The storyline is of a family who has a child with Down Syndrome. Chris Burke portrayed the son, and he did have mild Down Syndrome. I think I worked on one or two episodes in total. It was sweet to watch Chris becoming more and more confident as an actor and as a teenager.

Patti LuPone played his mother. It was her first TV series, and of course I had watched and admired her on Broadway. One day on the sound stage, I was singing *Don't Cry for Me Argentina,* from her smash hit performance in *Evita,* when I felt a presence behind me. Turning, I saw Patti catching up to me.

"Patti, I am so sorry. I just can't help myself sometimes."

"That's okay, let's sing it together."

Oh, my God. Patti LuPone and I singing together as we walked arm in arm down the hallway. A truly great moment for me.

This show had many firsts; they had hired a female director, Kim Friedman, for many of the episodes in their first year. Shows were starting to hire women, but many times not in the shows first season. She and I got along well, and in one heart-to-heart she told me, "They will never hire you to direct."

"Why?" I asked.

"Because they don't believe an AD can be creative and handle the actors."

This rang true to me and when another show called for my availability I left. I didn't care enough about that show, and now believing I had no future there, it was time to move on. As the show's title suggests, life goes on. However, I was beginning to feel adrift.

Twenty-nine

LET'S TRY SOMETHING NEW

All the shows I worked on until now were considered single camera, even though, at times, we'd have two, three, or even more cameras filming each scene. So, what is three-camera TV? Well, it's more like a stage show. Many are done in front of a live audience. You rehearse for the week, and then on a Friday (or any assigned shoot day), the audience comes in, and you shoot the show that night. Usually, there are three main sets, a living room or office – whatever the show needs to tell its story. They have three walls, and the front is open so the cameras can quickly move from one set to another. Three-camera is just a term used to describe these shows, primarily sitcoms.

Friends is one of the more famous three-camera shows. On shoot night, the director sits in a booth and watches the feed from the cameras. They can select the shots for editing later or call for another take. Live TV, such as sports events, are different as everything happens then and there in the control room, and snap decisions must be made. Either live or on tape, the AD stays on the "floor" with the cameras and the actors. We are connected to the director by our headsets; this way, we can carry out their orders to the film crews and even, at times, the actors. These shows are usually a half hour in length.

I met Penny Adams while co-chairing the DGA Women's Steering Committee, and we had become friends. She was hired as Producer on a three-camera show, *Doctor, Doctor.* This was a comedy created by the late Norman Steinberg. Penny arranged an interview with Norman, and I was excited to meet him. I stopped in the bathroom before our meeting, and while sitting on the toilet, I realized I had two different shoes on. I guessed I had tried them on to see which worked with my outfit and then forgot all about it. Now what was I to do? I dragged my coat over my feet as I walked into the office. Norman sat across the desk and started the questioning. Suddenly, he sprang up. "Let me sit next to you. This is too formal."

I cleared my throat and confessed, "Well, you see, I have to confess I have two different shoes on." He was already laughing. "I guess I decided on the blue but forgot to put the matching blue one on."

He loved it, and since this was to be a wacky comedy, I'd fit right in.

This show starred Matt Frewer, who had just come off a bizarre and way ahead-of-its-time series called *Max Headroom*. *Doctor, Doctor* had gotten a green light (go-ahead from the studio) before it was really cooked (thoroughly thought out). So, they were constantly changing and trying new things. I remember we had only done two episodes and then got notice we were to shut down and regroup.

Penny went on to a different show; in any case, my loyalty was to her, and I left the show, also. Besides, I had gotten a phone call asking my availability to AD a film to be shot on a location. Wanderlust always called to me. That was the end of my staying at home and having an almost normal life doing a nice three-camera TV show.

I signed on for that TV movie. It was to shoot both in South Carolina and North Carolina. *Night Walk* would reunite director Jerry Friedman and cinemaphotographer Thomas Burstyn—and me—for the first time since the fiasco of *Native Son*. He wanted to bring Thomas and me together to heal those wounds. Jerry told me that Thomas was reluctant to work with me, but he convinced him I was not the source of the insanity on *Native Son*.

Pre-production on the film was done in North Carolina, and then we traveled to South Carolina to shoot in Hilton Head. During the day, the beach was vast and relatively deserted. But shooting on any beach is challenging. Sand and saltwater get into everything. The changing tides can be a killer. I'm not sure how this happened, but no one had taken into account the tides, and they were extreme. I've never had to do a shooting schedule based on high and low tide. We'd start a scene, and by the time it was over, our actors were up to their necks, almost swimming in the ocean. This made for some grumpy actors.

I began to notice how white Hilton Head was. We'd return to the hotel around 8 a. M., sleep till around 4 p. M., and start again. Our hotel rooms were never made up, and the crew was complaining. We got to the bottom of the problem; the hotel workers were all Black, and in those days (1989), the last bus off the island left at 5 p. M. They were subjected to possible arrest if they were not on that bus—or worse.

We offered to help by providing transportation for the workers if they just stayed to clean our hotel rooms. They were too frightened to accept our offer. So, Jeanne Van Cott, our production manager, and I took the carts and cleaned the rooms ourselves. I hated Hilton Head and all it stood for.

The stars of that movie were Lesley-Anne Down and Robert Urich. Lesley's husband, Don FauntLeRoy, was the camera operator. This would be my first time working with Robert Urich, and I had little to do with him. For the most part, he ignored me. I sent our local PA, Cindy, in to fetch him when we needed him for filming. It didn't seem to me that he was a happy camper. Years later, Cindy told me that Robert had a crush on her, and she walked a fine line whenever she was around him. She is a very attractive gal, and now I'm ashamed I used her to make my life easier.

Jerry, Tom, and I went to a celebratory dinner the night the film wrapped. At dinner, we were finally comfortable enough to talk about *Native Son*. Tom related having seen Diane, the producer, once more. Well, he thought it was she. "I was waiting for my plane at LAX, and saw a woman who looked out of place. She actually looked like a homeless person, but she dropped her purse, and as she bent down to gather her belongings, there was something familiar about her. It was Diane, I'm sure of it."

None of us have ever heard or seen her since. I wish things would have been different.

A wonderful dinner was complete; we hugged and kissed goodbye. Parking the car in the motel lot, we faced chaos. There must have been four police cars with lights blazing. The wrap party for the crew was held in the bar of the motel. It seemed there was a good amount of drinking, and our star, Lesley-Anne Down, and her husband got into a domestic fight. Back in LA, the studio was already working on damage control. Everyone was stunned but not surprised. There were more police there than at a riot. The local press had also arrived. This wrap party had more drama than the movie itself.

The fighting was over, and the police were questioning our star and her husband separately. I joined the rest of the crew, dancing the night away at the bar. I've always taken refuge in dancing. I'm still a good dancer and love to shake and shimmy. While I was dancing, Cindy told me that one of the grips was watching me and wanted to dance with me. She encouraged him to ask me to dance. She relayed their conversation. It turned out she thought we'd make a good couple. He was shy about approaching me, after all I was the "boss."

"Will," I've changed his name, "you and Janet would be great dance partners. Go ask her."

He supposedly replied, "That's not all we'd be good at together."

Well, he was right about that. Will had watched me for over a month but never approached me. There is that pecking order, and I was closer to the top than he certainly was. And he was a good polite Southern boy. Well, that was my initial impression of him.

Instead of dancing, he walked me home from the party, and we talked for hours. Suddenly, my nose began to hemorrhage. He left me at my motel door and, within minutes, was back with an ice pack. I accepted the help, and we said good night. Before leaving, he asked if he could take me to breakfast the next day. I had the oddest feeling zooming through me, so I invited Jeanne Van Cott, our production manager, to accompany us. Not sure what I was protecting myself from.

At breakfast, the conversation was lively and intelligent. Then my nose gushed again, so much so that I had to lie on the restaurant floor while Will got more ice. He drove us back to the motel. I remember Jeanne had the correct reaction to the breakfast.

She mused out loud. "Well fuck me, here was this great guy all the time right here in front of us."

She was right. And I think she was a tiny bit jealous that he had his eye on me. Now we understood why he kept bicycling around the production office whenever I was there. I returned to my room to pack for my plane home the following day when a knock at the door changed my plans.

Will was there, offering to help me pack. "Well, okay. Come on in. I can use the help as I seem to be bringing back more than I brought with me."

Now, we both knew I didn't need help packing. And we both knew what was going to happen. What I didn't know was that this would be one of the shortest yet most intense weekends I've ever had. We got on beautifully, and I cannot say enough about the sex. He was a master. His very Republican family was coming Sunday morning to go to church with him. I watched him join them out my motel window and wondered what they would have thought of our time together. Will told me about his father, who was a local elected official. To his father, I might as well have been the Devil. I'm sure it was bad enough for Will to be in the film business but having sex with an older woman from Hollywood! And a Democrat at that!

A bit about my male radar: I had gone back into counseling with a new therapist. I told her about the various men that had populated my life so far. How I knew from a distance instantly who I'd be with. She suggested we take a look at how successful my radar was. I related one relationship after another, and it was clear I didn't have good radar when it came to men. I would try and work on that.

She suggested this. "Let's try something. Turn around and walk away whenever you get that feeling, whether through a wall, across a pool, or a parking lot. You have never learned what or who is good for you and who is not."

Will was my first example of a man that wasn't on my radar, yet it worked out just dandy. We stayed in touch a few times after the show, but I never saw him again. I jealously thought whatever woman got Will for a full-time lover was undoubtedly blessed. This blissful weekend would never have happened had I not opened my mind to see who he was. And maybe a few drinks and the dancing also helped.

Thirty

(OLUMBO

Even though this time in North Carolina ended with such a joyful rendezvous—and maybe because of that—once again, I came home exhausted. I pulled the blinds closed and took the phone off the hook. But not for long. I heard the answering machine recording a call from my friend Penny Adams, who had a new job for me. Penny was now producing the TV show *Columbo* and wanted to know my availability.

Patrick McGoohan was directing and also starring in that episode. He and Peter Falk were longtime friends. I had met Patrick before—well, sort of. *Ice Station Zebra* was the next film in the Cinerama Dome after *200: a Space Odyssey.* I had been booked for another *Snow White* tour, but I stayed at my usher job to help with the Hollywood-style premiere of the film. It starred Rock Hudson and Patrick McGoohan. I had no idea who Patrick was, but he fit the bill as a perfect Irish gentleman. Tall, handsome and ever so polite. I had never even heard of *The Prisoner,* the British series he was famous for. Now I was about to be his 1stAD.

Penny knew I had directed and wanted to direct again, so it seemed a good fit for Patrick. Many years had passed since Patrick both acted and directed two *Columbo* episodes. He was comfortable having an AD who also knew how to direct. It was important to him not to let his good friend, Peter Falk, down. So I jumped on board for this crazy ride.

Patrick's resume is a who's who of film and TV. He shared wonderful stories of Orson Welles during the stage production of *Moby Dick—Rehearsed*. Patrick said the cast rarely saw Orson. They would suddenly hear his voice from the rafters, directing them from afar. Orson Welles filmed this project and only 75% of it has been found. There are many stories about where the missing footage might still be. Patrick was dismayed that it was lost; he felt it was a fantastic project.

In pre-production and on the set of *Columbo*, Patrick was a complete professional. On the first day of filming, he confided in me that he had not directed since his sobriety and was afraid the talent was in the bottle. How Irish of him. So I knew I wanted him to have a perfect experience.

That first day on set during rehearsal, the director of photography would not stop talking to his gaffer (electrician), even after I asked for quiet. I went to him personally and explained that Patrick needed a quiet set.

"Don't ever tell me what to do on MY set."

I'm backing up as he's jabbing his index finger at me. It had been years since I was challenged like this. Oh boy, not another bully. I tried to be calm, "I'm just asking you to be quiet during rehearsal."

At this point, I don't remember what he said to me; what I do remember is he pushed me hard—his gaffer caught me from falling. Both the gaffer and I were in complete shock. I could have gone to the producers, and that DP would have been gone. But I was the newbie; he'd been there for quite a while. So, for the sake of the show, I kept it to myself.

There is an interesting relationship between some DPs and some ADs. The question is, who's in charge? Technically, the AD is in charge. All safety measures come from production; therefore, anything that goes wrong can be traced to the ADs not correctly informing the crew of the dangers. I would say this puts the AD in charge.

But egos are fragile, and I think the real problem for some DPs is that they want to direct. Quite often, they feel as though they have directed the show and not the director. I can agree with some of them on that. I did one movie where the director was new; it was the end of the day, and we were losing the light. We needed to get this one last shot. The director was taking his time in setting the shot up. Finally, the DP and I made eye contact and knew what had to happen.

Our frustrated DP snapped at the director. "Michael, why don't you sit down and let Janet and I do this shot?"

I think that director was happy we took over. But with some DPs, that would drive them crazy to do the work but not get the credit or the big paycheck. I certainly understand that feeling. Welcome to my world.

Shooting went on, and I loved Peter Falk. What a character. He'd wander off, sometimes into the street, mumbling to himself. We were in a parking lot in Pasadena when I noticed Peter in the middle of the busy main street.

"Peter, Peter, PETER!" No response.

I made it to the center of the road and found him mumbling to himself. I'm pretty sure it was his dialogue for the day.

"Peter, you're in the middle of the road. These are real drivers, not film people."

He looked up, looked around, then at me, "Don't worry so much. I'm OK. No one's going to hit me."

Maybe not, but now there were two targets in the road. "Peter, come back with me to the set." Then I added, "We are almost ready for you." That got him.

"Well, why didn't you just say that?"

We weren't ready. I think Peter knew that, but maybe he

began to realize the street wasn't a great place to rehearse.

I never wanted to lie to an actor about being ready when we were not. I once got in trouble with Kate Jackson while doing the TV version of *Baby Boom*. Whenever the DP said he was ready, I'd send my assistant for Kate. And she'd look over the lighting every time and tell them to do it better. After the 3rd time, she said she'd only come out if I went to get her. I made the DP promise he was ready, and off I went to her dressing room. Well, it still wasn't to her liking, and she then told them how to light it and left. I didn't last very long on that show—my choice. This work is so difficult; land mines on the floor and around every corner. If I saw them coming, I'd run. But really, is that my MO? Was there a pattern in both my work life and personal one? Perhaps.

One day, Peter asked if I wanted to ride with him to the next location. He had a black Rolls Royce, which somehow fit him even if it didn't fit his disheveled character of *Columbo*. He kept chatting and looking at me as he drove. All I could think of was, which was his glass eye? If it was his left one, then how did he see the road while looking at me sitting to his right?

On another day, I was standing by the camera, ready to shoot what was called a 2 T's. That is a shot from the breast to the head. Peter was ready to shoot and standing on his mark when I noticed his fly was down. No one else seemed to care, but I thought he might not know it and would like to know.

"Peter." How do I say this? I motioned to his fly. He didn't get it. "Peter, you are unzipped."

"Aah, who cares? The shot is up here." Slightly annoyed, he did zip up.

As pleasant as Peter and Patrick were, I still had to deal with Ray, our DP. My stomach was in turmoil all the time. He could see how Patrick and Peter felt about me, so he was careful while they were around. One day after rehearsal, he was unaware that Patrick was still on set and let loose with his garbage toward me. I was useless, annoying, talentless, and dragging the production down. Out of the shadows, Patrick appeared and came to me.

"How long has this been going on?"

I didn't lie. "Patrick, since day one."

Ray watched all this happen. Surely, he knew he had made a big mistake. Patrick marched upstairs to the producers, and we had a new DP by the afternoon. I was as surprised as the rest of the crew. However, before the DP left, Patrick let him have it before the whole crew.

When the filming was completed, Patrick gave me Stephen M. Silverman's book on David Lean. Patrick wrote an extraordinary dedication: "For Janet, My Friend, My Brain, My Number One, Love Patrick."

Recently, I received an email from Dene Kernohan, who works for the Library Authority of the County of Antrim, Ireland. She had found my name and wanted to interview me about what it was like working with Patrick. It brought back so many memories of such a wonderful man. I found him one of the most gallant and charming men I would ever meet. Peter Falk was not necessarily gallant, but he was indeed charming.

Thirty-one

WOMEN-IN-JEOPARDY MOVIES

My AD career was sailing along. There was no time wasted between *Columbo* and my next work call. Director Jerry Friedman and I were a good match. So, I signed on with him again when he was about to do the latest ripped-from-the-headlines TV movie. *Goodnight Sweet Wife* was a reenactment of Charles Stuart's brutal slaying of his pregnant wife and blaming an unknown Black man. We were supposed to film in Boston, where the murder was committed. But the Boston Police Department received terrible press on how they handled —bungled—the investigation.

Working on Stuart's accusation, the police rounded up hundreds of Black men, many of whom didn't even come close to Stuart's description. It was clear the production would receive no support from the city. So even though we scouted there, we could not film in Boston. Instead, we went to Chicago. I'm not sure how Jerry felt being back in the city where we filmed part of *Native Son.* Besides all the craziness of Native Son, what I remember about Chicago was how cold it was. This time we were to start filming in spring and last through summer. Ah, summer in Chicago.

TV was in the midst of what I called "women-in-jeopardy" shows. I can't even remember how many I worked on. So many that, at times, I'd forget what the show was called—or about. But *Goodnight Sweet Wife* was different. Its origins were from a CBS reality show, *Rescue 911*. A producer and camera crew would inhabit an ambulance or rescue vehicle and just ride around waiting for something to happen. They had been filming in Boston when a call came about a shooting. It was Charles Stuart and his then-pregnant wife who had been shot. The details weren't in as yet, and two ambulances were sent to the scene.

The filming crew was in the ambulance that carried Charles to the hospital; he had also been shot. In the ambulance, Charles asked the paramedics if he would have to wear a colostomy bag, as he was shot from the rear in his right hip area. After they deposited Charles at the hospital, the producer from the TV crew asked if that was a typical question for a layperson to ask.

"Heck no, never heard that before." The wheels started turning, and a TV movie was made.

Goodnight Sweet Wife starred Ken Olin, a man I deeply respected as an actor and later as a director. He was also very funny, and humor was needed at times. The Boston PD had fully bought Charles' story of a large Black man jumping into the back seat and killing his wife while wounding him.

Ultimately, there was no Black murderer. Charles had killed his wife and shot himself. After the truth was revealed, as well as the racism of the Boston police department, they wanted to erase the whole incident. Hence, we had to re-create Boston in Chicago.

One night we were shooting a sequence where the reporter, played by BD Wong, sets out to investigate Charles Stuart's route. It would be intercut with Charles and Ken driving the same path. Everything went wrong, not the least of it was that BD was a new driver, and he was having trouble navigating the car, the walkie-talkie, and his acting simultaneously. Ken kept his humor, but Jerry did not.

We had scouted this area on a Monday, and it was perfect— quiet and calm, easy to shoot a car sequence. However, we shot it on a Friday. Where did all these people come from? Why didn't the location department tell us this area was a Friday night hang-out? In addition, all the civilians had summer clothes on, and we were shooting for winter. I didn't have enough street help to stop folks from walking into our shot, and the traffic on the street meant that the timing I had laid out for the cars no longer worked. I had to regroup on the spot.

It was nuts. Jerry lost it. I turned around, and he was pounding his fists and screaming on the pavement. The crew backed away from the crazy man. That was it for me; it was me, after all, who was stuck trying to coordinate that shot. I threw my bullhorn to the ground and started yelling my head off.

The crew started to clear a path between Jerry and me. They were eager for a spectacle. Jerry got up from the ground, and the crew applauded me. Jerry didn't even notice that. He threw his arms around me and said, "Oh, now that felt good, didn't it?"

"I'm not acting, Jerry; this shot is killing me."

He just grinned and hugged me tighter.

The crew relaxed; no one wants to be around when Mommy and Daddy are fighting. We went on with the night and finally got the shot we needed. I have to add that Jerry is a great friend of mine. Sometimes, people go through hell together and come out hugging.

We were filming at Cabrini Greens, a housing project with one of the most violent reputations in Chicago. For a week, the residents watched us come and go. They were interested initially and then began to lose interest in us. Sixteen of Chicago's finest were assigned to guard us and our equipment. I had my cop following me to and from the set. I think this was not necessary and truly overkill—or I should say "overtime." Or perhaps because of their presence, all went well.

By the end of the week, the residents were glad to see us go. "You all work too hard." "You do this all the time?" "Shit, when are you going go home?"

It was a difficult shoot, but, in the end, we all made an excellent movie.

Shows like this need to have some real connection with the drama, or else they could be held liable. Whoever signs on to tell their side of the story, well, that slants the story a certain way. With *Goodnight Sweet Wife,* the story was from the perspective of the newspaper reporter who broke the story, so it was very plot heavy.

When I did *Casualty of Love: The Long Island Lolita Story,* we had the victim, Mary Buttafucco, and her husband, Joey, as our consultants. So it was their version of the shooting.

The set felt awkward and uncomfortable as Mary, Joey, and their family were with us the entire time.

Sly Stallone was a friend of our director, John Herzfeld, and he could be found hanging out with John and Joey during lighting set-ups. I was so tempted to remind him of his days as an usher, but he's a big guy; better off letting sleeping dogs lie.

All three networks wanted to do their version of this scandal. Our Lolita story was done for NBC, and we were in a race to complete it before the CBS/ABC version aired. Two were airing the same night, the other the next night. Viewers would not be able to get away from the Buttafucco family. Our producer, Diane Sokolow, and I hoped this rush to complete not one but three similar movies would finally end the women-in-jeopardy world of TV. The ratings came in and all three had way above average viewership. So no, that would not end these real-life soap operas on film. The TV viewers wanted more, and more is what we gave them.

Before I signed on to yet another of these movies, I knew I needed a vacation to a new Club Med in Huatulco, Mexico. It was a beautiful vacation spot situated just on the bay. I made new friends, and we kayaked around the bay to lookie-loo at Madonna's house. Besides the great food, warm water, and beautiful beach, the Club had an added attraction that week. A local LA radio station ran a contest—"Win a Week With the LA Kings." The team arrived and took over the Club. I'm not a hockey fan, so I didn't know who the Kings were.

Along with their arrival came a dramatic change in weather. The next day, we saw three ships from the Mexican Navy pull into the harbor. Wayne Gretzky was the big star hockey player with the Kings. We watched a limo pull up to take him to the airport or Madonna's house. I don't know which. I began to ask questions. Soon the word was out that a hurricane was headed our way. We all tried to get out, but the airport was closed. Hunkering down and wearing garbage bags to keep dry and warm, we were left to take care of ourselves.

The G. O. S (Gentle Organizers—what workers at the Club are called) were mainly from Montreal. This became their childhood fantasy, playing hockey with a professional team. The dining room was cleared out, and a foot of water sloshed around the floor, so it became water hockey. I sat on the ridge of the windowsill, watching what might as well be street kids playing a fierce hockey game. The G. O. S won. Then we went on to play all sorts of games like *Pictionary* with superstars Luc Robitaille and his teammates. I'm pretty sure we beat them at this, also.

The Club was built quickly and was now falling down just as fast. Crash, was that the bathroom or the main bar? It was a miracle that no one was seriously hurt. The hurricane and the Kings left the same day. My new friends and I had one more night, and it was a party to end all parties. Nothing like the threat of bodily harm to bring out the joy of living. All that was needed to turn this into a successful woman-in-jeopardy TV movie was for one of us, female only, to mysteriously have been swept away in the storm as her husband watched safely from the shore. Geez, I'm tired of these ripped-from-the-headlines stories.

Thirty-two

EQUAL JUSTICE/ MIDNIGHT CALLER

As soon as the plane landed, and before my tan could fade, I took yet another AD job. It turned out to be much more complicated than it should have been. Our director had also written the script. Disney had such hopes for this Sci-Fi that they also gave him a producing credit. Rarely can one person juggle all three jobs at once. And, for the sake of the show, I don't think they should. Fortunately, we had a great line producer, Ian Sanders, and we got along perfectly. This made my life so much easier as a 1stAD and a line producer are sort of the parents watching over the show. When Mommy and Daddy get along, as Ian and I did, then there is a good chance the show is running smoothly. Unless, for whatever reason they can't control the director.

Things were personally complicated as well. A crew member caught my attention, or I caught his. I think we were successful in hiding the budding relationship. And I don't think it ever crossed the line of interfering with the production. It grew and did continue for years until he ended it in a very personally dramatic way.

The one person that I never wanted to gain knowledge of this relationship was Ian. I could sense he was going to move up the ladder and I wanted to go with him. I confided in Ian how much I wanted to get back to directing. He believed in my talent and suggested I come to work with him on his next project: a new crime series, *Equal Justice.* If I signed on as one of the 1stADs, Ian would try and help me possibly get an episode to direct. This sounded great to me.

There was great potential for this series. Thomas Carter was producer/director and one of the first genuinely successful Black directors in TV. Sarah Jessica Parker was one of the young leads. Her then-boyfriend, Robert Downey Jr., sheepishly hung around. And my secret crush, Stanley Tucci, was a guest actor.

One directing slot was not filled yet; everyone knew I wanted to direct again. The prospect of getting this assignment was a carrot dangled in front of three of us; the DP, the script supervisor, and me.

I should have known that the script supervisor, who had worked with Thomas many times before, would be the front-runner. The DP knew enough not to try to knock her down, so what he had to do was at least eliminate me. He did this by sabotaging my relationship with Thomas. He would not tell me, even though I would ask, that he had finished lighting and was ready to shoot. Thomas would come on the set and ask when we would be ready, and Felix, the DP, would say we'd been ready for a while. Things like this would leave Thomas not believing in my ability. I could have taken my side of the story to Ian for support, but I sensed it was a losing battle.

There has been a lot written lately on abusive set behavior. It can border on violence, or it can be subtle and deadly. Previously on yet another woman-in-jeopardy TV movie, I'd had a director go crazy that an actor was not there for the scene we were shooting. It was all my fault, and he was screaming at me. He stopped shooting until that actor could come from his home and join us. I was equally furious, just without power. My assistant brought me the script to check that I was right. That actor's character was written, by that very director/writer, to be somewhere else at that time. When the actor got to the set, he asked me why he was there.

"I can't be here. I'm at the precinct. Why did you bring me in?" Now in his view, it was my fault!

Being right doesn't help when you don't have the power. In the case of *Equal Justice* and Felix—our DP—the crew misunderstood—or maybe not—Felix's motives for how he was treating me, and it was open season on me. This time the remarks were crude and sexual. I would drive to the set, sit in my car, and cry. I so didn't want to continue with this show. The tension was difficult, and my lifelong adventure with IBS (Irritable Bowel Syndrome) took over my body.

Ian and Thomas were shocked when I told them I was leaving *Equal Justice*. They wanted to know what had happened. I explained that the crew's vocal treatment of me was very vile. I stayed away from directly blaming Felix. One never knows who you will end up working with again.

I did have one pure moment of joy. I was sitting in my office prepping the next episode, which Eric Laneuville was to direct. Kevin Hooks was directing the current episode, and Thomas was in editing the prior episode. The three most important Black directors in TV in one room. They either trusted me or didn't even realize I was there. But I observed three friends who could drop all the Hollywood BS and just be guys on the playground with each other. I realized how hard it must have been for them to play the game white Hollywood expected of them. Then I realized I was playing a role also, just different from theirs.

Eric Laneuville had another show, set in San Francisco, lined up; my old friend Penny Adams was producing. Penny and I bonded over many things, but especially our dogs. Eric had told Penny how unhappy I was on *Equal Justice*. So, when they offered me a new job, I left and went with them to San Francisco to do *Midnight Caller*. There were no promises of directing, just being with wonderful people for six months in a great location.

Midnight Caller starred Gary Cole, whom I enjoyed working with. So much so that I recommended him for a TV movie I would work on. They also had the usual number of guest stars. One was G. Gordon Liddy, famous for his part in Nixon's fall from grace with the Watergate scandal. It was rumored that Mr. Liddy had participated in many brutal killings as an FBI agent. The crew walked lightly around him—until one day, some of them dared each other to put Post-it Notes on his back. Liddy had fallen asleep in a chair, and they did just that. All the stupid teenager tricks, "kick me," "kiss me," and one daring one, "I'm a killer." Oh, those crews!

Roger Daltrey from *The Who* also joined us. He was so charming, and I was smitten. He had not acted before and was open about what he didn't know about filming, which is always endearing. I had a crush, for sure.

I was truly flying high. I was spread out, living in three different environments. My home in Los Angeles with its poolside garden. Land and views of the ever-changing sky surrounding my small house in Santa Fe. And the high-rise I rented in San Francisco, a studio with views out to the Golden Gate Bridge. I was blessed to have a housekeeper in my LA home who loved Gracie and George as much as I did. I had three cars, one for each location. This was the Hollywood dream, at least on my scale and paycheck.

The show was pretty easy, and friends surrounded me. The office would go into a bit of a flutter when Lorimar's boss, Les

Moonves, came to visit. Otherwise we were happy campers. But, like all freelance jobs, the show ended. When your job is also your family, does the family end also? Sometimes they do coincide. When I heard my cousin Barbara's voice on my phone, I knew it wasn't good news. My beloved cousin Paul had succumbed to the ravishes of AIDS and had passed. I was grateful he was with Barbara full-time. He had such promise, so much kindness in him. And he was always great fun to be with. He held on hoping for a cure until his early 40s. I still miss him.

Unlike blood relatives that are never replaceable, there is always a new film family around the corner: some you will love and some you will hate. I hated leaving San Francisco but was welcomed back home by my friends Libby and Pamela. And, of course, many kisses from Gracie and George, the current dogs in my life.

Another string of women-in-jeopardy movies for TV followed *Midnight Caller.* Two solid years of them. They all seemed to blend. At one point, I turned to my trusty assistant, Cynthia Stefenoni. "I'll never do another show like *Heartbroken* again!"

She had a bit of a laugh. "That's not what we are working on. You turned that down."

"Really? Then what the fuck is what we are filming called?"

That's how interchangeable the stories were. But the networks loved the ratings they got.

Sometime during one of these films, I got a legal notice that came in the mail from New York City; they had done what they threatened to do and had taken guardianship of my grandmother. She had become a ward of NYC. They had removed her from her apartment in Jamaica and placed her in a home in Coney Island.

All the belongings in her apartment were disposed of. Simple as that. If there were any photos or letters, they were gone now.

Although I knew this would happen someday, it was still sad. I had tried to change the course her life was to take, but she refused my help. I'd found a senior residence that would take her, and I offered to pay for it. But she was not movable. She was 97 years old and had lived independently since her twenties.

Now, in my mid 70s, I wonder if I would give up the independence of living in my own home or if I'd have to be removed by some force or power. I like to think I'd never find myself in this situation. However, my genes are ripe for it. First, my father was taken out of his small apartment, and now his mother lost her independence. The fear that someday I will follow and take their path lingers. Could I end up roaming the streets with my shopping cart filled with my stuff? Whatever dog I had at the time resting atop that shopping cart, my new home.

Why had I chosen the life of a freelance worker when this looming doom, my shopping cart syndrome, playing over and over in my mind? What was I trying to prove, and to whom was I trying to prove myself? I didn't have a plan, and I didn't have anyone to guide me. I would continue once again putting my desire to direct behind me. Or perhaps I didn't believe in myself enough to forge forward and live out my dream of directing.

Thirty-three

THE EARTH SHOOK

In the early morning of January 1994, like everyone else in Los Angeles, I was violently awakened and tossed like a doll in my bed. This was the 6.7 Northridge Earthquake. I have never been as frightened as that. Within seconds the transformer near my backyard blew up and I thought: who were we at war with? Who rained bombs down on us? Then it came to me. This is the big one everyone in California waited for and dreaded.

After the initial assault, I grabbed my little dog George. I needed both arms to hold his trembling body, and I wasn't very steady on my feet. Gracie would have to stay on the bed until I could get back for her. Her little body was frozen, so I knew, or prayed she would not jump off the bed. I was so grateful to have hard-soled slippers at the ready. I walked over so much glass to get to the shelter of my doorway arch. I put George and myself by the front door and waited for the next jolt, which came soon.

That was a week of insanity, cleaning up and applying for help. My friend Pamela's house came down with her in it. After leaving the hospital she came to live with me.

Pamela was a producer then, so her plight made the trade papers. The phone rang often with well-wishers. But one call was for me—a lovely producer I had worked with who wanted to know my availability. Then and there I should have said that I was not in shape to work as yet. But my fear of ending up homeless always went before good judgment.

I drove to Santa Monica to meet with him and was introduced to the writer/director. I had such a good relationship with this producer that I was sure this would be the right fit. I was given the script to read at home but had no time to decide. They needed to start immediately, so I said, "Sure."

When I returned to the parking lot, I was greeted with a smashed window. My car had been broken into. This should have been a sign. I called the police, cleaned the glass up, and went home to read the script. I hated it. It read like a B movie thriller with many implausible situations. My reaction to the script should have been another sign not to take this job. But I had said yes, and my word is my word. Even with the slew of women-in-jeopardy films I had been doing, this was . . . well, it was trash to my thinking.

It was not just the usual freelancer's fear of never working again or my inherent fear of my DNA shopping cart syndrome that drove me to say yes to this film. It was more than that. It was the fear that I'd fall into a deep hole mentally and physically and I would not recover this time. I was frightened of being home and alone. Pamela was busy with insurance, relatives, friends and co-workers. I felt the need to be stable and not let on how frightened I was. This physical fear of the fragility of the earth I stood on was overwhelming. Yet, I had to force myself to get back in the saddle. As a woman working in this man's world, I had to be ready to work, be strong, and get on with it. That is a burden traditionally reserved for the male species. In either case, male or female, it's too much at times to keep on going. A freelance worker has to make difficult decisions. I was my best on the set, not behind a desk, even though that might have provided more security.

I would start work within days, so I went grocery shopping. Driving down my street, I turned the usual way, and as soon as I did, this feeling of being lost came over me. I didn't know where the store was; worse yet, I didn't know where I came from. I pulled the car over to calm down. I reasoned that I was driving east, so I must have come from the west. I turned the car around and slowly looked at each street sign. Tyrone Ave, "I live on Tyrone Avenue!" I heard myself exclaiming this out loud. I turned down the street, saw my house, crawled inside, and called my doctor.

Stress had brought on early menopause, and my doctor prescribed hormone replacement to even things out. This should have been an even bigger sign that I was not ready to return to work yet.

But no, I went to work on this movie, and of all the experiences I'd had, this was the most hateful. The only person I had worked with previously was the producer. The DP, the director, and the crew were new to me. Of all the actors I have worked with, the man staring in this film...well he and I definitely did not like each other.

I always wanted to give everyone the benefit of the doubt; since I was in no shape to work again, perhaps he was not either. Maybe he hadn't worked with a woman in charge before. There could be many reasons for our unpleasant relationship. I don't know what his were. I know he saw me as incompetent, and I will confess that I was not at the top of my game. But I also think there was something about my gender that bugged him.

We started on the first day of shooting at a nice, small LA hotel. The prop person came to me very upset. He told me our star would not give him back the prop gun at the end of the shot we had just completed and that he was walking around the lobby with said gun. Now, this may not seem like a problem, but it is. Gun safety on the set is essential.

Less than a year before this, I had been shooting *The Twilight: Zone Rod Sterling's Lost Classics* in Wilmington, North Carolina, when the ambulances flew onto the EUE Studio lot. Brandon Lee was killed when a blank bullet struck him. This should not have happened, but a sliver of metal inside the gun discharged with that blank, making it deadly. Everyone was jittery about actors and firearms. And here was our star wandering around a hotel lobby with a gun. It didn't matter that it was loaded with blanks. It was a working gun.

The prop person did not know what to do. I had an idea. Whenever there is a stunt, explosion, or gunfire, the 1stAD holds a safety meeting for the crew and actors to understand what will happen. With the weapons person, we go over exactly what the gun is loaded with, show the loads, or empty gun, and then proceed. It takes time away from shooting but is vital for everyone's safety. When he returned to the set for the next shot, I explained, " You are welcome to wander with that gun; however, each time you return to the set, you must give the safety speech."

He knew what I meant, but I continued.

"Just go through the whole thing, where the gun has been, show it's not loaded, etc."

He scowled but did that safety speech, once. When that shot was over, he returned the gun to the prop person, who was very grateful to me.

Was it this that made him hate me? Or was it the time the driver left him at LAX Terminal 1 instead of the International Terminal where we were shooting? We were on such a tight budget that the drivers didn't have walkie-talkies. When the driver who picked him up mistook our LAX designation and left him instead at the Southwest terminal, our lead was almost arrested. He marched through Terminal 1, thinking it was his film location. Without stopping, he barged through TSA, and he was stopped. He had a knife on him. I don't know how he finally talked himself out of this jam, but he was furious, and was just looking for something to blame on me.

When he finally arrived to join us at the International Terminal, he came straight for me, screaming. There was no reason to explain what had happened; he was over it. And really, so was I. I found the driver and asked him what the hell had happened, that's how I know the details of this story.

The next big mistake was on me. We were doing a drive-by; he was in the passenger seat, and Andrew McCarthy was driving. Andrew, by the way, was so lovely through all this.

I missed the cue. I forgot to ask if they were ready in the car, a basic mistake. It was not a stunt, just a drive-by, but still, I was wrong. In my early days, if I made a mistake, I would beat myself up, causing me to fall even further behind the action. Here I was, a seasoned 1st AD, making a beginner's mistake. In retrospect, I thought of the AD on *Hart to Hart* and how he started a stunt without checking if we were ready. Had I become that bad? All he needed to do was radio to me that he and Andrew were not ready. But he came ahead, and when he passed the camera, he made a stupid face, ensuring the shot could not be used. Shortly after, the producer called me into his trailer and fired me.

The worst part of this was ruining my reputation with that producer, who went on to produce a TV series I could have directed easily. Besides, I liked him and respected him. I was sorry to have caused him to lose face by vouching for me. I would have to take some time to rebuild my soul.

Cagney & Lacey: The Return: what better job to restore my battered ego? This made-for-TV movie reunited everyone. It was shot in NY and LA, making it doubly home for me. It was wonderful to be back with the gals and the whole gang. But like all freelance shows, it too ended all too soon.

I returned to LA and the ongoing construction to rebuild the city and my house. Pamela's insurance kicked in, and she rented a Malibu beach apartment. After the work on my house was completed, it was lovely. The pool sparkled and invited me daily for a dip. The whole yard bloomed in bright green and purple flowers. Now everything's in order and I began to feel ready for my next adventure. As my world healed, so did my soul; with it, the hope of directing returned.

Thirty-four

ᴰAMN IT ᴶANET

My friend Libby mentioned that there were times in my work life when no one knew where I was. She'd call Pamela, or vice versa. "Where is Janet now? I've forgotten which show she is doing," etc. She called them my nomad years. There were days when I'd wake up in yet another hotel, and for a moment, I wouldn't know where I was. Often, it's lonely, but sometimes it's freeing to realize that I could exist alone. I had a sense of freedom when driving around the country, with or without my four-legged companions.

Years ago, Lear Levin sent me to New Mexico to scout the Amtrak line and Taos Ski Mountain, and I fell in love. Born and raised in NYC, the vastness of New Mexico is hard to fathom. I would return as a tourist for years. In the late '8os I bought a tiny house—240 square feet—in Santa Fe. New Mexico was becoming home to me. This would be my resting spot. I could hop a on plane on a Friday night and be there watching the sun rise on Saturday morning.

I got a call from Ron Garcia, a DP I loved working with. He was going to work on a series that was headed to New Mexico to film. Ron was making me an offer that would be hard to refuse.

"Janet, you have a home in Santa Fe. Come for the year and do this series with me."

Usually, a DP has little, if any, say on the AD job, but Ron was so liked that I knew the producers would trust his recommendation.

I met with the producers, Tony To and John Melfi, and I liked them both immediately. It was a Sci-Fi series—*Earth 2*—about a colony forced to leave Earth, which was now disease-ridden, and find a new home. New Mexico was a perfect choice to shoot this dystopian vision. Only a few months had passed since the earthquake, and my Van Nuys house was repaired with the aid of FEMA and my insurance company. It was even better than before the quake, and I didn't want to leave it. But my friends had a better vision than I did and staged an intervention to show me the merits of selling my home and going to Santa Fe full time. After all, this TV show I was headed for could last for many years. They all knew how much I loved living in Santa Fe and so wanted me to be happy.

I said I would test the waters and put the house on the market, and if I got some interest, I might take it. I got an offer for the Van Nuys house right away. I still needed to be coaxed into taking the offer. This was my first house, and I argued it was all fixed up and perfect now. Once again my friends sat me down and gave me encouragement to accept the offer and start yet again another adventure. I took a deep breath, packed up, and put some things in storage. Piled George and Gracie into the car and drove off to Santa Fe. I was beginning to feel I had made the right choice. But driving away from the house was bitter sweet. I took one last look at the roses in the front yard—the roses I had buried my father beneath.

After arriving and settling into my tiny yet efficient house, I went early the following day to meet with Tony To and John Melfi to say hi. They were already filming the pilot; I would start work on the second episode. In TV a standard format is for the 1stADs to alternate episodes, just as the directors do. Lately this format has been changing, but this was the standard. You prep the episode, then shoot it while the other director and AD are prepping the next episode. This is one of the only ways you can shoot an ambitious TV series.

The famous Hollywood actress Greer Garson so wanted a film program in Santa Fe, the home she loved and had adopted, that she donated funds to build filming stages at what was then the College of Santa Fe. Her vision of New Mexico as a film state would take years to develop. *Earth 2* would be the first series to occupy the stages.

I pulled up to the Greer Garson Stages, and who was walking towards me but Felix, the DP from *Equal Justice*. A person I never wanted to see again. He came to my car window, and I'm sure he could read my confused face.

"Janet, we've had our problems, but we need you on this show."

We? Who are we? Was he admitting that I actually knew what I was doing?

He went on, "Please, I need you. This show is way harder than they realize, and we need someone like you on it."

I didn't know what to say or why Felix was even here. He had to go to the location where they were shooting, and he left me with, "Are we okay?" I nodded yes. I caught my breath and went inside to find the producers.

Tony and John's faces wore a very serious expressions as they sat me down for a chat. "Ron Garcia is not going to do the show. Instead, Felix is taking over."

It was a good thing I didn't know this in advance. I might not have made the move.

They continued, "We are aware that you have history, and we assure you that you will never have to work with him. After completing the pilot, he will go into prep to direct the third episode, and you will start on episode 2."

Well, this seemed fine to me. They asked if I would start the next day and take over the second unit. I was hoping for some time to unpack and get reacquainted with Santa Fe, but this was my job.

"Of course, I'll be here tomorrow morning, ready to work."

Second unit went very well, and soon I would be prepping the next episode. Once again, the Tony and John came to me with long serious faces.

Tony clears his throat. "Felix has a contract to direct two episodes. We were going to have him do 3 and 5, but we are moving him up."

They explained why they were changing his dates. After the two episodes, Felix would be gone.

John continued. "Now, we know we promised you that you would not be working with him, but you will have him as the director on episodes 2 and 4".

Gulp; me, AD for Felix. Visions of our time together on *Equal Justice* swirled through my aching head. Wow: life, especially in the film world, is so complicated. There was nothing I could do. This was the only show in New Mexico. I had sold my house, so there was no going home to LA. They dangled another compliment my way. "Felix needs your help." I was needed. Sometimes that's all I wanted to hear.

I am so grateful to have stayed the course. Felix did need my help, and he acknowledged it to all the producers. This time we got along very well. To this day, if you ask the crews who are still working there in New Mexico what was the most demanding show they worked on, they will say *Earth 2*. There are so many reasons why it was hard. Not the least of them is we started in temperatures in the high 90s, and then winter came—one of the coldest winters I've seen in New Mexico. Many a morning, it was below zero as I piled my well-padded self into my car.

July in Santa Fe is traditionally thunderstorm season. These storms are very dramatic and can be quite dangerous if you are in the wrong place at the wrong time. The locally hired crew understood the dangers, but the LA crew did not. Despite the warnings, a set was built high up a mountain. We arrived for our shoot day just as a torrent of rain hailed down on us. The set on that mountain was now at the newly formed river edge. It also hailed down on us.

The lightning from these storms could also become deadly. I had to take lightning classes to understand the weather and its hidden dangers. We'd go from sunny skies to dark foreboding skies filled with electricity and heavy water in moments. These storms could kill a crew member caught off guard. The shows were so hard, and the locations, weather, and simply the hours of available sunlight made the show a real challenge. Not one director was able to finish their assignment in the time given.

There were always second units to complete the episodes. And for the other 1st AD and me, this worked out great as we got to direct many of these second units. All the factors for this show lined up—the crews, actors, producers, and the place itself were in amazing harmony. It was just the best time. I mean it.

The opening three episodes had a villain who somehow had found himself on this new Earth. Dr. Frank-N-Furter himself, Mr. Tim Curry, played Gaal, our villain. For three episodes, he donned this long, crazy wig and wild outfit, all in the oppressive heat. Santa Fe has an added challenge to filming—the altitude. At over 7,000 feet, the air is thin, and one can run out of steam easily.

On one of our last days shooting with Tim, we were high on top of a cliff. The camera crew was on the ground below us; it would be a high and wide shot with Tim on top of an empty world. Sound, hair, wardrobe, and makeup were also with Tim and me. The camera crew below us seemed to take a long time setting the shot up. Finally, Tim turned to me and echoed his most famous line in a booming voice. "Damn it, Janet, when do I go home?" Everyone cheered.

The sound man said, "That's what we've been waiting for. Knew it had to come sooner or later."

The alternating 1stAD had worked with these producers before, so it didn't surprise me that he was scheduled to direct one of the episodes. The producers knew I had directed before and knew I was doing a good job directing the second unit, but I was not pushing for an assignment. One day John Melfi called me into the office where we kept the big board on the wall with the show's schedule.

Tony To had his body blocking the schedule. The whole office staff was standing around, just hanging out. I thought it was odd. My mind wanted to jump to a negative place, but they all seemed happy. Tony stepped away, and there was my name scheduled to direct episode 13. I admit I cried. It had been seven years since I first directed on *Cagney & Lacey*. I had almost lost hope that I would return to directing. I was grateful to finally get a second chance.

This episode would be shot the first week after the Christmas break, traditionally the coldest week or two in Santa Fe. When we first started shooting in June, I went to Tony To and asked him about the costume choices. The premise was that when the spaceship crashed, it separated from the part of the vessel that carried the supplies. While filming the pilot, I noticed the costumes the cast wore seemed to be the only ones they had.

"Tony, what will the cast wear in the winter?"

A blank expression formed. "Why are you asking that?"

"Well, Tony, we have four full seasons here, and it gets frigid."

Tony was not the one to select Santa Fe as a filming site. I guess whoever did thought, as many do, that being a desert, we have weather like Phoenix. He went off to check on what I was telling him. Now there had to be some help for the freezing actors. In the episode I directed, the space rangers find where the Gremlins (a harmless animal monster, maybe) have them stashed. Whoopee! They now had winter clothes.

We all needed those winter clothes. This January was surpassing tradition and the temperature hovered in single digits every day. Our shooting days were short on daylight and long on work to accomplish. Like the other directors, I could not finish in 7 days. After my official shooting days ended whenever I could, I would sneak away with a small camera crew and whatever actor I needed to complete, maybe only one shot at a time. I even still had the opening to finish. It involved three of the main actors and one Gremlin. There was enough work left to accomplish that I was given an entire second unit crew to work with. The excellent Dyanna Taylor was my DP. I brought my friend, Cynthia Stefenoni, in from LA to be my AD. An efficient and supportive group of talented women surrounded me. What a joy!

I didn't seem to have a vision for the opening shot. All opening sequences must grab the audience and ensure they continue watching the entire episode. I was nervous about this. I prided myself on being prepared. On the drive up the mountain, I tried to calm myself and trust the vision for that shot would come to me. It had snowed heavily the night before, and flurries were still coming down. When I got to our shooting location, I parked my car behind a mound of snow, and there it was—my shot. The actors would emerge full force from behind that mountain of white as the camera tracked them through the snow.

This was an Amblin Production, and one day we found out Steven Spielberg was coming to Santa Fe. Everyone was excited, but he skipped the set. After visiting with his ex-wife Amy Irving, with whom I had just worked with on the *Twilight Zone* movie. Instead he went to dinner with Tony and some other producers. We were disappointed. But not as disappointed as we all were when Universal didn't pick the show up for a second season. This broke a lot of hearts. We never got the whole story as to why we were canceled. Each week the show was doing better and better in the ratings.

Years later, I heard a rumor that it was a power play on Universal's part. NBC wanted the show back for another season; Amblin also wanted the show back, but Universal wanted changes. I suspect it was Spielberg that dug in. The New Mexico crew would have to hope another big production would come to town. I could not—would not—wait. Since I no longer lived in Los Angeles, I would have to decide where to go next. Whenever I worked in Wilmington, North Carolina, I loved the area. Who wouldn't want to live on Wrightsville Beach? The other choice was to go back to Los Angeles. Waiting it out in Santa Fe was not a practical option.

All the juice of directing was coursing through my veins again. Now was the time to make a dedicated effort to get another assignment. That meant LA. With the directing funds, and enough money saved I put a down payment on a spanking new condo in Studio City.

It was bittersweet packing to leave Santa Fe. Word got out pretty quickly that I was back in Los Angeles and ready to work. An offer came right away to AD a series. I didn't have enough courage to wait on a directing assignment, so I took that offer. *Courthouse* was another crime drama, and I saw it as a possible way to direct. It starred Patricia Wettig, who was married to Ken Olin. Ken and I had worked so well together in Chicago that perhaps it was he who recommended me to its creator Deborah Joy LeVine. It felt comfortable as I knew many people working on this show. It seemed like there was one person from every show I had ever worked on before. Cynthia Stefenoni would again be my assistant, so I was in good hands.

One of the funniest moments I've ever witnessed during a production meeting is when the call came from the network approving one of our female stars. Our director/producer, Bill D'Elia, took the call. "No, NO. Why did you approve Mia? We asked for Nia." Now he has all our attention. "Well, I don't care if you already booked her; unbook her." He gave the phone to Deborah Joy. "Here, you take care of this. They booked the wrong actress."

After a moment of silence, he held his head and moaned back and forth, "Mia, Nia, Mia, Nia, Nia, Mia; my career is down to three letters." Then he started to laugh, and we all joined in.

There is always some sort of conflict or drama on a TV show, maybe in every workplace. Each level has its infighting, just like a family. If the conflict is with the top management, it may never reach the crew level. If the conflict is on the set, it's a family affair, something like Mommy and Daddy fighting. Wherever it comes from, directly or indirectly, there is an atmosphere of unrest. It resembles a dry forest; a tiny spark can set it off. At first, Courthouse seemed a comfortable place to be. But then the cracks started to appear. This time it was evident that the producers had a different vision for the show than the network did. The network kept demanding changes, reshoots, long days and nights. After working on shows with little or no conflict, I didn't want to subject myself to the battle again. I'd had enough in my childhood for a lifetime.

My IMDb page suggests I did "unknown episodes" of Courthouse; that is an understatement. I have no idea how many I worked on. Annabeth Gish was an actor on the show, and she was from New Mexico. Her parents were professors at UNM, so she and I would fly back to New Mexico on weekends, exhausted from the infighting happening at the top. Every time I traveled back to Santa Fe, I realized how much I missed it. I longed for the peace I felt sitting in my small home watching the magnificent sunsets. So, it was natural when I got a call asking my availability for a show going to Santa Fe, and I jumped at it. Quitting *Courthouse* was so easy. Maybe too easy. You never know when you will run into an ex-DP, ex-producer, or an actor you've worked with before, and they remember you jumped ship. But in this case, I suspected that ship was going to sink. And it did after only one season.

Thirty-five

YOU WILL NEVER DIRECT ONE OF MY SHOWS

I had only a superficial relationship with Robert Urich while filming *Night Walk*. As I stated, I'm not proud to have used my PA, Cyndie, to communicate with Robert. Now I was to work with him again, and there was no Cyndie as a go-between.

The Lazarus Man was a western created by Robert Urich, specifically for him to star in. So, he had a lot to say about how it was run and staffed. In retrospect, I'm surprised he said yes to a female 1st AD. But the series was on CBS, and I had an excellent reputation there. Robert heard I wanted to direct one of the episodes. Pre-production went very well; it wasn't a difficult show. But once on set, you could cut the tension with a toothpick.

Sitting atop his horse, he looked down at me. "I hear you want to direct."

I responded, "I have directed other shows, Bob."

"Well, I don't think this is the right fit for you." However, his attitude told me it would be a cold day in hell before I got to direct one of his shows.

Since he didn't know me personally, I can only assume that working with a female director was not his cup of tea. In fact, of the 22 episodes, none were directed by a female.

He began to make my life hell, and not just mine. He seemed to alternate who he picked on in the crew. Many crew members were my friends from *Earth 2;* they didn't take kindly to how I was treated. Some actors can shut the entire world out when they are acting. Others have a problem seeing any crew in front of them during the shooting, even if everyone is perfectly still.

Early on, I made the mistake of wearing a red top while on *Murder, She Wrote.* Angela taught me a lesson then and there. Robert was in the no-see-um group. But he took it a step further. He could not stand anyone behind him either. It was a no-win for any of us. Sometimes the crew was asked to hit the deck and lie still on the ground. That was not going to happen on a snowy day!

It was a miserable set all the time, and I could see there was no future here for me. My working days would be one humiliating defeat at the hands of Robert. I wanted to quit, but I was back in my beloved Santa Fe. If I left, I'd again have to pack the dogs up, return to LA, and look for another job. How many times could I quit a show before my good reputation would be shattered? I had an appointment with my chiropractor, and as he worked my kinks out, he observed, "Janet, your body can't go on like this. What the heck is going on at work to make you this tight? My advice is to take care of yourself and get out."

On the drive home, that's all I could think of: get out. But it was Santa Fe, and there was only one other place I enjoyed working in as much. When I got home, Harry Longstreet, a writer I'd worked with, left a message. "I have a job for you, but it's on location in Wilmington, North Carolina." Yes, the only place I could see leaving Santa Fe for.

Perhaps it was divine intervention. The episode I was working on was finished, and I was sure they had another (male) AD waiting at LAX. I quit The *Lazarus Man* the following day.

Richard Lundin, our rough 'n tumble head wrangler (a wrangler works with the livestock, horses, etc.), called me into his trailer. He was in tears after he heard I had quit. He was angry enough to want to leave the show, also. This man so touched me. That was not what I expected from a rough-edged cowboy. History has a good defense for Robert Urich to explain his behavior. While on the show, he was diagnosed with cancer. He was in pain and, I'm sure, frightened. But none of us knew this at that time. His pain doesn't erase the memory of how ugly that show was for me.

Thirty-six

IF IT'S TUESDAY, I MUST BE IN...
WHERE AM I?

The Perfect Daughter was the movie I went back to North Carolina to shoot. It was an easy movie to work on. The crew was familiar to me, and we got along beautifully. But years had passed, and my nosebleed hero, Will, had moved on to other places in his life. I was disappointed that he wasn't around. I think continuing with him would have been fun

After that film was done, I flew home to LA with just enough time to pack my new dog Buddy, a rescue Yorkie, and Daisy, my rescue cat, and drive all three of us up to Park City, Utah, for a new assignment. I thought it best to leave George and Gracie behind in Studio City as they were older now, and I had an excellent house sitter who cared for them. I don't know where my career would have gotten to without all the helpers who kept my home alive for me.

Night Sins, a four-hour mini-series starring Valerie Bertinelli, would keep me occupied for many months. I had a great condo whose front door was the end of one of the ski runs. The official snowbird season was over, but there was still plenty of snow on the mountains.

This ski condo was a compact studio with walls covered top to bottom with mirrors. A huge jacuzzi tub was smack dab in the middle of the condo. It had bright green wall-to-wall carpet. Buddy loved the snow, and he'd get his tiny body lost in it.

Our offices were up the road from Park City, in Heber City. I'm sure this small town never had a film company there. We had many days where we drove to Salt Lake to shoot. I found the whole area both beautiful and fascinating. It seemed so white and blond to me.

Utah was having a small boom in filming, and the crew we had hired left us for a better-paying gig. That is not unusual for an out-of-town film. The workers feel, rightfully so, that they will never see you again, so go for the show that offers the biggest paycheck. Stuck without a crew, I suggested they bring in the New Mexico crews. Instead, the producers brought in a Chicago crew I had worked with before. Not much to say about the movie itself—other than now, the female lead, Valerie, was the law officer in charge. But somehow, she was still in jeopardy.

It was interesting to live among the Mormons of Utah. One night, we were filming at a farm outside of Heber City. We were nearing dinner time and invited the farmer's kids to eat with us. There must have been 20 blond children, all around the same age. It was freezing, and the farmer invited some of us to eat inside his warm house.

This was indeed a custom-made home. One big room had a kitchen, tables, chairs, and sofas. I brought my dinner to a table, sat, and had a good look around. There were maybe eight women of various ages, but they all looked similar. These were his wives. Then I noticed all the doors that surrounded the great room. Ah, they all had separate living quarters. Everyone was super friendly. My mind wandered to all sorts of scenarios. Did they have certain days that they alternated affections from, or for, the farmer? Did they enjoy their lives? For some reason the memory of the party in Tennessee when I was still acting in *The Drunkard* flashed before me. That was one woman and many men as opposed to this, one man and many women. Oh well, we all find ways to keep on going.

I had to fly back home one snowy weekend as my sitter told me George would not make it, and I needed to say goodbye. I carried her to the vet and kindly, with much love, let her go. There is so much guilt and sadness when one of my babies leave. Flying back to Utah, I realized how many people supported me throughout these years of traveling. Me shooting here and there, homes scattered around. It's no wonder why there are more men in the film business. Everyone needs a "wife" to keep things going. I relied on friends and folks I hired to keep me intact.

After the show wrapped, I took a much-needed vacation at a wellness spa on the Caribbean Island of St. Lucia. I could have stayed forever. The islands have always called to me. But there was work to be had.

Scattering Dad was a TV movie starring Olympia Dukakis. Joan Tewkesbury was to direct. It was a female-centered movie with many women acting and working on it. But most important, it was to film in Santa Fe. Pack everyone back up, Buddy the rescue Yorkie, and now his new friend, sweet Betsy, some sort of Poodle mix.

Sam, George, Gracie, Lucy, and Daisy were now precious memories. Some people mark the passage of time in their lives by significant events; marriage, children, and death. Since my work and living quarters were always so scattered, I'd have to think of my life by what animals I lived with, where I lived, and what car I drove. I often have to look myself up on the IMDb website to know what shows I did, and when I did it—a strange way to account for time. As long as there was someone to care for what I was leaving behind, then I could be the master of my life.

The TV movie, *Scattering Dad,* was just that. A journey to scatter the ashes of husband and father somewhere special. It brought back memories of my father. It was when I was working in Chicago on *Native Son* when he passed. I had his ashes shipped to my house in LA. My mail was being forwarded to me and I received a yellow slip from the post office saying if I didn't come and get my package, it would be returned to the sender—the funeral home in Brooklyn. I called Libby from my Chicago hotel office. "Libby, how are you doing?"

She answered with the usual, "Fine. What's up?"

"I hate to ask you this, but the post office sent me a notice that I had to pick my father up ASAP, or they'd send him back to Brooklyn."

"You mean.... Pick what up?'

"Him, well, his ashes."

Libby is always kind and rather polite. "Ah... he's at the post office?"

"Yup."

"Okay, but what do I do with him?" She asked me.

"Oh, can you just put him in the garage until I get home?"

She did, and when I got around to it, I scattered him under a rose bush in the front yard of my house in Van Nuys.

My neighbor saw me doing this and came over. "Is that legal?" she asked me.

I paused, "Humm, I don't know, but it's done now."

My mother is in a rose bush in Arlington, Texas. My grandmother is in a tree in Santa Fe. And my dad in Van Nuys, California. The dogs and cats are all over the place. Some are still in lovely little boxes waiting for me to free them. That's what I call a scattered family.

We had a great time filming *Scattering Dad.* Olympia was a great dame, funny and intelligent. The good shows do balance out the bad experiences. Once again, I loved living in my small Santa Fe home and wanted to stay put.

Luck would have it another miniseries set in Santa Fe came my way. This series would be directed by a woman I worked with years ago on *Remington Steele*. This is a business in which you never know who will show up in your life again.

I don't believe the woman starring in this movie had the acting chops for her part. I watched our female director pretend to love or truly love what this actor was doing. If she really thought that was good acting, well, in that case, I lost faith that she knew what she was doing. I had my hands full as her husband was also the DP, and they always fought. I think this was their MO, but it was disturbing for everyone to be subjected to it. Although I loved being home in New Mexico, I was glad when we finished shooting the series.

Ken Olin now added a directing resume to his long acting one. He called to say he was directing a pilot back in LA. *Push* was a story of Olympic hopefuls working out together. I loved working with Ken when he was the lead actor in *Goodnight Sweet Wife* which we shot in Chicago. I looked forward to working with him as a director. I packed the dogs up and drove back to my condo in Studio City.

I went to the table read—that is when all the actors, producers, writers, and some crew sit around and read the script. I wasn't there for the whole reading as I had prep work to complete. When I arrived, I could not tell which of the young men was the lead. I went to Ken and asked him, and he pointed out someone I never would have expected even to be an actor. Perhaps this goes back to *Caddyshack* when I couldn't find the lead actor.

I watched the filming for two days and then went to Ken. I felt we could be honest with each other.

"Ken, you really should spend more time with Bob. (I don't want to name the poor kid, so I'll call him Bob.) If you don't, I think you will be replacing him."

Now that's a bold thing to say to any director, but I knew it would be all right. Ken and I talked a bit more about the situation, and in the afternoon, that actor got a lot more of Ken's attention. The next day was a big one with hundreds of extras in a large college gymnasium. Stunt players were doing the acrobatics the actors could not do.

My walkie-talkie (always strapped to my side) went off.

"Janet, come to the producer's trailer."

I took the long walk through the parking lot to the trailers, knocked on the door, and Ken opened it. "You were right."

I knew what Ken meant, but no one else did. One of the producers got irate for some reason. How could a lowly AD know more than everyone who hired that actor? Being wrong never sits well with insecure people.

Ken proceeded to tell me they were firing Bob and asked me to get him and bring him to the trailer. That was the longest walk I ever took. Bob knew something was up and wanted me to tell him. That was not my business. However, in a roundabout way, I made it clear what was happening. I gave him platitudes to stay strong and know that things happen for the best.

I don't think this young man would have been happy staying in the business of Hollywood. I don't think he was cut out for how competitive it is. My ego puffed at being right about this young actor, but my heart broke knowing how crushed he was about to become.

As I opened the door to the trailer, I locked eyes with Ken, letting him know that Bob probably already knew his fate. I do hope he, and all the young actors that have had their dreams end in fire, find peace inside themselves. But it takes a lot of work and, in my case, it also took some time to heal. Giving up on a dream is very much like a death; one must take the time to grieve the loss. I count myself as lucky. I could never have ended the dream of stardom without a new dream taking its place.

Push became a series, and I stayed with it. We were filming in San Diego, and I rented a place in La Jolla, which brought back beautiful memories of my cousin Paul. He loved living in La Jolla, and I did, also. One of my best friends, Scottie Gisssel, took the job as my 2nd AD. We stayed until the end. We filmed, I think, seven episodes; maybe three of them were broadcast, and then it was canceled. Pack up once more, back to LA.

Thirty-seven

ANY DAY NOW

Friends who pass on leads and jobs are extremely valuable in Hollywood, just as they were in my waitress days. If one person can't do a job, or needs time off, they can recommend you to fill in for them. Cynthia Stefenoni had been my 2ndAD for many shows. Besides being such a good worker, she always found the time to be kind and generous. She was my fierce defender; if she ever heard a bad word spoken about me, she'd go right to the source and confront them. She annoyed me to no end by constantly reminding me to drink water, eat a snack, or just plain sit down for a moment. A new series for Lifetime TV was starting and she now had her chance to move up to 1stAD.

The only problem was that she was not available for the first episode. She asked if I could fill in for her for that one episode, then the producers would hold her spot open until she was available. It was four years since I directed on *Earth 2,* and I wanted to give it one last try. I had saved enough money not to need to take an AD job, at least for a year. But I loved Cynthia, and she had always been there for me. I wanted her to have her shot at being a 1stAD. I agreed to fill in for one episode on *Any Day Now.*

Cynthia did get her job back, but the producers also wanted me to stay on as well. That one episode I worked on was such a joy that I was tempted to say yes. I loved the cast, crew, directors, and, yes, even the producers. Topping it off, the show was unique and important.

Set in the Deep South, each episode's storyline alternated between the two women as young girls in the '70s, getting to know and understand the Black and white world they inhabited. Then it switched to the now grown-up women, facing today's racial climate. Annie Potts and Lorraine Toussaint headed an outstanding cast. I looked over their director line-up and saw one open spot. Could this be my answered prayer? I took the AD job and it turned into four happy years, and my way back into directing.

I had one conflict that I didn't want to change. I went to the producers and explained that I would not be available for one of the episodes mid-season. The Dalai Lama would be teaching a week long Buddhist workshop in Pasadena. I had signed up before production started and was determined to take this opportunity to study with this master teacher. That meant I could not AD the episode scheduled for shooting during that time. They were okay about it.

Oddly enough, it turned out to be the one episode that had an open directing slot. Our script supervisor, whom they had known for years, got that assignment. It was essential to me for everyone to understand that when I asked for the time off, I had no idea it would coincide with the script supervisor's first time directing. It was in no way sour grapes on my part. I would have gladly helped her out.

Maybe it was being in the company of many wonderful, prayerful people at the Dalai Lama's workshop. Perhaps just being in the presence of the Dalai Lama, who is such a force. But during that week and afterward, I felt freer than I have ever felt. I didn't feel any need to fight for my place in life. My place in life just existed. I must have even looked different when I returned. The producers had a surprise for me: the director scheduled for the next episode had to bail. Did I want it? Somehow it all felt just right.

I felt so comfortable even after a four-year absence. My best friend, Libby/Cinderella, was now heading the costume department on *Any Day Now*. Cynthia would be my 1st AD. Everyone seemed so happy for me. The actors were supportive: "Just tell us what you want us to do." Such support was all around me. This is how it all should be, and it so rarely materializes this way.

I had a ball. It all seemed so effortless and natural. The set was fun, productive, and the show was on schedule. The producers were impressed, and the show's creator, Nancy Miller, came to me. "How many directing assignments do you need to not AD anymore?"

I certainly didn't expect that, but I was in heaven. I gave her a number, and she increased it. I was home. Finally, I found a place where I was happy, proud, and grateful to go to work. I was 50 years old, and I'd been in "the business" for 33 years. To some, that might seem like a lifetime. But I know so many whose dreams never got close to these milestones. I was/am grateful.

One of the episodes I directed was titled *Lighten Up Rene*. This dealt with the prejudices within the Black community toward each other when their skin tones were different, light or dark, and everything in between. It was a new world for me to understand. Fortunately, our star, Lorraine Toussaint, is an excellent teacher. I learned a lot.

The show turned out wonderfully and was nominated for an NAACP Image Award. This brought me some attention, and I got an assignment on another Image Award nominee, *Soul Food*. I could not help but think back on people like Bill Mason, Gordon Parks, and all those outstanding Black directors I had worked with. I think they would be proud of me. I also wondered what my father would have thought of these shows.

We had four seasons on *Any Day Now,* and I believe we could have had one more. Once again, a power struggle erupted between the producers and the network. Lifetime wanted a scene reshot for a very specific reason. It was one I had directed. Annie Potts, our star, felt correctly that her character would never do what was in the script. The producer, writer, and I all agreed with her, and we shot it Annie's way. When Lifetime saw the dailies, they demanded we reshoot it, but Annie was not pleased. The reshoot didn't go well, and our showrunner, Gary Randall, commented, "She (Annie) put a nail in my coffin."

After four wonderful and essential years, *Any Day Now* was canceled. I was heartbroken. Yet I was filled with courage. My directing reel was filled with some wonderful work I had done. I had an agent, Janet Carol Norton, who believed in me. The world would now be my oyster.

Thirty-eight

MY ꟻATAL ꟻLAW SURFACES

How do I write the end? The four years I spent on *Any Day Now* was the happiest work experience of my life. I had sought fame, but I found success. I lived in the Hollywood Hills, had great friends, and had interesting and exciting work that was financially rewarding. I still had my small home in New Mexico, which was now a restful weekend getaway. I was riding so high that I could not envision any bumps in the road. To top it all off, my agent, Janet Carol Norton, called to say I was booked for two new directing gigs.

The first of the two, *Soul Food,* was shot in Toronto, Canada. The episode I was scheduled to direct was to shoot in the dead of winter. Before I left LA, I got a call from a friend and fellow director, warning me about the show's producer. "Felicia knows what she wants the show to be, and every decision has to be approved by her."

That sounded okay. He explained further. "No, I mean every little thing has to go through her. The only way to succeed on that show is to let her do it all." He ended the conversation by saying he would never accept another assignment on that show. Wow, now that was a warning.

When I got to Canada, the producer I had been warned about was directing an episode. It would be her first time directing. I'm sure she felt she had directed most of the episodes. That sounded familiar to me, having been an AD for many directors who were sometimes lost in their quest for a good product. I'd done work that was certainly out of my job description. Her show was running over by many days. My start date was put off almost by an entire week.

I spent a few lovely, fully paid days in a great hotel, sightseeing in Toronto. When I got to the stages to prep, needless to say, she was not in a good mood. I do not know how much pressure the studio brass put on her. A general rule of thumb is that the parent company, the studio, never wants one person to have as much power as she already had. Now as a DGA director, she wielded even more control than I suspect they wanted her to have.

I should have realized how vulnerable she felt. Creating and running a TV show carries a heavy weight, especially if that person is a female and Black. That doesn't excuse her bad behavior. At production meetings, she questioned everything I suggested, and did it in such a way that it enlisted giggles from the others attending the meeting. I've never had someone roll their eyes at me, at least to my face, as she did. One thing I prided myself on was my ability to lead. If I ever had a problem with someone in the crew, I'd always try to address it on a personal level. Otherwise it creates too much tension. And this was a very tense set.

If she had genuine concerns about my work, she never once even try to take me aside and talk to me. The crew seemed to me to be miserable working for her. You could feel the tension the minute she visited the set. Or perhaps it was only the hairs on the back of my head standing at attention. But the actors loved her. She was their goddess.

Before we started shooting, she left for LA to attend the NAACP Image Awards. Doesn't matter if I was doing the job as AD or director, the first day of shooting is nerve racking. The actors and crew stand around waiting to see if you know what you are doing. My tummy would always churn and digestive juices flowed up and down my body. On this first day of shooting things became harder than they should have. I laid out the shot, and the actors rehearsed. I gave a note to one of them and got this from her: "That's not the way Felicia wants the scene directed."

What!

The actor went on. "I spoke with her last night, and she told me what she wanted, how she wants the scene to go."

I had a choice. For my soul, I chose the right one. For my career, I chose the wrong one. "Well, I'm directing, and that's not quite how I see this scene."

I'd been warned, yet here I was, showing more bravado or stupidity than I should have. Felicia, the producer, returned from LA, and *Soul Food* had not won the award, and neither had my beloved *Any Day Now*. I could not have been in a worse situation. I could have avoided this situation by taking my director friend's advice and letting her do it all. But I'd left my acting skills behind me. But it was my ego I should have left at the door.

The final product was good, and Showtime, the Network it ran on, was happy. I flew home, hoping to put this experience behind me. I should have known better. My agent, Janet Carol, had already gotten calls from Canada regarding my work. I called production manager to try and heal the situation, he was direct. "Janet, you will never work on this show again."

Not wanting to shake my confidence, Janet Carol didn't immediately share the details of the phone call she had gotten regarding me.

With only slightly bruised confidence, I marched on to my next assignment. I was overjoyed. *Judging Amy* would reunite me with Tyne Daly. The memories of *Cagney & Lacey* will forever hold a deep space in my being. And I was very familiar with how Tyne liked to work. I was sure this would be a success for me, and I would regain my confidence in my abilities. However, Tyne would be the only actor I knew. As for the crew and producers, they were equally new to me.

I'm always asked to explain what a producer does. With each passing year, it gets more and more complicated. Here is my best breakdown of this show's producers. Barbara Hall was the creator, along with Amy Brenneman, who was, of course, Amy. The concept was their idea, and they sold it to CBS. Joseph Stern was the executive producer. On a feature film, the executive would quite often be the money person. On series TV, they would still be the money person, but they answer to the studio whose money it is. Daniel Sackheim was co-executive producer/director. It was his responsibility to ensure the guest directors understand the show and how it works. Keep an eye on the day-to-day events and troubleshoot when needed. Of course, trouble might be in the eye of the beholder.

I first met Daniel when he was directing some of the *Earth 2* episodes, but I was not part of his team, so we did not have a relationship. Maggie Parker was my 1st AD, and having a fellow female with me was great. There were many more writers/producers working on the show, but these are the ones I'll focus on.

I received the script, and it was terrific. It was an important one containing a plot point that would carry on to the future. Dan Futterman, who played Amy's brother, Vincent, was leaving the series. He was taking time off to write and produce his award-winning script, *Capote*. I was aware that there was a lot of, shall we say, energy surrounding this particular episode. Maggie and I carried on with our prep location scouting at LAX and Downtown LA, and it seemed all was going well.

A few days before you start photography, all shows have a final location scout. This is where all the departments determine what you plan to shoot and prepare for it. The scout bus dropped us off at a park in Downtown LA, and Daniel Sackheim proceeded to the right. Maggie and I went to the left. That is where I had planned to shoot. Unfortunately, because Daniel had the producing power, the crew followed him. I was furious. This was not normal. Something had gone wrong between Daniel and me, but I didn't have time to figure it out then and there. I did not handle it well. Maggie and I joined the crew, and I proceeded to tell Daniel that I was shooting on the other side of the park and to please follow me to that location. Had I learned nothing from my time on *Soul Food?* Oy vey, what did I just do?

This started a power war. One I was never going to win.

We were to start shooting on September 12, 2001. On the morning of our final prep day, September 11, my friend Pamela called me in tears. "Turn on your TV." There it was. The Twin Towers exploding and falling to Earth. It was my hometown. I fell to my knees as I watched in horror.

I remember the World Trade Center as it was being built. For some reason, my mother was fascinated by this towering wonder rising before us and wanted to see it in person. I remember meeting her in Manhattan to walk down to the building site. She'd never lived to see it completed—or destroyed.

Judging Amy was shot in Century City on the 20th Century Fox lot. Of course, no one went to work that September 11th. The episode that was currently shooting had to finish up a day late on the 13th. So, we were pushed and would start shooting on the following Monday. Our first day of shooting was to be at LAX. That would not happen, and our schedule had to be changed. Everything about our lives changed forever on that day.

Everyone was regrouping. Many studios got word from Homeland Security that they were on a list of targets put out by the terrorists. Overnight security measures went into place. Barricades were put in at the entrance, and they reminded me of the ones I'd seen in Egypt. They forced you to drive no more than 3 miles an hour and zigzag your course to the gate. We reported to the security office and got new employee badges. Dealing with this new reality was going to be a challenge. The physical challenge was one thing, but the emotions—the current of fear that ran through everyone's bodies—were undeniable.

The 1stAD is in charge of safety on the set, and the director sets the pace for the show. I was determined not to have long shooting hours. I knew the crew wanted to be home with their families as soon as possible. For this reason, I designed a very tight shooting schedule and was prepared for each day. However, each day brought with it a new challenge. Tyne and Amy wanted prayer time in the morning for the whole crew. This took time from the shooting schedule. We could no longer shoot at LAX, and a set had to be constructed, one I would only see hours before we filmed it. A new experience each day.

On the first day of shooting at that park in Downtown LA, Tyne came to me with what she felt was a problem with the script. Something I was so used to from our days on Cagney & Lacey. I saw her point, and I called the writer.

"Tyne knows the rules," he said.

"What rules?" I asked him.

"The 48-hour rule." Huh? "She knows that if she has a problem, she has to tell us 48 hours in advance."

Oh, great, my first day of shooting this show, and I must return to the set and tell Tyne his reply. I think we could have actually used this rule back on *Cagney & Lacey*. I shot it both her way and as it was written. Her way was a tiny bit better. Even with that, we wrapped for the day at 3:30 in the afternoon.

On the second day, we were back in the studio. The executive producer, Joseph Stern, came to the set to talk to me. There are times in all our lives when we can remember every inch of a scene from our lives. This was/is one of those moments. "Great job yesterday. And you wrapped the crew so early!"

I felt so proud and excited my new road was before me. But something in the air was not right. I caught a glimpse of our director/producer, Daniel, standing behind Joseph, and he did not look happy.

As the brass left the set, I turned to Maggie, my AD. "What just happened?"

This is her report. "Last night, I reported to Daniel the time we wrapped, and he didn't believe that you had gotten all the work done or done well. I told him we did, but he said he would call Joseph to get him to watch the dailies."

"Oh boy, that's not good."

Here was another point in time I could have changed the course we were headed on. Maybe it was too late already. Nevertheless, I did nothing to create a good relationship with Daniel. Part of me was too busy to worry about it, but a larger part was stubborn and self-righteous. My need to show everyone how good and talented I was continued to rule my life. Circumstances had changed from my 1st-grade experiences, but I was still that little girl trying to prove she was good enough.

Every day I felt my work and my judgment was in question. To add to all this drama, Joseph's wife became ill, and he was not to be seen again. The show's creator, Barbara Hall, had a family member who worked at the World Trade Center, and she was not to be seen again either.

On the last day of shooting, the set for LAX was ready. The art department did a fantastic job. The scenic backdrop the crew had hung outside the set's windows made it feel like we were actually at the airport. Everyone seemed to notice that among the planes sitting on the tarmac on the painted backdrop was a United plane, just like the one from 9/11. A sad reminder that things were not normal and may never be again.

Things boiled over. Daniel and I had angry words over a shot I wanted that day. He thought it was unnecessary. I knew we had time to light it as Amy was off doing a telethon and not returning for hours. But I should have given in and not asked for that shot. It would be one of the last things I ever was to shoot. EVER!

I have a dear friend who started directing around the same time I did. She became a huge success. We had a heart-to-heart one day, and I mused how easy it seemed for her to get work. I'm not naming her, but this is her quote, "Janet, when they come to me to change something or request I do it their way, I just say yes and do it. You fight them on it and want it your way. It's their shows, not yours. Just do what they want." I wish we'd had this conversation earlier, but would I have listened?

The producers screened the edited episode for the crew at lunchtime. I was invited. Joseph was back and asked me, "Are you happy with the episode?" That seemed such an odd question, and I should have replied, "Only if you are." But I stammered, and I'm not sure what I said. I just knew something was very wrong. The shot Daniel and I came to blows about was not in the final edit. He was right. It wasn't needed.

My agent, Janet Carol Norton, called me. "You have damage control to do."

That meant the word was out. I was talented but difficult. Maybe I was. I don't know how many men I've heard that about, and they still worked consistently. How do you even do damage control? Deliver cookies to producers?

In retrospect, I could have gone to the source of the complaints and begged forgiveness. Forgiveness for being good at what I did. Forgiveness for not recognizing power. Forgiveness for never fully understanding the game. Years earlier, when I applied for a job as the 1stAD on a movie, the director told me he didn't want to work with a woman.

"Why?" I asked him.

"Because women take things personally."

I know this is true for me. But do I want to live in a world where slings and arrows are to be sloughed off as not personal, that they just come with the territory? There was some part of me that wanted out. That didn't want to go on the apology tour. In the past, when I didn't want to go to an audition, I would call my mother with my complaints and fears. I wanted to call her again, "What should I do, Mom? I've worked so hard to get here, and it's slipping away from me."

I realize now that each new show was yet another audition. I'd been either an AD or director for almost 30 years, yet each time I went on set, I was auditioning for the actors and the crews. Auditioning, proving myself, asking, and hoping to be accepted. I thought I had left all that behind me.

My agent was right about damage control; I was in what we call "Hollywood jail." It's a term when someone is untouchable for whatever reason. Sometimes it's a permanent expulsion, and sometimes you can emerge after your sentence ends. I have no idea who decides your fate. Finally, someone might rescue you and give you another shot.

Daniel did not return for the next season of *Amy,* and a new director/producer was installed. James Frawley was a director I had worked with many times on *Cagney & Lacey*. I asked him to find out what the noise was about my directing. Months later, I got a call from him. "Joseph said that the crew didn't like you."

Wow. "Jim, we've worked together for years. You know how the crews feel about me. And since when does a producer care what the crew feels?"

"Well, that's what they told me. Sorry; hey, keep the faith."

I was crushed, I liked and respected Jim, but it didn't sound like he stood up for me. Sometimes Hollywood courage is only on film. I realized a female director was scheduled after me, which I heard the crew complain about. They outright didn't like her. So, was I being confused with this woman? *Judging Amy* had more female directors than any show I knew of. Were we still interchangeable? Still "that fucking woman" from the producer's mouth when I was doing *Remington Steele*? Working as part of a crew for years, I knew many a male director the crews hated with all their being, and these men never suffered from this. I told Tyne what was being said about me. She shook her head. "It's never what they tell you."

If it's not what they tell you, how do I ever find out how to change my behavior? I went to other female directors I knew and asked for advice. No one seemed to have an answer for my current situation. They were all fighting to hold on to their place in line and could not entertain failure for themselves or me. I felt I had become untouchable.

I knocked on the doors of the producers who had done *Any Day Now*. Together, they had started a new series. What I got was, "Oh, you don't want to work on this show."

That's an excuse that goes back to my early days interviewing for AD jobs. "I see you live in the Valley. Wouldn't you rather work in the Valley?" Even with all the credits I now had, it seemed nothing had changed. I don't think any of these producers thought their not giving me a show would end my career, but it did. Or I did. Was I that difficult? Or was I not the talent that many people gave me credit as being?

If they, the producers who I knew liked me, would not hire me, who would? My rise took almost 30 years, but my fall in Hollywood happened in moments. You're in one day, out the next. Wait it out, or get out? Try to make sense of it all, or just accept it? Added to all that, I was still a woman in a man's world. Things change slowly.

Power and control. Was I still fighting with the ghost of my father for some sort of validation? Most of the people in the film business who had power were men. If I were to put the men who helped me in one column and in another the ones who didn't, it might be equal. I have no idea how I might have been thwarted or supported behind my back. The people I've written about—I knew how they felt about me. Only a few of these men might have hated women, and working with a woman was sometimes something new for them. The times were changing. Not fast enough for the women and minorities in the film industry, but too fast for too many of the white men in power.

The #MeToo movement has shed a bright light on men and the power and control they have abused. The cases that make the headlines deal with the sexual aspect of control. No man I ever worked with laid an unwanted hand on me in a sexual context. Just as my father never raised a hand to me.

My damage was all internal, a result of the doubting and criticizing of my abilities and talent. My constant need to prove myself. The sound effects of my thoughts drained my soul. It all felt like a broken record, from my father's opinion of my talent to producers questioning my choices. Power and control; I have been experiencing this since childhood. It spilled over into my personal life. My inability to choose and stay with a healthy male relationship. How many times would I have to replicate this drama before I could honestly deal with it?

I look back to my seven-year-old self, stopping my family's heated argument by screaming at them to "STOP IT." Then my collapse, the loss of my ability to walk, and their love and care to bring me back to health. They were the ideal parents for that short five-day period. Their only thought was for me to be healthy. I can't say that my life would have been different if those five days of peace and harmony had been how I was consistently raised. I had been parenting myself for so long. But what was I using as a road map?

In my life, I have regrouped and risen from the ashes so many times. School. Acting. Producing. Assistant directing. Directing. Could I do it again? Did I want to do it again? What were my options? I ruled out going back to being a 1st AD. Directing was slipping away from me. Even worse I was losing faith in myself. I was becoming my father's child. The one who wasn't good enough.

Thirty-nine

A THANKSGIVING GIFT

Over a year had passed, and my ego wasn't the only thing taking a beating from not working. My savings account was rapidly dwindling. It was Thanksgiving, and although I felt I didn't have much to be grateful for, I went ahead and took my yearly trip to New York to see friends and visit my Aunt Violet. Violet, my mother's youngest sister, was my last connection to my mother. Violet and Uncle Louis had a home in Candlewood Isle, Connecticut. That is where I learned to swim, water ski, and play wicked games of cards with my cousins. Louis had passed, and now she was alone-the last of the Gardner girls.

My dear friend Leslie McNeil lived nearby, so it was always a joyous visit. After spending the day with Leslie, I returned to my aunt's house. I opened the door quietly, as I was sure she'd be sleeping. Curled up in a Lazy-Boy, she was sound asleep. I went to the refrigerator to get some water, and there was writing on the refrigerator door—"Shirley MacLaine called"—and her number. By now, my aunt was up and wide awake, and like an excited teenager came to the kitchen. "I was afraid I'd fall asleep before you got home, and I wanted you to know that she called. Do you know Shirley?" My aunt asked me.

"No, I've never met her, but I know she lives in Santa Fe."

"Well, there's the phone," she is pointing to the freezer door, "call her back." Now she's gone to get the phone for me.

I was dying to but, "Violet, it's late."

"Nope, she said whatever time you got back to call her."

"Well, since there is a two-hour time difference between here and Santa Fe, she's probably still up. Okay, I'll call now."

I called Ms. MacLaine back. She said in that very recognizable voice, "I've heard about you."

What had she heard? That I was difficult?

She continued, "We have a new governor here, Bill Richardson, and I want to talk to you about the film business and New Mexico."

Wow, this was out of the blue.

She went on, "Can you meet me here in Santa Fe in the next couple of days?"

"You bet I'll meet with you."

I quickly changed my ticket to make a stop in Albuquerque and left the next morning for the airport. I called the pet sitter in LA and told her it would be a few more days before I returned.

Violet stood behind the screen door as I drove away, waving goodbye. I gasped. There was my mother. The last time I saw my mother, she was waving goodbye through the screen door in Texas. I smiled and waved back at Violet, then once out of sight, I pulled the car over and cried. I knew I would not see my aunt again; she passed shortly after that. Anything I would want to discover about my mother, I would have to do on my own. There was no one left to answer my questions. But all my searching would have to wait. I was off to meet THE Shirley MacLaine.

I still had one of my cars at the Albuquerque airport; I drove to my house in Santa Fe and quickly freshened up. I met with Shirley at her home, a large condo on the mountain close to the Santa Fe Opera. Her then assistant was with us and we had tea with some pastries. Chatting away she and I hit it off quickly. She made me an offer that would once again alter the course of my life. "Come to New Mexico and work with me to create a film industry here."

After so many twists and turns in my life and my varied careers, I didn't expect there to be yet another corner to turn. This offer was exciting, a new and different venture for me. Working for the government meant I had to be a full-time resident. I finally had gotten the perfect Hollywood Hills home with views of the Valley; leaving it would not be easy. That home, and its lifestyle, was a dream come true for me. A home that spelled success.

I had to face the fact that I had tumbled out of favor. I searched out everyone I had ever worked for to see if there was a way back in. The one thing I could have done was go to the producers of *Judging Amy* and plead my case. If they could give me another try, I would do better, be better. To this day, I don't know why I didn't take that avenue.

The decision I had to make was more than just giving up a home. Would I be giving up my dream also? I saw before me two options: go back to being a 1stAD, or take the job with Shirley in New Mexico. I didn't want to AD again, and I wasn't sure what director would want an AD that, in her heart, was now a director.

After weighing the pros and cons, I saw no reason to hang on. I sold the house in LA. And to make a new start, I also sold my house in Santa Fe and bought a lovely new home nearer downtown. If I were to make this change, it would have to be a totally new life. I piled Buddy, Betsy, and the latest rescue cat, Buddha (I had to stay in the B's), into the car, and with a dear friend, Barry (curiously also a B), drove to my new life as Shirley MacLaine's administrative deputy for the New Mexico Film Commission.

I loved the times I worked in New Mexico and genuinely wanted to help create a profitable film industry for the state. I saw a vibrant film industry as an excellent avenue for the talent there, for growth and prosperity. But I knew the fallen angel in me had a different reason for saying yes—one so out of proportion to reality that I hate to confess it. I wanted New Mexico to take work away from the people in Hollywood that I thought had hurt me.

My evil side didn't consider the loving and supportive people I knew in Hollywood whose living depended on the film business staying in LA. I fantasized that one of the people from my past that I held accountable for the demise of my career would want to film in NM, and I would hold all the cards. I could say yes or no to them. I was still repeating the lyrics from my audition song: *everybody knew my name.* How hurt and wounded was I? Would this move heal that hurt or sharpen its edges?

I had now entered what I would come to see as an even deadlier arena than Hollywood—politics. I was now a state government employee. Hollywood is a very political place. Not just the politics of the industry itself but state and national politics as well. The talk at video village, where the actors and directors waited for "action," often revolved around politics. As a young girl, I loved history and always got an A. My dad loved history, and my mom always read, cover to cover, whatever paper we got delivered. These were good attributes handed down to me.

For one brief moment, I thought I would go into politics. In 1992, I had served as an elected California State Delegate and went to Sacramento to attend the Democratic State Platform Convention during the Bill Clinton administration. This experience deterred me from wanting to work in government. And clearly, I sucked at the politics of Hollywood.

New Mexico had flirted with the film business for quite some time. Governor Richardson saw some real financial gains by implementing a tax rebate for film companies to work in the state. This idea had its supporters and more than a few skeptics. He needed to roll it out with a splash—a flourish—to make it work. Shirley MacLaine certainly could provide that for him.

But Shirley is her own person and was serious about making filming in New Mexico viable and successful. Being a figurehead never appealed to her. She and I discussed many scenarios to make this work for the state. I had my views on how to attain success. She liked what I proposed. The growth method I championed was different and challenging for the powers in charge. But I had seen it work in Canada. I suggested a viable training program for above and below-the-line film workers. The most prominent voice opposing my ideas was the local head of the IATSE union (International Alliance of Theatrical Stage Employees).

The reason he had to fight my program made sense to him. Spending funds to train above-the-line talent would take money away from the workers he protected. Shirley and I felt his lack of vision was shortsighted. The governor went along with the union view—train crews only, no funds for above-the-line training.

But that program would not create a film industry. The rebate for hiring New Mexico workers would simply supply a less expensive way for Hollywood to finish their films. We would be suppliers, not creators. All above-the-line talent would still come in on a plane from Hollywood. To have a real film industry, you must invest in training producers, writers, editors, and directors. Training crews is great, and it has served New Mexico well. But Shirley and I knew there was so much talent in the state waiting for their chance to be a filmmaker and tell their stories.

Shirley had no patience for what seemed to be a naive approach to the film business. She was used to just getting things done. I remember the head of the film office calling me into his office one day. "Shirley keeps going directly to the governor. Why can't you control Shirley?"

I have a feeling his inside voice was screaming "that fucking woman." Ha, so Shirley and I had this problematic women syndrome attached to us. This showed me how much he didn't understand how Hollywood works. When you are a star of her magnitude, you are not controlled by anyone. Everyone knows her name!

Word spread in Hollywood of her quest to make a film industry in NM. Our newly created film office would take calls from many a big-name producer. Unfortunately, the gal answering the calls was lost. They had pulled her to work in this new film office from, I think, the Motor Vehicle Division. When the likes of, say, a Steven Spielberg would call, his name meant nothing to her. Why should it? The calls were left unattended and sometimes only an afterthought. "Oh, some guy called for Shirley."

"What, some guy?"

"I wrote it somewhere. I think, like maybe Steven, last name starts with an S."

"Spielberg?"

"Yeah, that's it."

She'd leave these VIPs on hold for so long that many gave up and called Shirley directly. This drove Shirley and me crazy. It was not this gal's fault. She was thrust into something as foreign as speaking a different language. Hollywood language: you'd better learn it if you want to move up. She did not want to learn it. Good for her. I think it is great when people know what they don't want as much as what they do want in life. She went back to the MVD.

Shirley and I toured the state, looking at possible film locations. We met with the leaders of the various Native

American tribes to push how filming could financially help them. But after three diligent months, it seemed we were getting nowhere. Governor Richardson and the unions wanted the film industry, but selling it to the legislature was a lesson in patience. Patience that neither Shirley nor I had.

At a late-night meeting, Shirley and I were giving our pitch one more time on training above-the-line NM talent. We were on one side of the table, and the governor's folks sat on the other. Their position was that all the funds the legislature had allotted to the film office were approved and earmarked. Perhaps they could/would bring spending additional funds up in the next session. The art of give and take, wait and see, and tomorrow's another day were not in Shirley's vocabulary. We both could see their words had little conviction. Even the newly appointed head of the film office didn't seem to agree with us. It got pretty heated, and Shirley had enough. I could sense she'd reached her limit. The following day she called me.

"Janet, I've been crying all night. I can't continue with this."

Even though I knew the call would come, my heart still skipped a beat.

"I feel terrible. I brought you here." She asked me, "What will you do?"

I had so many emotions running through me that the only response I could come up with at that time was this: "Well, they are going to fire me. I'm your person. I don't think I came here to work in politics. Something else will come around for me." Was I saying this for Shirley or did I believe it? Now, I really can't say. Once again I'd have to regroup. Gather all my scattered pieces and go forward.

I met some incredibly talented people during my brief time at the New Mexico Film Office. Deborah Johnson, like me, was a transplant from Los Angeles. She had office space in Santa Fe but also had acquired a ranch quite a bit north of Santa Fe.

Her plan was to turn this into a film studio. It was a wonderful property set along the Pecos River. In 2006, I took a meeting at the ranch and was introduced to David Hilliard. I had no idea who this man was. I knew he was in New Mexico for the year teaching a Black Studies program at UNM. At the meeting, I got a brief and exciting history lesson.

David was a childhood friend of Huey P. Newton, and when Huey took the reins of the Black Panther organization, he brought David along as his chief of staff. In 1967, when Huey was arrested, David briefly took over the leadership of the Panthers. Until he, too, was arrested. David and I hit it off. I was fascinated by his strength and believed in his commitment. He had a dream, and somehow, he felt I fit in.

His dream was to salute the women of the Panther movement.

"David, why me? I know little, if anything about the Black Panthers."

"You don't have any preconceived opinions regarding our history. Everything you do will be from your observations."

I told him I'd think about it, but I was intrigued.

Overnight, I tossed and turned about the prospect. I thought of my father and his wanting that baseball bat to scare the new Black neighbors who weren't neighbors after all. It's ironic that so much of my life—performing for the kids, White and Black, working with some of the most successful Black directors, working on *Any Day Now*—seems now to have had such a direct purpose. Was it all leading to this? I would be a documentary filmmaker—this is the title we came up with— *Growing Up Panther, The Women and Children of The Black Panther Party*. I called David in the morning and agreed to help him with his dream.

It's interesting about dreams and fulfilling them. One has to be careful and understand whose dreams you are following:

your parents' dream, your classmates dreams, your significant other's dream, or your own. I do better when I can feel
passionate about the project. It's a rush to work on something
I feel is significant. I so wanted to feel that rush again. That is
probably the reason I took the documentary on.

To produce *Growing Up Panther,* David and I formed our own
production company, For Giving Productions LLC. For me, the
title means two things: one, the more I knew about these women,
the more I wanted to give their stories a proper place in history.
And two, for me personally, I dearly wished to forgive any of the
past wounds I might have suffered or inflicted while I was coming
up in Hollywood. I wanted to forgive myself for being frightened
and walking away from my home in LA and, ultimately, my career.

I saw the documentary was something I could throw myself
into, and I could believe I was still part of the film world. I had
business cards made with the company logo and my name, Janet
Davidson, Producer/Director. I set out to learn as much as possible
about the Black Panther Party's women and their children.

Back in California, David had a garage full of Panther
memorabilia, including hundreds of the newspapers they had
printed. Many other historic items had already gone to various
universities and archival museums. David helped me set up
meetings with many of the women and their children who were
still available and wanted to talk about their past.

I traveled to New York to meet some members of the East
Coast Panthers. A few needed to be convinced to meet me. David
was not their favorite person. When imprisoned, word went
out that David was part of our government's "COINTELPRO"
Counterintelligence Program. Many believed this, and he was
painted as a traitor to the Panthers.

Every so often, a deeply scarred memory would cross David's
mind and I would see the fighter in him. But mostly, he was a

gentleman who truly believed these women's stories had to be told. The stories I heard made me realize how brave these women were. They weren't just fighting the government but, in many cases, the men within the Panther organization. I saw that many of the women I interviewed were done fighting and wanted to just get on with their lives. Yet, others still had that fighting spirit.

Wow, I had been in the trenches on a much smaller scale. I was proud of my work fighting for women's rights in the film industry. The DGA's Women's Steering Committee, founding New Mexico Women in Film, being on the board of Women in Film and TV International…yes, I can call myself a fighter.

I believed this documentary was my next adventure. I knew I'd need to spend some of my own money to make it happen, so I took an early retirement from the DGA. Thank God for unions. They had taken money from every check, and now I had a good amount I could take in a lump sum or monthly. I chose to do both. I will forever be grateful.

To sell the proposed documentary, I took meetings at a level I had never been invited to before. For the most part, the response to the idea was positive. However, I kept getting the same question asked of me: why me? Why was I bringing this project to them? My responses began to be muddled and unclear, even to me. I was spending my own money and losing sight of the finish line.

Why had I said yes to David? I could rationalize all my past experiences as compelling evidence that this project was right for me. Or be brutally honest. I saw it as a way back into Hollywood. I still wanted to be a Hollywood player.

Ultimately, I spent a good amount of that lump sum. And I had to remind myself that I didn't have any work on the horizon. So, I bowed out of the adventure. Sadly, the documentary was never made.

The Panthers I met were very much a family. Their shared experiences bonded them together for life. My whole life seemed now to be a long series of bouncing between different jobs and different men. Ghosts began to appear to me. It seemed that the information stored on my IMDb (Internet Movie Database) pages was the sum total of my life. The Black Panther story was not mine to tell, but what was my story?

I would continue to tell other people's stories. Walter Dilts, a theatre producer in Santa Fe, heard of me and asked me to direct a play. I took him up on it, he and I were great partners. I had the joy of directing a dozen wonderful theatre pieces. I got to choose anything and anyone I wanted to work with. Walter left me in control. He trusted me, and once again, I trusted myself. I worked with some great New Mexico talent. I was in heaven. For me, it was the most creative time in my life. It was a call back to my early years of being in love with theatre.

Although directing and producing theatre was an emotionally rewarding time, it was a disaster financially. Walter passed away, and I started paying to produce the shows myself. As with the Black Panthers, I realized my pockets were not deep enough to continue without financial assistance. Then Covid hit, and all theatres closed their doors.

Writing started as a project just to occupy my mind. That's what I told everyone. But I knew I needed to understand all my pieces. They seemed scattered all over the map, the roads I took and the ones I avoided. Besides the goal of being a star and becoming famous, I never had a plan. I never took the time needed to do an excavation of my life. What drove me? What fed me, and what was poison to me? Now it seems so clear. I had issues. I thought mine were centered on power and control. But with all my highs and lows, there might be something else controlling me.

Forty

THE STORY/MY STORY

On my last trip to meet some women from the Black Panthers, I was curious to see my childhood home. I parked my rented car across the street. Taking in my surroundings, they seemed strange but also familiar. 196th Street, in Hollis, Queens, seemed smaller and narrower than when I roller-skated and bicycled up and down that street. I took in the house I'd grown up in; it looked so different now.

Gone was the front porch. That was one of my favorite spots. When I was very young, it was where I would wait for my father to come home, pick me up and hug me. That's when he still had a job in Manhattan. I remember my mother bathing and putting me in a fresh dress to greet him. That's when she didn't have go to work to keep the roof over our heads.

The front yard he had taken such pride in was now cemented over. All three of us would sit on the porch and delight in catching fireflies. Put them into a jar with little holes on top and watch them light up the night.

The attic, where all my childhood treasures were found, now had what looked like bedroom curtains on the window. That attic had held many a secret. Soon after my mother had passed, my Aunt Violet and I climbed the wooden stairs to sit and discover whatever treasure my mother had buried there. That's how I found two letters from Mrs. O'Rourke, my 1st grade teacher, hidden in a trunk.

"Janet is too restless and uncontrollable in class. She disrupts the learning process. I think she is still too young to enter the 2nd grade."

I remember being restless, constantly moving around, chatting with my friends, and telling silly jokes. Jokes a five-year-old can come up with. Mrs. O'Rourke would often move me to a different area of the room, thinking that would quiet me. But no, I would just make new friends and entertain them with the stories I'd make up.

Of course, I did not know about these letters when I was five. So, I didn't know why my mother helped me put together a puppet show. I already had the puppets, and she made a stage for them. We went to work stapling cardboard together and painting it. She even sewed small curtains so my puppets could make a grand entrance. Then we carried the small stage to the classroom. She stood at the back, listening to the class erupt in laughter as the show continued. I was in heaven. The show was successful, and I could see that my mother was proud of me.

After the puppet show, a second letter from Mrs. O'Rourke appeared. "I didn't know Janet was one of those children, talented and gifted. Of course, she will be promoted to the second grade."

All I needed to succeed was to be someone else. Perform, entertain, and shine my light. Was this the start of my need to act? Perhaps. Was it also the beginning of my need to be in control of my life? I would not fail. Here sitting in a rented car, parked in front of my childhood, all I could think of was, I did fail. I had reached for the stars, lived there briefly, then crashed.

I snapped back from these thoughts when a neighbor in a sarong came out. She had a thick Indian accent and seemed angry. She came right to my open window. "What are you doing here?"

"I grew up here, right across the street."

"I don't think you did; move on, go away before I call the police."

Hollis had changed and was indeed a melting pot, and she couldn't believe this white woman had grown up there. Now, I was out of place.

"Sorry, I just wanted to see the house."

"Go, go, go."

I put my foot to the gas, turned the key, and left. Nothing but ghosts were there for me—although I would have loved to know if the willow tree my mother and I planted in the backyard was still there. Or the swing set with its iron chains that I'd foolishly stuck my tiny fingers into and lost the tip of my thumb as I fell off one day.

Was my father's tomato garden still there? He took such pride in it. He was always competing with my Uncle Louis for who grew the biggest, juiciest tomatoes.

Was there a little girl living there now who played grocery shopping with her mom from the back door to the front?

What might have happened to the afghan I knitted for my mother? While on tour as Snow White, I started knitting to pass the time between cities and states. I'd do little squares and sew them together to make an afghan. I think of all these stories as squares in my blanket. When I started writing, it was only about the war stories of my life in Hollywood. Soon, I realized I had my personal war stories that needed to be told or examined as well.

I realized that each of my experiences told a story of power and control. I could not examine my relationship to this power and control without contemplating the source, my parents— the people who had, even in death, the most power and control over me. I'd have to start with them.

What memories could I imagine my childhood home would tell me? I would start in the attic. It was too hot in the summer to play up there, but a great place at other times. Up there, I could not hear their arguing. I remember opening an old trunk and finding treasures. Flamenco dresses, flapper gowns, costume jewelry, suits, and ties were sized right for my mother. I wish I had asked her why she had all these costumes. Now I wish I'd asked her so many questions. Leading the pack, why did you marry HIM?

In the trunks there were many pictures of my mother before she met my father—happy images with her friends, snow skiing, roller skating, and dancing. I'd never seen her dance. Sometimes, when she was with her sisters, I would glimpse that happy face I saw in the pictures of her youth. But just around the corner of her beautiful blue eyes lay sadness and despair.

She had a softness about her, and strangers everywhere would bare their souls to her—on a bus, train, or standing in line at the market. She always listened. I would get annoyed, as I didn't want to share her with anyone. I needed all of her, and she willingly gave herself to me. My father was excluded from this mother-and-daughter club we had. She pushed him out, and I locked the door.

Like most couples, my parents fought over two things: money and sex. When the fight was about money, I could clearly hear them both. When it was about sex, I could only hear my mother's voice. I could hear her yelling "No," over and over. She must have known I was listening. What picture was she trying to paint for me? I grew up in a highly charged sexual atmosphere. No "sin and be sorry" passages sent to me would ever explain anything. I lived in confusion and in a fog of my own growing physical feelings, countered by the emotional shame they brought on.

It was clear that she was exhausted. Making sure the mortgage, car payments, and my classes were paid fell to her. I tried to help with the cleaning and cooking. My mother would leave notes for me as to how to prepare dinner. I spent my childhood trying to protect her and hoping to make her life easier. I was, at times, the parent. It pains me to confess this, but her death when I was 23 years old, in many ways, freed me to move forward with my career and explore who I was, especially as a sexual being. I would never have left NYC for California while she was alive.

I resented being the good little girl. I was frightened of doing anything that was considered to be bad, or evil. A rage would take over me, and since I was my mother's protector I would never show her what anger coursed through my veins. The direct object of this rage would be my father and his mother. Without them, life would be perfect. That's why I thought I'd just kill him. If I'd had a gun, I would have, but that small paring knife I was holding would never have worked. Only when I performed, danced, and sang did my rage have an outlet. The harder I danced and the louder I sang, the demon inside would escape from me. I'd let it fill the room as long as my father wasn't home. When I heard the car pull up, I'd turn the record player off and go to my room. Thus, I'd escape his negative comments.

Keeping my rage inside is, I'm sure, one of the reasons my face broke out so badly. How could I show my anger when my father's rage filled every room? I'm sure my mother saw in me the man she married, both the good and the bad. I even looked more like him than I resembled my mom. I wonder how she felt about that.

She left this world confident that I would give up acting, use my accounting skills, get a "normal" job, meet a loving man, marry, and have kids. That was all I think she wanted for me. I can't blame her; that was the fate most women of her generation wanted, and many in my generation as well. She couldn't see, nor did I want her to see, that the example she and my father set for me would never support a happy marriage.

Most of my life, I blamed my father for being the sole source of her pain. Yet now I recognize that something hidden in her past, other than her choice of a husband, caused her sadness. I have to be content with the mystery, as there are no clues to follow in order to understand her more fully. That afghan I made for her has literal and figurative missing squares. I can't make it whole with any factual knowledge of her life. Instead, I can accept her imperfections and know how much she loved me. I can hold onto our beautiful times, especially when we'd go to Manhattan, have lunch, shop, and see a play. It was during these times that I also saw happiness on her face.

I never knitted an afghan for my father. I didn't think he wanted or needed anything from me. But now I know I needed to try and sort his life out. Not for him, as he'd been gone for years, but for me. I thought it would be as difficult as finding out about my mother. I was wrong. Many of my father's secrets were easily uncovered.

I started searching *Ancestry.com* and *23 and Me* for answers. It didn't take long to find a treasure chest of information facilitated by Stephen Higham, who in 2019 had taken on writing the history of Trenton, NJ. He found me on *Ancestry.com* and sent me many news articles from *The Trenton Times* that included my father's family. The first article he sent me, dated 1902, was about a certain *"James Hartigan, a modest man who would soon be traveling back to Tober, Ireland, to collect a fortune left to him."* These stories introduced me to my great-grandfather, James Hartigan, and my great-grandmother, Bridget Delia Cavanaugh Hartigan.

Hartigan; I remembered the day, as a child, that I first heard that name. My father was arguing with his mother over her name. She said that since she was divorced from Davidson, she was once again a Hartigan. I never could imagine her even married.

"No, it doesn't work that way," my father insisted.

Then the voices got lower. I could not hear clearly, but now I believe it had something to do with my father's father, D-I-L-L-O-N. My mother was not in the room during this particular argument but was still in the house. I assume that is why my father hushed his mother up. My mother never knew the story of my father's birth father, James Dillon. I guess he was too ashamed that he was "illegitimate" to share that with her.

I realized my grandmother had some Irish in her; I didn't know until I had my DNA done I was 68% Irish. My Dad is 100% Irish. For years, for reasons I didn't understand, my heart called me to attend the Dublin Theatre Festival each year in late September. Now I had the time and money left from my retirement lump sum to embark on this adventure. Nearing my 70th year, I became a time traveler.

Armed with information from the internet, I would go to the festival and then search out the Hartigan family. Tober is in Wicklow County, so I visited the genealogy society there. A lovely woman helped me find the birth and marriage records, but there was no phone number or address for any Hartigan. Her suggestion was to go to the local pub and ask.

I was staying with actress Lorraine Toussaint. We bonded during the filming of *Any Day Now*. She was shooting a TV series in Ireland and lived in a romantic apartment with moody views of the Irish Sea. Lorraine is a tall, beautiful Black women. Sitting in her small kitchen having our morning coffee, I asked, "Lorraine, you want to help me look for my family?"

"That sounds exciting." She's already getting up from the kitchen table and with a giggle in her voice and a twinkle in her eyes she continued on. "Let's do it! How do we get started?"

"We're going bar hopping."

Tober was not even a village; it consisted of a few houses on a single-lane road. The closest pub was in a small town, Dunlavin. It was a typical Irish pub with dark wood, marred bar tops, sawdust on the floor, and the smell of a hundred years of stale beer, cigarette smoke, and red-faced men drinking at noon. I felt like we were walking into a scene in a movie. Everyone turned and stared at Lorraine, clearly it was not often that a beautiful Black woman entered this bar.

I cleared my throat. "Hi. Does anyone know the Hartigans?"

There was much musing and chatting among the patrons, and then they called out for the pub manager to see if he could help. "Tommy, get out here." A note about the Irish accent: many times, I didn't understand what was being said to me. I'd stammer and say, "Excuse me." I'm sure they thought I was the daft one.

Tommy, the manager, was younger than most of the men drinking at the bar. He was stopped in his tracks seeing Lorraine and me. We filled him in on our quest. He thought for a moment and then said, "Oh, you mean Christy's kid? Yeah, they live around here." He then asked the others at the bar, "Anyone know where Christy's kid lives?" Blank stares.

That was disappointing, but Lorraine, now thoroughly engaged in my quest, would not give up. She and I went to dinner at a pub in Baltinglass, a larger town several miles down the road. This pub was very different; first off, it smelled great. We were hungry from just the aroma wafting from the kitchen. A sweet young lass took our orders. Lorraine was on a mission. No time to waste. She asked the waitress if she knew any Hartigans. "No, but maybe my boss does. I'll get him."

A tall, well-dressed man came out from the kitchen and came to our table. Lorraine spoke right up, "This is my friend Janet, and she is searching for her family. Do you, by chance, know a John Hartigan?"

"Sure, I know John Hartigan. He is my plumber. I'll get his number."

Bingo! We had a name and a phone number. He even let me use the bar phone to make the call.

A lilting voice with a heavy Irish accent answered the phone. "Are you John Hartigan?" I asked.

With a bit of suspicion, he answered, "Yes."

"You don't know me," I said, "but I am James Hartigan's great-granddaughter from America."

To my relief and delight, his response was warm. "Oh! The family always wondered what happened to James when he left for America. My father, Christy, told me of James leaving."

John Hartigan and I agreed to meet the next day back in Dunlavin. Lorraine and I drove back to her apartment, and the following day she wished me well as I set off to meet my distant cousin. I met John in the town center, really just a building in the center of the road and some shops on either side. John was parked in his plumber truck right in the middle of the road. He got out and came to my car. I saw that the "kid" the pub manager referred to was easily in his 60s. He had an easy smile and was quick to laugh. I could see some of the better parts of my grandmother in him. We drove to his home in Tober, just up the road, a lovely modern house. Not sure what romantic fantasy of thatched roofs I was hoping for.

Sitting in the kitchen over tea, John and I peppered each other with questions. I told him a sad story from the *Trenton Times*—how James Hartigan, my great-grandfather, had taken the loss of his promised windfall badly, and was in the hospital for reasons the paper didn't mention. That left his wife, Bridget Delia Cavanaugh Hartigan, my great-grandmother, with six little girls to raise. A plea for charity in the paper said she was a worthy Catholic woman. John speculated that there had been money left for James, but another cousin might have appropriated it and lost it all gambling. Ah, what a familiar story.

With a sweet, joyous feeling of genuine connection, John Hartigan and I promised to do more research on the family and stay in touch, and we have done so.

My time in Ireland was coming to a close. But I knew my DNA was buried in that ground I walked on with John. I was ready to learn more about the Hartigan blood that ran through my father and into me. When I returned home I dug deeper into our history.

In 1910, at seventeen, my grandmother, Margaret Hartigan, married Thomas Davidson. She must have been pregnant when they married, as Thomas Jr. appeared in no short time. Only months after the birth of Thomas Jr., she became pregnant again. When William, my father, arrived, Thomas Sr. knew this baby, my dad, was not his. He abandoned the marriage and left my grandmother with two small boys to care for. He still visited his son Thomas Jr., brought him presents, and took him places while my father stayed alone. My father must have felt he was being punished for something. He was just a child and from birth his world was nothing but chaos. The church and his Catholic school also knew about his bastard standing. As immigrants, they lived in a crowded tenement, and in such close quarters, every floor knew the situation. They also knew who my dads' birth father was. James Dillon.

Babies born out of wedlock are probably more common than anyone knows. But the Irish have a religious history of treating mothers, and their babies, especially cruelly. Ireland was filled with homes for the unwed and cemeteries for their babies. My Father wore the official label of "bastard."

My mind went to the day in the car when I asked him about my grandmother's confession. The small pieces he did share made sense now. James Dillon seemed unable or unwilling to be a father. He'd promise things and then disappear. Sometimes the police had to be called to find my father waiting on a corner for an anticipated day out. James Dillon was a dead end for me. He lived with his parents and then his brothers until he died in 1966—he remained unmarried. Was there some mental or physical problem we should have known about?

My father seemed to have a deep, almost hatred—or fear— toward the Catholic church. I was never allowed to go to a dance at our local parish. One day, he did explain that the very pious nuns when he was growing up in Trenton would make a point of treating him as different. They punished my father often and, according to him, without reason. From birth, the sins of his parents were vested upon him. His brother, Thomas Jr., seemed to be the good boy and escaped the nuns' wrath and the neighbors' gossip.

But the sadness of my father's childhood only took a darker turn. The *Trenton Times,* April 18, 1920: *Thomas Davidson Jr., nine years old, was accidentally shot and killed yesterday morning by Julius Bushgerber, nine years old. The shooting occurred at the Bushgerber home, where the dead boy and his brother William, eight years old, were waiting for their friend to go to mass. The Davidson brothers found an old revolver lying on a sewing machine and began to examine it. The gun exploded; the bullet entered the boy's left side and penetrated his heart.* This confirmed the story my father had only touched on in the car that day. The news article is also confusing. The Davidson boys were playing with the gun; was my father holding it?

More facts shared by the Times. *Upon hearing of her son's killing, Mrs. Davidson was taken by ambulance to the hospital.* She spent two years in a mental hospital. My father lived in the Bronx with his beloved grandmother during that time. She was remarried and had two small children. To my Father, Bridget Delia Cavanaugh Hartigan Kelly was the only person who ever loved him.

I have a few great memories of my dad. We loved roller-coasters. Perhaps that is why I took refuge there while filming in Santa Cruz. When I was very tiny, he and I were mid-screaming ride at Coney Island when I almost fell out. The force he grabbed me with to pull me back into my seat hurt. But I knew he had saved me. The happy time he spent with his grandma Kelly was not enough to pull him back into a safe seat, as he had saved me.

I see the pattern of my father's life that shaped my childhood. He competed from birth with his slightly older brother Thomas. Even though my father grew tall, handsome, and had many friends, it would never be enough to fill the hole of being stigmatized as illegitimate. He spent his life competing for the crumbs of love as a second-class citizen in his own family. That didn't end when he married and had a daughter—his wife simply loved me more than she loved him. I saw it all so clearly now. All those times he compared me to someone else, told me that someone else had a better voice, danced better, and was far more talented—it was never about me. It was always about the ghosts of his childhood.

My father lived his life through the eyes of his wounded inner child. His tantrums, babbling, gambling, insatiable need for love, and constant competitiveness, with not just me but his dead brother. These were all symptoms of a neglected childhood. Indeed, the choices he made were not healthy ones.

Even his choice of a wife. He chose a woman who could not love him, not how he wanted to be loved—fully, emotionally, and physically.

Wow, so much drama in his life. He was addicted to it. The highs and lows. The winning and losing. Was his father an addict also? What might his father have been addicted to? Was that the reason he never married, and why had he stayed with his parents his whole life?

Am I an addict?

Am I? And was I always, my father's daughter? Have I lived my life through the eyes of my wounded childhood? I made relationship choices that rarely seemed healthy. I am competitive beyond what is even comfortable for me. My need to be right, to never make a mistake, drove me to be good at what I did. But the dark side of righteousness is that recipients don't like it, and sometimes they fight back. I've had my share of tantrums. I don't gamble—wouldn't dare—and I don't babble. Well, I hope I don't. But my need for acceptance and love is limitless. And yet there is a part of me that would not compromise to accommodate this need.

Had I set myself up to constantly succeed/fail, climb back, only to fall again? As I picked at the pimples on my young face, I was told (by my father) to stop. But I carried on. It was punishment for the high of gratifying myself sexually. It was a high to hear "you've got the job." And tears spent over losing a job would bring me down to depths of despair. Falling in love, only to be rejected. How on the moon I felt as the audience applauded, only to be dragged down by a bad review. As I fought with producers, I knew they had the power. And yet I entered into the struggle willingly. On occasion, I would win the fight. That's a massive high. I'd won a battle, but not the war. One producer compared me to a terrier. "You grab onto my pant legs and won't let go until I see things your way." Terriers can be very annoying.

I could see how my father felt winning at the track, bringing home cash for my mother and me. Then the next week, losing the money for the mortgage, car payment, or my acting classes. His highs never would balance the depths of his despair.

I am content with not fully understanding my mother's life. By understanding my father's life more fully, his addiction, I see my own patterns. I think it's useless to say that I wished things were different. Or that abstaining from any situation that might present a challenge to my addictions will foster a happy life. Hell, I've written this book. That's a huge gamble. If it's a success will that bring me that high I miss? If it fails will that supply me with enough pain to last the rest of my life? I hope I've gained enough wisdom to ride yet another roller-coaster and enjoy the ride differently.

I am compelled to say something that I could never say before: "I love you, Dad; I understand and forgive you. In fact, I thank you. Yes, perhaps I have inherited some of your problems. And even though all I wanted, or thought I wanted, was for you to leave us, you never did. What made you stay? You said you treated me the way you did because you felt I needed courage. Well, I became courageous and passionate. I believe you loved me, but my heart was closed to you from a very early age. For this, I am sorry. I don't blame Mom; I can't blame someone for loving me so much and wanting all of me for herself. But I would have loved to know you, William Harold Davidson—Dillon. I think you might have been an interesting person. I think you might have thought the same about me."

I grew up in conflict, and as an adult, I tried to protect myself from it, but I ended up in a world that spun on drama, conflict, and competition. Every film has to have its high points and its lows. It's an entire industry that depends on emotional highs and lows. There can't be a happy ending without the messy journey the hero must take. Boy, my journey was undoubtedly a mess sometimes.

My odyssey began with a puppet show in first grade, which garnered me the label "one of those children"—I was a child with a gift to entertain, a pretty child who sometimes got away with bad behavior because I was considered "talented but difficult." The catchphrase itself is a high and low. Ah, talented but difficult! Is there an age limit to finally facing these aspects of my being that had lasted all these 70 plus years?

I started investigating this life, my life, as the Covid19 pandemic hit. A mask would cover my face. The blemished face on which I blamed so much of my heartache and loss. Wearing that mask, only my eyes were left to communicate with the world—my mother's and father's combined beautiful eyes that everyone said were special. But what is remarkable is what I realized I had seen through these eyes.

Traveling the country performing for children, waiting on tables, ushering at Broadway theatres, working for a famous hairstylist, climbing the ladder in the film world, politics, Black Panthers, the men in and out of my life, and finding my love of theatre again. Every step was a lesson. The people I met along the way—friends, colleagues, lovers, and some enemies—what an exceptional collection of souls.

I have now had the luxury to travel back in time to understand and learn to love the flawed but beautiful mother and father I had. To forgive them and me, and perhaps also some folks along the way—people I might have stepped on or those that consciously and unconsciously put a foot on me.

It has not been an ordinary life.

I can still hear all those young voices screaming to save Snow White as the poison apple is offered to her. "Don't eat it." They would grow more passionate as the apple came closer to my mouth. "DON'T EAT IT!" And that one young man in the upper rows, louder than the other voices, demanding, "OH EAT IT, SNOW WHITE!"

I'm glad I took the bite.

ABOUT THE AUTHOR

Janet Davidson held five union memberships reflecting her varied career: AEA, SAG, DGA, IATSE 100, and the Hotel and Restaurant Workers. She was DGA 1st AD on many iconic TV shows: *Remington Steele, Murder She Wrote,* and *Columbo,* then director on *Cagney & Lacey, Any Day Now,* and *Judging Amy.* Janet co-chaired the first DGA Women's Steering Committee, started New Mexico Women in Film, and was vice-chair of Women in Film and TV International. She played a role in establishing a new film industry in New Mexico. Currently, Janet is retired and resides in Palm Desert, California.

Printed in the USA
CPSIA information can be obtained
at www.ICGtesting.com
LVHW020821271123
764914LV00024B/168